Comparative Approaches to Program Planning

Comparative Approaches to Program Planning

F. Ellen Netting
Mary Katherine O'Connor
David P. Fauri

WILEY

John Wiley & Sons, Inc.

To the courageous planners who are willing
to risk the hard thinking necessary
to design human service programs that will
truly better the world for us all

Contents

Preface   **xiii**

Acknowledgments   **xxiii**

Chapter 1   Differences Between Lines and Circles   **1**

Lines and Circles as Planning Metaphors 5

A Brief History of Lines and Circles 7

Planning Theory: Both Lines and Circles 16

Examples of Planning Approaches 20

The "Surety" of the Line and the "Tentativeness" of the Circle 24

A Conceptual Framework 25

Summary 27

Discussion Questions 28

Chapter 2   Programs: Containers for Idea Implementation   **31**

Programs and Projects; Services and Interventions 32

Programs and Projects 36

Services and Interventions 38

Programs in Organizational Context 39

Program Planning 43

Mandates and Initiatives 44

Planning Different Types of Programs 46

Summary 48

Discussion Questions 49

Case Exercise: Chronic Pain 51

Chapter 3   Rational Planning and Prescriptive Approaches   59

Case: The Mayor and the Street Educators 61

Introduction 69

History of Rational Planning and Prescriptive Approaches 71

Dimensions of Rational Planning and Prescriptive Approaches 75

The Logic Model 75

Assessing Needs 78

Defining and Analyzing Problems 80

Selecting Intervention Strategies 82

Writing Goals and Objectives 87

Program Design and Decision-Making 91

Accountability in a Prescriptive Approach 96

Accountability Challenges 97

Information Systems 100

Budgeting 103

Rational Planning 104

Mind-sets 104

Skills 106

Strengths and Challenges of Rational Planning 110

Summary 112

Discussion Questions 114

Chapter 4   Interpretive Planning and Emergent Approaches   **117**

Case: The Invisible People and the Area Agency on Aging 119

Introduction 126

History of Interpretive Planning and Emergent Approaches 129

Dimensions of Interpretive Planning and Emergent Approaches 133

The Logic of Emergence 133

Engagement 138

Discovery 144

Sense-making 146

Unfolding 148

Accountability in an Emergent Approach 155

Accountability Challenges 156

Accountability Options 157

Interpretive Planning 162

Mind-sets 163

Skills 164

Strengths and Challenges of Interpretive Planning 165

Summary 166

Discussion Questions 167

Chapter 5   Knowing When to Use Which Planning Approach   **169**

Case: AIDS Orphans and the Pig Intervention 173

Similarities in Planning Approach Challenges 176

Gaining Entry 177

Becoming Oriented 179

Engaging in Critical Thinking 181

Making Ethical Decisions 187

Comparing Program Planning Approaches 192

Comparing Dimensions 192

Examining Accountability 198

Thinking about Mind-sets and Skills 201

Decision Issues for Approach Selection 205

Summary 208

Discussion Questions 208

Appendix: Comparing Planning Approaches 210

Chapter 6   Program Planning in Diverse Cultural Contexts   **213**

Culture and Context 216

Defining Culture 216

Elements in Culture Development 217

Cultural Competence 220

Skills of the Culturally Competent 222

Challenges to Culturally Competent Human Service Programming 225

Understanding Empiricism 225

Recognizing Realism and Interpretivism 227

Responding to Accountability Demands 229

Cultural Competence and Program Planning 231

Planning with Sensitivity to Difference 233

Planning with Sensitivity to Inclusion 238

Planning with Sensitivity to Context 240

Planning Across Multiple Organizational Settings 244
Issues When Practicing Internationally 245

Summary 247

Conclusion 249

Exercises 250

Glossary **253**

References **271**

Index **281**

Preface

One of the basic assumptions of the rationalist school is that decisions precede an action, a belief that has entered popular folklore in the exhortation: "look before you leap." This is, of course, good counsel. But suppose you don't know how to leap? The inability to leap or, more generally, the ability or inability to implement a decision is rarely taken into account in the process of decision analysis.

—John Freidmann and Barclay Hudson, *Knowledge and Action: A Guide to Planning Theory*

GENERAL APPROACH TO THE BOOK

"Program planning" is a construct that can make complex situations more manageable. In a world in which change is a constant, program planning approaches that provide an illusion of being in control may be comforting. In fact, the certitude of knowing how to plan something from beginning to end is a desired skill set for those who want to "look before they leap." This certitude is designed by professionals who want to demonstrate that they have something to offer and who might want to be hired as a program coordinator, grants writer, or manager. Many a professional has carried a copy of a plan or grant proposal with them to a job interview to demonstrate their ability to design a program.

Based on our understanding of students' aspirations and needs, for years we taught program planning with the assurance that if a goal could be established, and if measurable objectives could be articulated, then somehow or some way their program designs could be implemented in a reasonable manner. Yet many programs that looked doable on paper were anything but doable in real life. Even though our graduates' facility with "logic models" wowed employers and even potential funders, when it came to implementation many were often surprised to find that program designs did not always unfold in the envisioned manner. In fact, we learned in this process that excellent, precise, evidence-based designs could win accolades from professionals *and* funders, but that the process of enacting plans revealed unexpected gaps and barriers for staff tasked with implementation. Ironically, while some funded programs were not always creatively designed for addressing complex situations that needed alternative approaches, staff of community-based programs that appeared to work could not always articulate why and how their programs did work. They could not discuss their planning experiences in terms that could be grasped by exacting professional audiences. Our challenge, then, became to prepare our students to think and talk in the established language of program planning, as well as offer them alternative ways of planning, thinking, talking, and surviving. They needed to be facile at entering the established world of program planning while also knowing when to use different approaches. Most of all, they needed to recognize that there was no one best way to plan. With this came a necessity to accurately assess the situation for which they were planning and, from that, determine the appropriate approach for the circumstances at hand. To accomplish this, we had the stimulating challenge of determining how to impart the needed knowledge, skills, and attitudes. Our students have told us that we have been able to meet the challenge.

Therefore, we decided to write this book with the purpose of comparing and contrasting different ways of program planning. We do so out of a belief that there are multiple ways of knowing, and that there are multiple ways of planning and doing. Because these ways are different does not make one superior to others, and we have found that recognizing that there are differences can be freeing. It allows the purpose of the planning process to drive the methods used, rather than the methods driving the design. This goes a long way toward facilitating professional program planners in acquiring resources for planning and having increased flexibility for functioning in varying social, economic, and cultural settings.

Our book is geared to future program planners in master's programs in social work, public administration, nonprofit management, public health, community psychology, applied sociology, human services, and related fields. It may also be useful in required senior-level courses on large systems change offered in baccalaureate programs. In social work, community psychology, applied sociology, and human services programs, where many students expect to perform "direct service work," it can increase understanding of direct service programs. Courses in program planning, macro social work practice, program evaluation, organization practice, policy implementation, and related subjects will benefit from using this book for creating expanded applications of program planning strategies, tactics, and skills.

Reasons for all practitioners to become familiar with the skills offered in this book will be central in the pages that follow. All practitioners both impact and are impacted by programming at some stage in their direct service delivery work. They are also sometimes alienated by the language and techniques of traditional planning, thinking that planning has nothing to do with their efforts in relationship building and problem-solving with their clients. We believe that an alternative, nonlinear approach to planning that takes into account intuition and serendipity and creatively capitalizes on complex circumstances is sure to make sense to many students who are turned off by more traditional, prescriptive planning approaches.

We are aware that some people prefer to have a greater sense of order, and that they believe there is a preferred way to plan a program, through precise, linear thought. For these planners, linear reasoning is a priority. This book is designed to show that nonlinear (sometimes called nonrational or circular) thinking is not only useful in reasoning, but that it supports an alternative type of interpretive planning called an emergent approach.

Interpretive planning translates different ways of knowing and understanding into the "doing" aspects of planning human service programs. Linear planning models can be compared with alternative, nonlinear approaches, and it is possible to assess the costs and benefits of each approach. Ideas about when differing approaches are used most effectively are offered here as a guide for program planners faced with situations that do not always resemble the clean, clear opportunities for which rational, prescriptive planning is usually discussed. Ways to systematically approach messy situations (e.g., when you are called on to begin to plan in the middle, not at the beginning, of a project; or when you are asked to help in situations in nontraditional or non-Western cultures with differing approaches to logic) will be addressed while applying reasonable ways of assuring and accounting for quality in human service programming, regardless of the context. Our emphasis is on planning and design, with implementation and evaluation of the results of planning also recognized. This is a flexible conceptualization of the planning process that can be useful regardless of the culture, mission, or goals of the human service setting or organization within which planning occurs. Through different approaches, alternate ways of knowing are introduced into planning processes, facilitating programs targeted to meet needs in traditional or alternative contexts.

ORGANIZATION OF THE BOOK

The book is composed of six chapters, successively building both understanding and competence for good program planning. End-of-chapter discussion questions and exercises focus on skills development derived from material in each chapter. Practical application of planning concepts is made through real-life case examples intended to be of help in thinking about the issues and the way they are presented, and to assist those not yet engaged with the challenges and opportunities of complex problem-solving in program planning. A glossary is offered to aid thinking along the way and to clarify our use of terms.

Conceptually, we examine two types of planning based on different worldviews: rational and interpretive. These worldviews are joined by two approaches to planning: rational planning, which is tied to what we are calling prescriptive approaches; and interpretive planning, which is connected to what we are calling emergent approaches. Throughout the book we refer to problem-solving as a process that can be undertaken through prescriptive approaches, in which a goal is predetermined, or through emergent approaches, in which plans unfold in an unpredictable manner. We have carefully chosen our terms, in hopes that they will provide the reader with viable conceptual frameworks and languages in which to communicate about program planning.

In Chapter 1, we introduce the possibility that the need identification for a social program intervention may come from choices raised by different ways of conceptualizing an opportunity or problem, that there are choices in program design. Some of these choices are strongly cognitive, but others have affective and power dimensions. Through an exploration of the difference between a line and a circle, Chapter 2 also seeks an evenhanded understanding of the differences in these choices and the processes by which programs are designed and planned. This subsequently takes us into how to know and understand differences between induction and deduction and positivist/rational and interpretivist ways of knowing. We think aspects of rational and nonrational thought (as opposed to irrational thought) are at the basis of the acceptance of both traditional and nontraditional ways of planning. Through the discussion of induction and deduction, as well as positivist and interpretivist ways of knowing, we present in detail the different assumptions that are part of linear and more circular thinking problem-solving processes and how those differences are important to the planning process. While these different notions may be based in rational and nonrational thought processes, the intent is to distinguish both from irrational thinking.

Chapter 2 provides an overview of the elements that constitute a program; it introduces planning terms and identifies categories of stakeholders that will appear throughout the text. Here we describe how programs differ from projects, services, and policies. The various sources of needs identification and the programming ideas developed to meet those needs are discussed. The chapter also emphasizes that social programming is dependent on authorizing and funding sources, from policy enactment to needs assessment to government or other funder mandates to grassroots demands, all of which reflect how differently programs can be thought about, designed, and planned.

Chapter 3 is devoted to traditional rational program planning, based on the prescriptive approaches such as planned change and logic models. Building on the work of well-known scholars in planning and administration, we review the logic model that moves from needs assessment and problem analysis through hypothesis development, goals and objectives setting, and designing programs that are monitored and evaluated using traditional methods. The pros and cons of using prescriptive approaches are introduced, as are the specifics of how these approaches work and in which situations they would likely be most valuable.

Chapter 4 focuses on interpretive program planning, based on emergent approaches to problem-solving. To date, textbooks on program planning have focused on rational planning and prescriptive approaches, stopping there, assuming that program planners would not need alternative models and might not draw on creative, fluid aspects in their work. Using an interpretive view of planning, the chapter outlines a collaborative, less reductionistic, approach to decision-making in program planning. Politics, goals, problems, solutions, and political reasoning and pragmatic thought focus and guide the reader into opportunities and challenges of using an emergent approach, as well as the specifics of how it works and in which situations it would be valuable.

Together, Chapters 3 and 4 outline the details of the traditional planned change or logic model approach based on rational thought and the more interpretive methods of an emergent approach to planning based on nonrational thinking. Both chapters use a critical lens to discuss when each approach is most useful, so that in Chapter 5, the reader can engage in an assessment of both the costs and benefits of each approach in order to develop the skills necessary to determine when and how each works best. The comparative aspect of the textbook is pursued in Chapter 5. We invite readers to critique the two planning approaches, based on what they learned in Chapters 3 and 4, helping them to clarify the questions that should be asked and answered in determining when each approach works best. We also elaborate on critical thinking and ethical decision-making, and explain how to assess the unintended consequences of planning choices in program implementation and evaluation. Examples from practice experience are used to compare the different approaches.

Using a global, culturally sensitive perspective on the program planning process, Chapter 6 assists the reader in exploring the sociopolitical benefits of having more than one approach to planning, regardless of cultural context or organizational tradition. In this chapter, we briefly return to the philosophy of science dialogue introduced at the beginning of the book as a way to choose appropriate responses to cultural needs, so that the planner can demonstrate skills in cultural competency. The goal is to signal the possibility of considering an alternative way. Our hope is that the reader will take advantage of the opportunity to consider and evaluate alternative planning approaches and not assume that some situations only reflect a lack of competence for engaging in planning. Chapter 6 is intended to assist the reader in identifying consequences of cultural context aspects of planning and recognizing both the challenges and possible benefits of embracing alternative approaches for successful program planning.

The material in this text is intended to help readers manage the difficulties of teaching and learning a linear process of planning while they are experiencing the serendipitous, sometimes nonlinear, nature of the human service environment. It also helps them address planning in a systematic way when the actual process is not strictly a linear one. All of us should all want to encounter, manage, and enjoy planning in varying cultural settings, and compete positively and effectively in a global human service marketplace in which designing culturally sensitive programs means being able to adapt to the ways of varying cultures. It should also aid us in creating and maintaining human service organization cultures that continually evolve standards for operationalizing cultural competence within our organizations (see, for example: NASW, 2001; U.S. Department of Health and Human Services, 2001).

At the beginning here, we indicated that, conceptually, program planning may be employed to cast an illusion of being in control of a process that is often not as linear as it is often conceptualized. Professionals can be comforted by that illusion, as we have at times. In this book, we hope to convince the reader that comfort can also come from recognizing the inevitabilities of difference and from having a repertoire of skills to be used as needed, rather than using only one established way. In our classes, students are heard to exclaim, in effect, "This is hard, and my head hurts!" Our response is usually something like: "This is not an easy cookbook approach, and your head is hurting because you are thinking so hard. If program planning were easy, it could be done without skills, and you wouldn't be in school. If you master the variety of program planning skills allowing you to work in diverse situations, then you will make a real difference in the real world of social program design and implementation." Thus, we hope the following pages will make your head hurt in good ways!

Acknowledgments

We are indebted to colleagues and former students around the country and in various parts of the world who have talked and debated with us throughout the years about program planning. We are especially indebted to colleagues and former professors who have guided us and who are the real pioneers in writing the books on program planning that have provided incredible insights into the planning process. We are particularly thankful for Peter M. Kettner who has always supported our efforts to push beyond rational approaches, to Roger Lohmann, Edward J. Pawlak, Donald E. Chambers, and Bob Vinter who taught us or worked with us on program planning in the early days. We appreciate as well the efforts of a number of anonymous reviewers who provided careful and thoughtful assessments of our ideas, including Felice Davidson Perlmutter, Kathy Byers, Paul D. McWhinney, and Jon E. Singletary.

To our editor, Lisa Gebo, we do not have words to express our appreciation for the faith you have put in us as collaborators. You are an inspiration to us in so many ways. To our dear friend and former editor, David Estrin, we are grateful to you for always listening to our ideas, smiling appropriately, and then carefully giving us advice about who might be willing to listen to what we have to say.

To Frank R. Baskind, our Dean, we thank you for always supporting us in whatever direction we have decided to go, for being interested in our work, and for your willingness to read (and even use!) what we have to say. To our colleagues at Virginia Commonwealth University School of Social Work, we thank you for your continual support and for your enthusiasm when we chatter about what we are writing.

Most of all we thank our students and our graduates/community practitioners who have inspired us to write this book. It is through the many classroom experiences we have had with you that we have truly learned what it means to plan for practice. You have asked the tough questions and helped us conceptualize what alternative planning would look like when we did not have textbooks to guide us. Your willingness to push the envelope has provided us with rich examples of what can happen when one trusts emergence.

F. Ellen Netting
Mary Katherine O'Connor
David P. Fauri

CHAPTER 1

Differences between Lines and Circles

Our romance with deliberate strategies has blinded us to the reality that all strategy is a pattern in a stream of actions involving both intensions and emergence.

—Henry Mintzberg, as paraphrased in *Getting to Maybe:*
How the World Has Changed

Chapter Outline

Lines and Circles as Planning Metaphors
  A Brief History of Lines and Circles
  Science and Reason
  Positivism versus Interpretivism
  Rational and Nonrational Thought
  Rational and Nonrational Problem-Solving and Decision-Making
Planning Theory: Both Lines and Circles
  Examples of Planning Approaches
The "Surety" of the Line and the "Tentativeness" of the Circle
A Conceptual Framework
Summary
Discussion Questions

Assumptions upon which the chapter is built:
- Reason can be linear and nonlinear (or circular).
- Circular reasoning, sometimes called nonrational thought, is different from irrational thought.
- Both rational and nonrational thought have a basis in the history of decision-making and planning.
- Both rational and nonrational thought bring strengths and challenges to the program planning process.

Practitioners have many different experiences with planning *programs*. Starting new programs from the beginning is often the task of founders, and provides a unique set of creative challenges. Many programs are inherited, making it necessary to simultaneously redesign or make changes at the same time that one is carrying out current plans. Smaller organizations may have only one program, which means that planning the program is organization-wide, whereas within larger organizations various programs are units representing a range of sizes. These programs are siblings within a larger setting. Public programs are typically *mandated* by law and come with various regulatory strings attached. Yet other programs come to life from the grassroots up, being designed to address felt needs. Programs come in all sizes and forms, and some are considered *models*, *demonstrations*, or *pilots* as various constituencies watch to see if and how they "work." Others are planned as replications of existing or earlier efforts. Programs can be described as being mainstream, alternative, hybrid, direct service, advocacy, and a host of other terms.

Thus, planning programs is not one unique set of activities that move in one specific way. For example, in a study of fourteen social programs, Goldberg (1995) found that no single approach to practice could be found and that "effective programs were developed with a variety of methods" (p. 614). We see program planning as an unlimited number of possibilities for creative thinking. For example, have you ever been in a situation in which someone said, "We're spinning our wheels," yet in the process something new and interesting emerged? What was that about? Conversely, have you ever participated in something that was highly planful, in which a very specific set of goals and objectives was guiding the effort, but it simply did not work no matter how close one stuck to the plan? In the former situation, "spinning our wheels" is a metaphor for going in circles. In the process new ideas were emerging even though it felt redundant and unfocused. In the latter situation, having a detailed plan and placing it over a changing context might have meant that no one (no matter how skilled) could have preidentified how things would unfold. The program planning process unfolds in different ways, depending on its unique context. One *approach* does not fit all situations. We believe that both are useful and that the skilled practitioner must learn when to use different approaches. Both can be based on evidence in a world that is smitten with evidence-based practice. As you will see, the evidence used may be somewhat different in what, where, and when data are collected and analyzed.

Over a period of years a case management project was funded by a large private foundation. A health administrator, a social worker, a physician, and a nurse collaborated in responding to the request for proposals (RFP) to evaluate the project. There were eight project sites around the country, all of which had received funding to implement their case management interventions in physician practices in their respective locations. Each site was embedded in highly respected health care systems with dedicated, competent staff. The evaluation team began traveling to each site to assess these projects—each designed within its specific contexts. Each had measurable objectives, and on paper every project looked feasible. However, given local preferences, different practitioners performed case management.

Some were nurses, others were social workers, some were physician assistants, still others were nurse practitioners, and some had mixed disciplinary teams. Every site used a different assessment tool, based on the current instruments used in its health care environment. The work location of the case managers were different, given that some were colocated in physician offices, others were in adjacent buildings, and still others were in a central location from which they moved between physician offices on a regular basis. As the evaluation team interviewed various participants in these projects, it became increasingly clear that the projects were "apples and oranges," and the interventions were not the same, even though all were doing case management. Each project had its own culture, structure, and norms of intervention.

The team recognized that each project had to be evaluated based on its own objectives, not the overall objectives of the foundation because the projects were really not comparable. This was fine; but what they soon realized was that each project had its own challenges. A few were moving toward their objectives in what seemed to be a consistent way; however, the majority of sites were in constant flux given the changing nature of the health care field. Staff came and went; physician practices merged; patients' needs shifted; interorganizational relationships changed—and on and on. Original objectives became obsolete as project needs altered. Further, patient input during the intervention revealed a whole set of needs that had not been originally identified. Yet the foundation held the projects accountable to the original plans they had proposed in their grant applications because that was what the projects had contracted to do. The evaluation team had difficulty remaining detached. In fact, every time the team made a visit and asked questions, new issues and concerns emerged about how a project had or needed to change to make it responsive to patient needs.

In this example, very well-written plans were still on file in the foundation offices, but many of them had become obsolete in the process of implementation. Being tied to these plans became a dilemma for staff and for the evaluation team. Without the latitude to change in midstream, it became clear to the evaluation team that these projects were propelling forward, actually "doing" things differently but "pretending" that the plans they had submitted were what they were carrying out. How many times have practitioners found themselves in situations where they remain tethered to obsolete plans because the plans did not allow for flexibility? How many times do experts write plans that do not consider client needs or the views of various stakeholders, feasibility, or context? How often do program coordinators inherit plans that look logical on paper only to find that they do not hold up in "real life?" How often do funders require a particular format that demands up-front *outcomes* when the "real" outcomes have to emerge in process? If any of these questions ring a bell with you, then you may find what follows to be useful.

LINES AND CIRCLES AS PLANNING METAPHORS

Some scientific thought distinguishes no difference between a line and a circle. This is supported by the idea that if you make the line long enough, it ultimately becomes a circle. Senge asserts that, "Reality is made up of circles but we see straight lines" (1990, p. 71). In this book we are concerned with lines and circles and what they have to do with how one thinks about and does program planning.

Metaphorically, lines and circles conjure up different images. Being linear includes moving in a concerted direction: upward, downward, backward, forward, or sideways. Circles also have directionality, but they go round and round, reconnecting with themselves. While linearity implies the ability to move in different directions, circularity means reiteration. Some things work better using lines, whereas other things work better using circles, and yet others work better using lines and circles at different times. For example, seams need to be straight. The seamstress who sews only in circles cannot make a seam! Yet wheels need to be circular in order to roll. A linear wheel could not exist or work, yet a circular wheel propels one forward in a splendid manner. Sometimes to roll things forward, the attention needs to move from the wheel to the axle (a line) that connects two wheels. The basic premise of this book is that program planning can be linear, circular, or a combination of the two—lines and circles. The key is recognizing when it is appropriate and feasible to plan in which of these ways.

It is helpful to look at the differences between lines and circles based on what they can represent symbolically in Western thought and what they have to do with program planning. To understand the choice-making patterns in *decision-making* that go into seizing opportunities and/or *problem-solving* of any sort, it is necessary to understand differences between linear (deductive) thinking and circular (inductive) thinking. Reasonable thinking can include either and may include both.

To make the distinctions, we will take a quick look at the history of reason in Western thought and how it has influenced what is considered acceptable rigorous thinking for knowledge building. This history reveals what has happened in the tension between *induction* and *deduction*, as ways of coming to know. It may also help clarify the basis of the scientific controversy between *positivism* and what has come to be known as *interpretivism* (in postmodern research). This discussion should provide the building blocks for the focus of the chapter, the differences between *rational* and *non-rational thought* in the influence of planning theories and the resulting need to distinguish approaches to program planning.

Now hold your breath a moment because we are going to take you on a brief but complicated historical journey. When you come up for air we hope you have a deeper understanding of how lines became privileged over circles. You will see differences between a line and a circle when it comes to planning, the costs and benefits of deduction and induction, and rational and nonrational thought. This will also lead to distinguishing differences between nonrational and *irrational thought* approaches and identification of when rational or nonrational approaches to problem-solving will best serve your needs. If there is bias in our presentation, it is that both rational and nonrational approaches need to be privileged in order to skillfully plan quality programs.

A Brief History of Lines and Circles

Science and Reason

As early as the 1700s, debates raged about human nature and the development of knowledge. Philosophers known as *Continental Rationalists* took the position that what is known about nature could be reasoned by using one's intelligence, while other philosophers, *British Empiricists*, took the position that knowledge about the environment came from experience, or sense data. Philosophers such as Locke, Berkley, and Hume struggled with ideas about what constituted science. Was it based on physics and mathematics, or did the true basis of scientific knowledge rest on empirical verification rather than personal experience?

At the turn of the twentieth century, the Vienna Circle composed of scientific thinkers like Schlick, Hahn, Carnap, Ayers, and Wittgenstein extended the thinking of the early empiricists in influencing the development of *logical empiricism* and *logical positivism*. Logical empiricism asserted that the true basis of knowledge rests in empirical or evidence-based verification rather than on personal experience. The Logical Positivists believed that the task of science is to clarify basic concepts, rejecting the abstractions of metaphysics and meaning in favor of findings grounded on empirical evidence. Keys to this position are familiar aspects of the *natural sciences*: logic, methodology, and validation procedures.

Thanks to Comte and other Positivists active in the nineteenth and the early twentieth centuries, these methods were transferred almost without question (for an exception, see the life work of Karl Popper) and applied to human agency, later known as social science. It was Comte in *The Positive Philosophy* (1855, trans 1974) who first coined the term "sociology" and saw it as being the most complex of sciences, a naturalistic one that can both explain the past development of humankind and predict its future course. With this, the application of positivist ideals to social phenomena was almost complete. The belief that all true human knowledge is contained within the boundaries of science became the accepted norm in Western thought. Humanity was to be studied in the same scientific manner as the world of nature, through observations, development of hypotheses, and experimentation.

Induction, defined as making inferences of a generalized nature from particular instances, became the preferred method of consolidating the observational link between science and reality, not only for the natural, but also for the social sciences. This is in contrast to deduction, a method by which knowledge, inductively generated, is applied to situations not yet observed. Induction, going from the general to the specific, became preferred over deduction, going from the specific to the general.

Embedded in this philosophy about what constitutes science, including the study of human nature, is the assumption of the role of *reason* in human behavior and human understanding. For the most part, the Empiricists and Positivists were also Rationalists who, according to Fay (1996) explain human actions by providing their rationale; "to show how [these actions] were the rational thing to have done given agent's beliefs and desires" (p. 92). From this, it should be clear that the belief about *human agency* is that humans engage in certain inferential processes (think induction) and act on that basis. Rationalists, then, assume that any act based on a reasoning process where the premises do not warrant the conclusions (think deduction), is a product of irrationality. The idea is to use reason to reduce information to its most elegant or simplest form. Based on the *reductionistic* goals that developed as positivism developed, the only "real" reasoning became linear reasoning. Rational thinking became understood as linear thinking and, thus, became accepted as reason. Linear thinking became the "gold coin" of thinking until the more recent postmodern critique of positivism gained momentum. With that critique came an opening for more interpretive approaches to human understanding. Mid-twentieth-century postmodern philosophy of science with its roots in continental rationalism has embraced nonlinear thought as a valid way of systematically coming to know.

Positivism versus Interpretivism

As we develop the idea that there are a variety of respectable ways of reasoning, it is also important to understand the difference between positivist and interpretivist ways of knowing. Traditional positivistic scientific thought favors exclusively rational (think linear) conduct of research and data analysis through carefully defined variables, sample frames, and data collection mechanisms based on the belief that prediction and control of events and variables are of interest and are possible. Good science will result in powerful generalizations about human behavior comparable to those found in natural science. This positivist frame assumes that any social phenomenon has real existence outside the individual and that knowledge is hard and measurable. What is of interest is the *objective* nature of social reality and relating to what is (Rodwell, 1998).

The modern approach to positivism, including *Post-Positivists*, tends to be *realist, determinist,* and *nomothetic,* or attending to the rule-governed nature of reality. Positivism seeks to provide rational explanations of social affairs. While being pragmatic and problem-oriented, it continues to apply the reason, models, and methods of the natural sciences to the social sciences out of an assumption that the social works, like the natural works. Both are seen as composed of relatively concrete empirical facts and relationships that can be identified (Burrell & Morgan, 1979). Once identified, these facts or artifacts can be studied and measured through reductionistic approaches, providing an *etic* or outsider's/expert's perspective. For positivists, a more linear reasoning would be most appropriate to accomplish their goals.

In contrast, the interpretive approach seeks understanding, rather than description or *generalization* (Imre, 1991; Tyson, 1995). Systematic inquiry is used to develop rich understandings of a situation. Mainstream, objective, controlled, or experimental quantitative methods are not preferred, as they are unsuited for deeply probing into sociobehavioral phenomena. Objective social reality is rejected in favor of deep, contextualized understandings from the participants' or actors' *emic,* or insiders' points of view. Interpretivist approaches to knowledge building are acknowledged to be a mix of the rational, serendipitous, and intuitive—allowing many learning opportunities in the effort to understand. This perspective assumes that while producing accurate but not objective (in the positivistic sense) information, processes and products can be warm, full, and artistic with meaning for both the planner and the user (consumer) communities.

Operating from an interpretive perspective asserts that the world, as it is, can be understood, but that understanding happens at the level of subjective experience. Individual consciousness and *subjectivity* are basic to understanding (Dilthey, 1976; Polanyi, 1958), and reality is actively created from this understanding (Gadamer, 1989; Merleau-Ponty, 1994). The social world is an emergent social process created by the participants. Universal laws are rejected in favor of highly individual, unique, and *emergent logic*. Social reality is little more than a network of assumptions and intersubjectively shared meanings among those participating in the social construction. Multiple realities or truths, rather than a single reality or truth, replace that which can be known, making reductionism an impossible goal for interpretive approaches. There is no generalizable truth, so the point of reference is toward understanding ongoing, ever changing processes (Burrell & Morgan, 1979). Realities, then, can only be studied holistically, making prediction and control impossible. For Interpretivists, a more circular approach to reason is appropriate and useful.

Essentially, the basic *ontological* (what is real) and *epistemological* (how we come to know it) assumptions of the positivist and interpretivist perspectives are fundamentally at odds. History would suggest that the perspectives do not so much differ as they compete (Deising, 1991), making it impossible to hold certain positivist assumptions while also holding interpretive assumptions without living in a state of paradox. One cannot assume both single and multiple realities at the same time without experiencing a paradox; nor can the planner and the object of inquiry both be at an objective distance while also entering into supportive interaction. One cannot produce both nomothetic (rule governed and generalizable) knowledge while also viewing knowledge as idiographic or individualized. Unfortunately, for many who are comfortable with a more holistic, intuitive approach to knowledge building, in the philosophy of science competition regarding "real science," positivist approaches favoring controlled experiences involving quantitative data collection have become the gold standard for good science, over the more emergent and more qualitatively oriented interpretive approaches. Positivism, reason, and linearity have shaped the scientific discourse.

In terms of the program planning process in the foundation-funded medical case management project described earlier in this chapter, the issues are no different. Differing assumptions were present in varying ways of problem-solving, based on different assumptions in each project about reality or *Truth*. The foundation embraced the objectives in the proposals submitted by each of the eight sites as "Truth," and whatever outcomes were developed became the only outcomes to be pursued. Such linear, rational thinking is more congruent with the positivist position. The sites, on the other hand, experienced the need for engaging in circular, nonrational thinking, which is more congruent with interpretive approaches. This does not mean they would not have eventually come up with new outcomes and different plans, but they needed the flexibility to take what was learned in process and mull it over (spin their wheels) until new, feasible, context-based directions emerged. However, due to the positivist/interpretivist science competition, these alternative approaches to rational thinking are rarely discussed or recognized as legitimate for program planning, and the foundation was not open to entertaining them. Thus, the various participants in this large multisite project felt they were not using their energies well when they were not able to move forward in a linear way. In actuality, we think this was productive planning. It was just different from the dominant view of how planning should occur.

Rational and Nonrational Thought

A basic premise for this chapter is the existence and use in problem-solving of both linear and circular thinking, both of which can be important to the planning process. To understand how both rational and nonrational thought serve the planning process, it is important to understand the basic premises of each. It should not be surprising to see that rational thought is congruent with the positivistic assumption that there exists a single, immutable truth that can be discovered.

Based on this, rational thought extends to include the idea that most decisions can be made through a series of well-defined steps that follow a predictable or fixed linear sequence, moving toward a predetermined goal. Decisions are made through a reductionistic assessment of the most benefit for the least cost. The decisions conform to objective and determinant rules to forecast costs and benefits after completing assessment of alternatives, including their positive and negative consequences. Linear reason helps to make appropriate selections among alternatives geared to minimizing objections while maximizing benefits. A comparison of rational and nonrational thinking is provided in Table 1.1.

Table 1.1
Rational/Nonrational: Comparison of Thought Processes for Planning

Rational	Nonrational
Single truth	Multiple, competing truths
Thoughts constructed through series of well-defined steps	Thoughts must include multiple understandings
Steps follow fixed sequence	No fixed sequence of analytic steps
Process linear	Process nonlinear
Based on market (biggest bang for the buck)	Based on power and politics
Most benefit, least cost	Context is everything
Decisions based on objectivity and determinant rules	Decisions based on influence
Goal: prediction based on objectives, alternatives, consequences	Goal: getting what is "good" and avoiding what is "bad"
Decisions from selecting alternatives and minimizing objections	Making sense of paradox and politics
Reason as the basic building block	Reasoning by metaphor and analogy
Decisions made with assumptions of precision and linearity	Decisions made with clarity and reason, but more fluid and circular

Adapted from Fauri, Netting & O'Connor, 2005, p. 105.

The nonrational approaches, in keeping with interpretive assumptions, recognize a multiplicity and complexity of truths where understanding, rather than control, is possible. The thought process is context-embedded. It is attentive to all things, including power and *historicity*, that serve to influence processes, so that no fixed design or set of analytic steps can be predetermined or asserted to be useful at all times. Instead, a fluid notion of thought, one using both analogy and metaphor through both induction and deduction, allows a holistic view of the situation to emerge. This provides clarity about what might be best in a particular situation while avoiding what might be bad. Reductionism is not appreciated here because everything and anything may be important and should be considered and questioned in order to make the best decision for the moment. This sort of *satisficing* conclusion can only be achieved through a comprehensive, amorphous, circular thought pattern.

Though rational thought might be seen to be more appropriate for controlling unexpected influences in problem-solving in a *hierarchical*, expert-driven manner, the nonrational, emergent approach has the capacity to attend to the political and the contextual in a more *collaborative* or *hermeneutic* way. In cultures steeped in rationality and positivism, rational thinking for problem-solving may be assumed to be the only way to achieve good decision-making. In other cultural contexts with linguistic and cultural patterns that are more circular, the nonrational thought patterns may be assumed to be more natural. Looking at the differences that accrue when rational or nonrational thought is applied to problem-solving, we move closer to articulating an alternative to the traditional prescriptive program planning approach currently dominating accountability standards throughout the world. Our concern is that without considering the possible need for alternative approaches to problem-solving and decision-making, we unthinkingly would be using rational planning, regardless of the ontological, epistemological, and linguistic assumptions undergirding thought patterns within the environmental or organizational contexts in which planning occurs. This would create challenges for culturally relevant and technologically appropriate programming worldwide. It is our suspicion that even when there is a high degree of positivistic influence, nonrational approaches to problem-solving and decision-making are enacted in secret, with a sense that they are not quite legitimate. This is what happened when the eight health care sites in our earlier example did one thing, but pretended to be doing another.

Rational and Nonrational Problem-Solving and Decision-Making

Most existing decision-making and planning approaches are based on rational models (see, e.g., Kettner, Moroney & Martin, 1999; Netting, Kettner, & McMurtry, 2008; Pawlak & Vinter, 2004). It is as if the only way to problem-solve is to do so rationally with a predetermined goal in mind. However, rational problem-solving is not without critique. For example, Hasenfeld (2000) sees the rational model as "theoretically weak and empirically untenable" (p. 92). His position recognizes the uniqueness and complexities of organizational situations in the face of the multitudes of goals, agendas, and problem-solving and service technologies. This understanding of organizational realities makes the reduction necessary for successful rational planning all but impossible.

The nonrational approach to decision-making makes that reduction unnecessary. The logic of this problem-solving process is not so much nonlinear as it is circular, allowing for the consideration of even the most tangential aspects. Knowledge will include multiple understandings reached through no fixed sequence of steps. If the process were to be characterized, it would look like the child's toy known as a Slinky, with its energy moving back and forth through circular loops of tempered steel wire with directionality, but no linearity. With no linearity, there is no possibility of reduction to one best way.

Our point in examining this brief and complicated history of how lines became privileged over circles is to distinguish two very different and respectable forms of problem-solving and decision-making. We hope we have made it clear that both ways of thinking have identifiable form and potential function in the planning process. In later chapters, we look more closely at the types of planning each approach will produce. For now it is important to see that rational and nonrational thought can be described, their processes articulated, and their consequences derived.

It is clear that nonrational thought is not irrational. Nonrational thought is as much based on reason as rational thought. It just uses reason differently and produces different results. Irrationality, on the other hand, does not have an identifiable logic or consequences that can be derived. Care must be given not to confuse irrationality with nonrational decision-making. Doing so limits the possibilities of applying nonrational thought processes in program planning and the potential for achieving, in certain situations, possibilities of another brand of guidance and clarity.

PLANNING THEORY: BOTH LINES AND CIRCLES

In 1979, Barclay Hudson compared planning theories that he identified as *synoptic* (rational), *incremental, advocacy, transactive,* and *radical.* The comparison remains relevant, especially in regard to the dominance of synoptic planning with its rational base as reflected in today's human service program planning texts. For example, Kettner et al. (1999) build their effectiveness-based program planning model on rational planning, which assumes that there is an expert planner, or at least someone who will guide a problem-solving process. Similarly, Pawlak and Vinter (2004) discuss service program planning as, "essentially a *rational* decision and an activity process carried out in successive stages of work. Planning is rational in that it is means-ends-driven process" (p. 11). The synoptic planning tradition is particularly relevant to publicly mandated programs that have explicit regulations and guidelines attached to them. These programs must be carried out to the letter, or they will not be continued. A rational process fits well with this type of programming. In light of our previous discussion, it should be obvious that synoptic, or rational, planning has a distinguished history.

The other planning theories in Hudson's comparison (incremental, advocacy, transactive, and radical) developed in reaction to what was seen as limits to the synoptic tradition. One can quickly see how this would happen, given the differences between rational and nonrational thought. As we investigate their respective underlying assumptions, you will see clues to program planning differences. It is within these theoretical perspectives on planning that the possibilities of alternative approaches to planning are grounded.

Incremental theoretical approaches involve compromises between competing groups in which the "most politically expedient policy rather than the best plan is adopted and implemented" (Hardina, 2003, p. 256). Incremental planning fits well with planning pilot or demonstration projects because of its short-term nature. For example, a common strategy used by persons with new ideas is to develop a pilot project instead of creating a fully conceptualized program. Why? Because if the idea behind the project is controversial at all, there is a good chance that decision-makers will agree to support a temporary pilot project, whereas they would not even consider a long-term commitment to a program. This allows the project to demonstrate its worth and buys time for the initiators to negotiate and bargain with persons in power. For example, Chambers and Wedel (2005) talk about *pilot projects* as "likely to be the loosest type of demonstration program and the ones whose objectives are most subject to change. A pilot project searches for unexpected outcomes, and the program design is changed on a simple trial-and-error basis 'to see what happens' as a result" (p. 71). Charles Lindblom (1959) is associated with incremental planning because of his famous article on "the science of mudding through" in which he criticized rational planning traditions for their insensitivity to the politics of planning in a free market economy and a democratic political-economy. As we will see later, one might even call Lindblom one of the "fathers" of the emergent approach to planning we introduce in Chapter 4.

Advocacy, transactive, and radical theoretical approaches to planning engage various groups, sometimes referred to as *constituencies* or *stakeholders*, in the planning process and stress inclusiveness as a precursor to large-scale change. Advocacy planners respond to group interests, recognizing pluralistic needs and demands. This assumes involvement of multiple groups with different interests, making the process cumbersome and complex. These approaches are very interpretive in their historical roots. In the case of advocacy planning, the planner's skills in managing power dynamics take precedence over technical planning skills. Advocacy programs draw on this planning tradition, as do emergent planning approaches, to be discussed in later chapters.

Transactive planning focuses on maintaining as much face-to-face contact as possible in which mutual learning occurs. It is very relationship- and process-oriented, assuming that fundamental change can only be secured in this way. Advocacy and transactive planning are helpful approaches in planning programs of capacity building and sustainable community development in which buy-in by various constituent groups is essential. Transactive planning is also essential to the consensus building about both *problems* and solutions so necessary in more interpretive forms of planning. The adage that how the problem is defined in great part determines the solution very much fits here.

Radical planning theories assume the system in which planning is occurring is oppressive, and collaboration among all stakeholding groups is rarely possible due to power inequities. Here the focus is on empowerment of the oppressed so that transformative change assures oppressed groups share in the fruits of the system or engage in planning for systemic-level change. Planning and enacting plans guided by the radical planning theories require huge amounts of time, and generally involve conflict. To enact the full change process and the solutions proposed (when guided by radical planning theories) may not actually be feasible, certainly not at the programmatic level (Hardina, 2003).

Hudson (1979) points out that these schools of planning theory are not mutually exclusive, and each has something to contribute to the other. In rational planning, the intent is often to develop services, or gain access to services within existing systems, not to alter the fundamental nature of the system itself. Incremental planning guides project development so that ideas can be demonstrated and powerful parties can be appeased, building programs one step at a time and even retracing one's steps if one runs into difficulty. Advocacy planning, on the other hand, seeks to broaden the scope of whose voices are heard, perhaps bringing subjugated views to the planning process. Advocacy planning can be the beginning of moving toward systemic change. Similarly, process-oriented transactive planning can move participants in desired directions and is actually very interpretive in its nature, since the focus is as much on inclusion as it is on results. Therefore, transactive planning is a way to collect consumer-sensitive needs assessment data for developing personal service programs. It employs a more circular process and is highly relevant to interpretive or emergent approaches to planning, the focus of Chapter 4. Conversely, depending on the planning intent, transactive planning could be used as a beginning step in moving toward transformative change. Obviously, radical planning is most closely aligned with the intent of system transformation. It requires not settling for needs identification without altering the very mechanisms that exist to respond to those needs, which is often seen as maintaining the status quo that allows oppression to continue.

Table 1.2 provides an overview of these planning theories and the approaches to planning that come from each school of thought. Note how different ways of thinking will lead to different approaches.

EXAMPLES OF PLANNING APPROACHES

Hudson distinguished types of planning theory in 1979. Since his work, a plethora of efforts have been made to modify planning. Most pertain to entire organizations, even to communities, but are relevant to programs as well. We will provide some examples of the planning approaches that are useful because they reveal the continual process of trying to find approaches that "work" in an increasingly complex world.

Most readers will have some familiarity with *strategic planning,* which is a very rational, goal-oriented process often adopted by nonprofit and public organizations, although it was birthed in the business sector. "Strategic management is seen as a way to design and guide a course of planned change" (Kloss, 1999, p. 73). At the program level, strategic planning would be a very intentional process in which a program's mission is scrutinized, goals and objectives designed to fit hand-in-glove with the mission, and *strategies* and *tactics* identified to follow suit. This type of planning reflects the reductionalist nature of assumptions built on rationality.

Table 1.2

Planning Theories Having Different Approaches

Synoptic (rational) planning:
Is synonymous with a prescriptive type of problem-solving model.
Is based on linear thinking, with predetermined goals.
Assumes that it's possible to collect sufficient knowledge so that the best
plan is chosen.
Sees planner as expert.

Incremental planning:
Is based on Lindblom's (1959) approach to incremental decision-making.
Has policy and program plans determined through interest group negotiations.
Compromises may be mediated by government through satisficing.
Sees planner as pluralist decision-maker to gather information, use social
networks.

Advocacy planning:
Assumes policies and plans are determined through interaction of interest groups.
Planners work on behalf of specific groups involved in the planning process and
use methods best suited to represent the views of these groups.
Role of planner is to develop ways to equalize the decision-making playing field
and to advocate for a particular constituency group.
Is described as a pluralist approach that takes place in an atmosphere of
competition.
Success is more tied to use of power resources than to having technical skills.

Transactive planning:
Is carried out face to face with people affected by decisions.
Planners and participants engage in a process of mutual learning.
Both expert knowledge and knowledge acquired through experience.

Radical planning:
Focuses on social movements and grassroots community action.
Traditional planning is viewed as supporting the current capitalist system.
Planner's role is to help oppressed groups understand restrictions imposed on
them by the current system.
Focuses on the status quo as harmful and that action must be taken to address
social problems.

Based on Hudson, 1979.

Kloss (1979) describes *scenario planning,* which is based on a theater/play metaphor in which a script or story is developed. She credits a military strategist with the Rand Corporation in applying the term "scenario" to various projects in the 1950s and its subsequent successful use by urban planners in Paris during the 1960s. Rather than simply forecasting one way of things unfolding, scenario planning has been used to spin different scripts based on alternative narratives of what could happen in a particular process, essentially telling somewhat elaborate stories about the future. Three schools of scenario planning have emerged: (1) an intuitive school in which it was assumed that decisions are highly qualitative, with complex intellectual processes about understanding a multitude of internal and external factors; (2) a quantitative school using rational tools such as time-series analyses and traditional techniques of forecasting; and (3) a hybrid school in which mixed methods for analysis are used to propel future scenarios. Note how the privileging of various "evidence" in each of the three types may facilitate the spinning of different scenarios.

The concept of the *learning organization* is credited to Aries de Gues, a businessman involved in implementing scenario planning into a French company. The insights learned from scenario planning "suggest that one learns by observing and reflecting on the results of our experiences. Reflection allows to deduce new patterns and trends that we did not perceive before and to form new mental models and theories. We then apply these theories and test their implications. We observe and reflect on the results of our experiences, thus beginning the loop once again" (Kloss, 1999, p. 74). If this quote about scenario planning sounds vaguely familiar, it may be because it describes the Slinky of interpretive thinking. If you are thinking that the foundation in the example introduced early in the chapter would have done well to have allowed the eight case management projects to engage in a bit of Slinky-like scenario planning, rather than being bound by only one scenario, you see the usefulness of this approach.

The *Search Conference* has been used as a participatory planning model; it is closely aligned with advocacy and transactive planning. Its intent it to begin with a wide-open funnel, pulling in all possible stakeholders, so that the planning process is totally inclusive. "The Search Conference is like solving a jigsaw puzzle. The focus is on putting the right puzzle pieces of strategy together that will produce the desirable future. In a search conference, each person contributes knowledge about some pieces of the overall puzzle. The idea is to get the right people in the room—those whose presence is critical for doing the job" (Rehm & Cebula, 2000, p. 2). Based on following principles rather than recipes, search conferencing is a democratically oriented planning process in which every voice is heard. As you can see, this type of planning is very different from an individual or small group of founders initiating a program.

A *feminist model of planning* was proposed by Ellsworth and her colleagues (1982) to assist women in planning services for and with other women, either in traditional or nontraditional environments. Aiming to demystify the planning process, the model assumes that all women can and should be involved in planning, that there is a need to eliminate the expert/nonexpert dichotomy. Recognizing the central importance of power, they forgo rational dominant models of planning with clear differentiated steps and move toward cooperative processes that value "multidimensional thinking, intuitions, and feelings [as] viable options" (p. 151). Using coalitions of constituencies, the planning model includes "process orientation; divergent thinking; consumer input throughout the process; an open statement of values, biases, and assumptions; the collection of qualitative as well as quantitative data; criteria for service delivery that address the elimination of sexist, racist, and class-biased practices; integration of the principles of empower-ment; the use of process and outcome evaluation; and a commit-ment to the self-determination of all women" (p. 151). It should be clear to the reader that this approach is another example of an attempt to move toward nonrational and interpretive planning.

The "Surety" of the Line and the "Tentativeness" of the Circle

So what is the real difference between a line and a circle? For us it is the difference between being sure and the tentativeness of never knowing for sure. Each position has its attraction and each has great consequences for the program planning process. Each also has its role in program planning.

The rational *problem-solving model* has the surety of a beginning and an ending just the way a line begins and stops. Planned change and strategic planning models are built on surety. It is in keeping with the tradition of top-down hierarchy and bureau-cratic models of organizing, steeped in the tradition of the Indus-trial Revolution whereby factory overseers and managers found the one best way to get from raw material to a finished product. The line shows the way to get from point A to point B with the least interference possible. A line is precise, clean, clear, and effi-cient. A line can be comforting in a complex world because it helps one know where to go next.

However, the efficiency of linear planning approaches may or may not be effective. The reductionism in linear thinking may cause the planner to overlook or underemphasize essential information needed for effective decision-making. The planning may be glori-ously precise and clear but impossible to enact because of inatten-tion to the vagaries of the *conditions* at hand, just as some of the sites in our case management example discovered.

Nonrational problem-solving, by virtue of its high sensitivity to power, politics, and contextualized particulars, provides no assurance of a "right" answer. There is no way to be certain, just as there is no way to determine where a circle begins or ends. You start where you can and end where you must. What works for here and now may not work tomorrow. What seems right now may need to change in response to new information. The circle, even when closed, continues to reverberate with more actions and reactions. It is much more tentative in nature than the rational linear alternative.

Note the metaphors used in more circular planning models— the scripts of plays having multiple scenarios, searching for the puzzle pieces—but most importantly note the broad-based inclusiveness required. Perhaps staff at the foundation in our case management example felt overwhelmed by eight sites, all with different constellations of stakeholders, emerging in different directions. It certainly overwhelmed the evaluators who spent a good deal of time trying to make sense of the situation. In Chapter 4, we will talk about sense-making, which is a very interpretive process. In the meantime, we hope that Chapters 2 and 3 will help you to make thoughtful decisions about how to plan for relevant, effective programs.

A CONCEPTUAL FRAMEWORK

Throughout this chapter we italicized words to indicate they are terms defined in the Glossary. We will continue this convention throughout the book as we introduce new concepts. We recognize that some of the words we are using are defined differently, depending on the source. Therefore, we encourage you to refer to the Glossary as a reminder of how we define them in this work.

In this chapter, we presented a conceptual framework that moves from different ways of knowing (philosophy) to different ways of

Table 1.3

Hierarchy of Key Concepts

Ways of Knowing (Philosophy)	Positivism	Interpretivism
Ways of Thinking (Thought)	Rational	Interpretive (nonrational)
Ways of Doing (Approaches)	Prescriptive	Emergent

thinking. In Table 1.3, we list key terms that form the conceptual framework for the book. The broadest terms are positivism and interpretivism, ways of knowing that lead, respectively, to rational and nonrational thinking. Thus, we are using rational and interpretive (nonrational) planning to distinguish between ways of thinking about planning. In later chapters we will move along the hierarchy to different ways of approaching planning that logically flow from different ways of knowing and thinking.

In Chapter 3, we will focus on rational planning and prescriptive approaches such as the logic model, problem-solving model, or planned change model (step-by-step processes leading to predetermined goals). Note that the term "model" is only used with prescriptive approaches because a model is defined as a conceptual structure consisting of various dimensions or parts that can be used to guide a particular type of practice in a regularized direction. This is a rational process.

In Chapter 4, we will focus on interpretive planning and emergent approaches in which goals are not predetermined. Emergent approaches attempt to remove barriers to innovation through intense interactions, networking, and information exchange among those with a stake in change, based on the assumption that they should be empowered to create and re-create as new discoveries occur using nonlinear, unpredictable strategies.

This language of rational and interpretive planning, prescriptive and emergent approaches, will be repeated throughout the book. Table 1.3 sets the stage for things to come.

SUMMARY

Programs start in many ways, created by founders, inherited by others, responding to initiatives, and/or mandated by decision-makers. Some resemble lines, conforming to a rational, linear approach in which a predetermined goal is targeted. Others resemble circles, with planners starting wherever they can in an ongoing, fluid process. Still others move from one approach to the other, and vice versa, depending on the circumstances.

A brief history of lines and circles as metaphors for how one views the world points out the historical privileging of rational over nonrational (which is different from irrational) thought. Rational thought is inductive; what is observed in the larger world is used to inform planning (going from the general to the specific). Nonrational thought is deductive, requiring planners and participants to learn in process, going from the specific to the general. Positivistic ways of knowing lead to rational approaches; whereas interpretive ways of knowing lead to nonrational approaches.

Five planning traditions are recognized: synoptic (rational), incremental, advocacy, transactive, and radical. The latter four emerged in reaction to the dominance of the rational tradition. Examples of recent planning approaches are introduced, including strategic planning, scenario planning, search conferencing, and a feminist model of planning.

In this chapter, we are making no assertion of supremacy of one way of problem-solving in planning over another, just as there is no argument here over whether positivism or interpretivism is better for knowledge building. At issue is how well the assumptions of a perspective, and the subsequent type of logic, fit the context and the need. Neither way of problem-solving in planning is better than the other. Each is different, capable of producing different kinds of information for knowledge building and planning. The challenge for the planner is to determine congruence with the broadest goals and values in the context of the planning process in order to produce a relevant product with utility for the task at hand.

DISCUSSION QUESTIONS

1. This chapter describes lines and circles, but others have used different metaphors. What metaphors come to mind as you think about different approaches to planning programs? Think about programs you are either involved in or familiar with: what metaphors best describe how they are planned?

2. What assumptions do you bring to the program planning process? Did this chapter make you rethink any of these assumptions? If so, how?

3. This chapter included a lot of technical terms. How might language be important in the planning process? How might you use certain terms to actually implant values into program planning? Can you give examples?

4. Locate a description of a human service program. You might look in program proposals, grant applications, or agency annual reports. What assumptions are embedded about planning in this description? What values are projected?

5. Select a program with which you are familiar and explain how you would plan for change in this program using a rational approach. Now use a nonrational approach. How do they differ? What felt most comfortable to you in the particular situation of the program?

6. Of the planning theories identified by Hudson, are there ones that you would like to use? Ones that you would probably not like to use? Why or why not? What might you gain and what would you give up in using each theory?

7. Can you think of other adjectives used to describe planning (e.g. contingency planning, continuity planning) with which you are familiar? How might the basic assumptions of the types of planning you have identified be applied to program planning? What would be their advantages and disadvantages?

CHAPTER 2

Programs: Containers for Idea Implementation

The term "program" has been used in social services for decades, and in many ways it has been taken for granted.

—Peter M. Kettner, Robert M. Moroney, and Lawrence L. Martin,
Designing and Managing Programs

Chapter Outline

Programs and Projects; Services and Interventions
    Programs and Projects
    Services and Interventions
Programs in Organizational Context
Program Planning
    Mandates and Initiatives
    Planning Different Types of Programs
Summary
Discussion Questions
Case Exercise: Chronic Pain

Assumptions upon which this chapter is based:

- Programs come in many forms and types.
- Programs and projects are not the same.
- Services and interventions give life to programs and projects.
- Programs are usually contextualized in organizations, but some programs constitute their own organization.
- Program planning will differ depending on the impetus for the program.
- Different types of programs also require different planning approaches based on their assumptions and theories.

In this chapter we provide an overview of what constitutes a program, and how programs and *projects* are interrelated. We consider programs to be the structural containers for long-term commitments usually composed of services and/or interventions designed to both directly and indirectly address human needs. Program designs can be as diverse as creative thought allows, and their development reveals how opportunities and problems are identified and pursued in many ways. We also place programs in context, reflecting on the consequences of being tethered to organizations and/or groups.

PROGRAMS AND PROJECTS; SERVICES AND INTERVENTIONS

We introduce the concept of programs as containers because containers come in so many forms and have varying characteristics. Rational program planning at its extreme implies that programs are like airtight containers in which the contents remain the same, no matter what happens. A secret is that containers may be anything but airtight. Conversely, nonrational program planning views programs as highly versatile containers that are expected to change and be used for varying purposes. When program plans do not fit with a group's expectations, regardless of which approach to planning has been undertaken, it is like trying to place an ill-fitting lid on a container. No matter what one does, it just doesn't work well. Another container may be needed.

Like ideas, programs come in all sizes and forms. Some have large sets of interconnected services with complicated regulations and guidelines attached. Others are quite simple and straightforward. The term "program" is so much a part of common parlance that it is often taken for granted. Yet program roles are complicated and powerful. They are the critical units or components within human service organizations. They translate organizational mission into action. They are the pivot points of evaluation and outcome measurement. Program success, or failure, affects organizational survival and individual, community, and even societal change (Netting, O'Connor, & Fauri, 2007).

For example, the Medicare program is a complex federal initiative, with multiple parts administered through thousands of staff members in offices throughout the United States. Conversely, small grassroots single-office health programs serve only a small area, but their efforts may be just as important to local participants. The Smithville Friendly Visiting Program, designed to reach isolated elders in a rural community involves just 10 committed volunteers and a half-time supervisor in carrying out its interventions. The structures of the "containers" are incredibly different in scope and complexity for the national Medicare program and the Smithville Friendly Visiting Program, but they have a great deal in common. They both focus on the needs and potential needs of older and disabled citizens. Both are built on thoughts, aspirations, and processes that have moved beyond the idea stage. These ideas have come alive in the real world of implementation, and the resulting actions are intended to create change or betterment in human living conditions.

Programs have been defined as prearranged sets of tasks designed to achieve a set of goals and objectives (Netting, Kettner, & McMurtry, 2004, p. 327). Pawlak and Vinter (2004) view a program "as a composite of linked services that constitute an integrated enterprise" (p. 5). Netting and O'Connor (2003) identify three types of programs that are often part of the human service landscape: direct service, staff development and training, and support programs (p. 296). Let's take a brief look at each.

Direct service programs focus on clients. Pawlak and Vinter (2004) call these *human service programs*, "designed to provide specific benefits of some kind to particular persons who are believed to have distinctive needs and problems" (p. 4). Usually, they are administered under the *auspices* of a formal nonprofit or public agency, with the appropriate staff to deliver the services in a particular location with a particular set of goals.

Staff development and training programs target staff by providing additional knowledge and skills for better direct service provision or for performing at a higher capacity. Essentially, they are capacity-building-focused, investing in staff skills and abilities. They may not directly benefit clients or consumers, but the assumption is that if staff members are appropriately nurtured and trained, they will be equipped for better practice, benefiting clients. Clients are the ultimate beneficiaries, even though staff are the immediate target. In truth, the ultimate beneficiaries in any social program should be the clients in need.

Support programs are intended to assist direct service or staff development and training programs (Netting and O'Connor, 2003, p. 296). Examples of these are research and development or fundraising programs, in which ideas about how to increase resources are the focus. When one hears complaints about the infrastructure in an organization, it is typically because support programs are not adequately developed. *Advocacy programs* are support programs because they are geared to "systematically influence decision-making in an unjust or unresponsive system" (Schneider & Lester, 2001, p. 64) by facilitating either *case* (individual) or *cause* (collective) problem-solving. Their intent is to make things better by persuading decision-makers and persons with power to take action or allow action to be taken for the betterment of human need. The program types just discussed are summarized in Table 2.1.

Unrau, Gabor, and Grinnell (2001) spend an entire chapter of their book, *Evaluation in the Human Services*, on "What Is a Program?" (p. 33). They identify four ways that programs are named, based on: *function* (e.g., respite program, family counseling program); *setting* (e.g., housing program, day care program); *target population*

Table 2.1

Types of Programs

Program Type	Characteristics
Direct Service	Focuses on client or consumer-based care provision. Designed to provide specific benefits to specific people. Typically administered by a human-service-type agency. Hires clinical or direct service staff.
Staff Development/Training	Focuses on staff who need specialized knowledge and skills. Is capacity building. Assumes that once staff are developed/trained, they will be able to perform better.
Support	Focuses on assisting the work of the organization or group. Comes in multiple forms (e.g., advocacy, research and development, fundraising).

(e.g., elder services program, child care program); or *social problem* (e.g., child abuse program; crime prevention program). The emphasis in this *typology* is on the combining of functions, as organizing principles, with program delivery. "Like an agency, a program is an organization that also exists to fulfill a social purpose. There is one main difference, however; a program has a narrower, better-defined purpose and is always nested within an agency" (p. 42). In small agencies, it may be that there is only one program, and that program and agency are actually one and the same.

Programs and Projects

The terms "program" and "project" are often used interchangeably; yet they are defined differently in textbooks. "Projects are much like programs but have a time-limited existence and are more flexible so that they can be adapted to the needs of a changing environment. Projects, if deemed successful and worthwhile, are often permanently installed as programs" (Netting, Kettner, & McMurtry, 2008, p. 329). In the previous chapter, we noted that Chambers and Wedel (2005) are very specific about the definition of a pilot project as the "loosest type of demonstration program[s] and the ones whose objectives are most subject to change" (p. 71). Thus, projects can be viewed as one-time operations of shorter duration (Pawlak & Vinter, 2004). It could be said that projects are miniprograms or pilots that test out whether ideas will work in the real world. Then, projects rise to program status, *if* they are viewed as working well and are seen as relevant to problem-solving.

Some programs have cycles, such as after-school programs, that ebb and flow with the academic year. Others have a sense of constant flow, such as hospice programs in which people in need of support in the dying process are encountered throughout the year.

Regardless, all programs are seen as ongoing—at least until they are no longer needed or discontinued.

Assumptions are embedded in current definitions of programs and projects. First, programs are assumed to be "prearranged," implying that someone has the capacity to predict the future or at least reasonably determine what needs to happen. One can quickly identify how rational this assumption is. In contrast, an interpretive view would assume that prearrangement is illusory, and as the planned arrangements are tried, the need for other arrangements will emerge.

Second, there are, alternatively, either sets of tasks or linked services. Linked services assume complexity in which various elements are connected and must occur, rather than a single set of actions. Linked services may have to be flexible rather than fixed and occurring in a specific order. Cohen-Mansfield and Bester (2006) provide an example of a dementia care program designed at the Adards nursing home in Australia. Rather than having a lockstep set of tasks in this 30-bed unit for persons with various dementia and behavioral problems, the guiding principle in program design is flexibility. "Flexibility in regard to residents is manifested in their ability to control the time they get up, eat, go outdoors, and go to sleep. Therefore, different residents eat, get dressed, and are active at different times of the day" (p. 541). Valuing flexibility has implications for everything that happens, including hiring extended-care assistants on floating time schedules, rather than having traditional nursing assistants tied to three specific shifts; providing specialized training for staff; encouraging families to come in at any time, rather than having regular visiting hours; and working with residents to accommodate to their schedules and needs. Cohen-Mansfield and Bester see the use of a flexible approach to fit well with "new business paradigms. Whereas the old paradigm stressed hierarchy and centralization of control, formal rules, and strict separation of private life from work, the new [approach] allows self-organization, more complexity, and more responsiveness and respect . . . " (p. 544). This example reveals how a nonrational approach to program planning might be used, rather than rationally planning for a single set of tasks to be performed.

Third, actions are targeted to "a set of *goals* and *objectives*," the achievement of which reveal that the program "works." The proliferation of books on program evaluation attest to effectiveness-based (or performance-based, or outcomes-based) program planning, which requires determining *in advance* where a program is going and what it is to achieve. For example, Unrau, Gabor and Grinnell state that, "Programs are born via program logic models . . . plausible and logical plans for how programs aim to produce change for their clients" (p. 42). But in the example of Adards nursing home, the goals and objectives might have to be flexible as well, changing as residents' needs change, but also changing as new technologies to deal with dementia emerge. In that situation, there might be alternate ways to be effective, rather than simply one best way.

SERVICES AND INTERVENTIONS

If programs are composed of sets of tasks or, alternatively, linked services, then it is important to know what constitutes *services*. Service means directly intervening to address human need. For example, an adult who is having difficulty coping with life issues seeks counseling at child and family services (CFS). Counseling is a service, among others, offered by CFS, and it is provided by professional social workers trained to use cognitive restructuring methods. This intervention will hopefully help the client address life issues in a different way and, ultimately, be better able to cope. But let's assume that this client is a recent immigrant with limited English language skills. Coping has an entirely different meaning in this situation, and unless the counselor is culturally sensitive and able to intervene in a culturally competent way, he or she will not be able to address human need in this case. It would behoove CFS, therefore, to have a staff development and training program in place to keep its counselors up to date on methods used to work with diverse population groups as the composition of the local community changes, especially if the agency case load is shifting in this direction.

Some services are interventions to address human needs directly, while others indirectly impact human need; and these are equally important. *Macrointerventions* are sets of coordinated or linked actions, often engaging numerous participants in organizational, community, or policy arenas. These interventions, often called macro-level strategies and tactics, are programmatic as well, and are often performed in tandem with direct service intervention. For example, if the same counselor who was seeing a recent immigrant began to find his or her caseload swelling as many new immigrants arrived in the community, not only would the counselor's need for development and training increase but he or she might begin to see patterns. Patterns might include an influx of people who are struggling to adjust to the culture, parents who are having difficulty finding jobs, and children who are forsaking traditional cultures from their homelands for American lifestyles. In addition to providing direct services, interventions might include advocating for sensitive policy change and participating in community outreach.

PROGRAMS IN ORGANIZATIONAL CONTEXT

Programs should not be confused with *organizations*, which are generally understood to be "social unit[s] with some particular purpose" (Shafritz & Ott, 2001, p. 1). From our perspective, in human service organizations, individuals usually gather together to serve a particular purpose, and that purpose is served through operationalizing programs. Organization goals are achieved because programmatic tasks are completed by a collection of individuals able to achieve something more and better than that which could be achieved by a single individual. For the most part, programs develop within the cultural and technological context of organizations; and, of course, organizations develop within larger cultural and technological contexts, which sanction or approve their purposes.

Jewell, Davidson, and Rowe (2006) identify what they call "the paradox of engagement" in which political, organizational, and evaluative demands impact the planning, development, and delivery of community mental health services. Their findings from a well-controlled study of peer staff in community health teams reveal a scenario in which the expectations of policymakers and the realities of program planning diverge, resulting in a stalemate of opposite assumptions about program implementation and ultimate success. This study underscores the importance of recognizing when different assumptions and expectations collide in what appears to be rational program planning. Although their analysis reveals that the community mental health program has a positive effect on many clients, they:

> focus on why such a promising programmatic change was perceived as a political failure . . . while all actors . . . were concerned with improving outcomes for persons with mental illness, varied interests and pressures from different groups led to unintended and often unacknowledged disjunctures between political expectations and program capacities. . . . This paradox encompasses contradictions manifested in three areas: (1) which clients received services, (2) how the peer specialist's role was structured, and (3) how outcomes were evaluated (p. 5).

Programs do not always develop in response to organization-based mandates. Sometimes, programs are planned in response to a need, and evolve prior to the creation of the organization in which they are eventually housed. To some degree, then, a distinction between a program and an organization is the degree of structural complexity that surrounds actions geared toward "the enhancement of the social, emotional, physical, and/or intellectual well-being of some component of the population" (Brager & Holloway, 1978, p. 2). In other words, some programs are containers, nested within larger containers. In other programs, one container holds the organization and the program in homogenized fashion.

There is a chicken-and-egg kind of dilemma surrounding creative programming, in which some programs become organizations and others are placed within existing organizations. We recently witnessed this phenomenon in a study of 15 exemplary faith-related programs (Netting, O'Connor, & Singletary, 2007). This study revealed that founders placed their visions in viable contexts using four different strategies: (1) developing new organizations in which to place their programs, (2) temporarily incubating them until a new organization could be formed, (3) tethering them to congregations, or (4) birthing them in well-established faith-related agencies with deep historical roots in the community. These different strategies were used by various founders so that their visions would have the potential to become full-fledged, stable programs. The consequences were not only delivering the envisioned services but also influencing the identity of the programs' organizational homes, as well as the images of those homes held by the larger community. One example is a program for fathers that had started as an outgrowth of a community center. Attempting to create supports for fathers recently released from incarceration, to help them to be reunited with their children, the part-time director developed a board of committed men and then incorporated the program so that it became a one-program organization in the local community. The hope was that it would be seen as a place of refuge for men who had no other program directed at their needs, and that it would be trusted because the services were provided at the location of the public social service agency.

Programs are housed under the auspices of grassroots groups, voluntary associations, coalitions, nonprofit organizations, public agencies, and a host of others. Many times, the clients for whom programs advocate may be controversial, making the organizational base very important in providing an element of stability. All funded programs require at least some formal organizational structure to serve as a legal conduit for funding. Organizational auspices are important to the context, but it is the programmatic activity through which implementation of service vision comes alive.

Practitioners are often professionally affiliated with an organizational structure or structures—whether they are private practitioners within the confines of a small group practice or public officials within a complex web of bureaucratically entangled relationships. In their work practitioners encounter multitudes of organizations within their communities, regardless of where they perform their roles. They work in and with organizations, interfacing with a multiple network of organizations, all of which will have distinctive cultures. Throughout this book you will see the important role culture plays in all aspects of organization practice, to the degree that multicultural skills have become an important cornerstone for effective practice (Netting & O'Connor, 2003).

Organizations have been viewed by some theorists as situated in uncertain, turbulent environments in which they are constantly responding to *constraints* (things they can not change) and *contingencies* (things about which they have to compromise and negotiate). Yet it is not just the environments in which organizations operate that are uncertain and turbulent; organizations face internal uncertainties and turbulence as well. Organizations are dynamic, changing entities that are situated in dynamic and changing communities. Given the organizational linkage, this means that programs are like that as well.

It is important for practitioners to know how the organizations within which they practice are put together. One often hears the term "formal" used to describe an organization. This implies that there are also "informal" organizations. It is not always easy to define clear boundaries between what is a formal and what is an informal organization. For example, a group of committed citizens may organize to provide services to persons in need. In the process of organizing they may develop a statement of purpose, rally the support of volunteers, and structure their services. They are, technically, an informal group. But what happens when they decide to form a nonprofit corporation so that they can receive funding from outside sources? If they are incorporated, they are formally recognized as a nonprofit organization. They may still have the same purpose, continue to use volunteers, and structure their services the same way. Yet they are no longer just a "group"; they are an "organization," with very particular legal responsibilities. Perhaps there are degrees of formality. We cannot tell clearly when a group becomes a formal organization or when service delivery becomes formalized. Boundaries between organizational practice arenas are not always clear and distinctive (Netting & O'Connor, 2003) which may also mean that programs are not always clear and distinctive.

PROGRAM PLANNING

Program planning, regardless of organizational auspices, is about moving toward idea implementation and achieving the intent of the many stakeholders to the planning process. The genesis of planning for a program comes from many different directions, including public mandates and private initiatives. Stakeholders can be those with good intentions, those who have an idea of betterment, those who have the problem that the program is being designed to address, or those who participate primarily to gain something for themselves or their organization. In short, programs grow from planning, the impetus of which may be quite complicated.

MANDATES AND INITIATIVES

Program planning may begin when an enacted social policy faces implementation. For example, national policy mandates have led to the Food Stamp Program and to the Senior Nutrition Program. A combination of federal and state policies mandate and direct emergency food distribution to those eligible for food stamps or senior nutrition programs; whereas state or local policies may extend the mandate to include feeding programs for the homeless. Too often, policy advocates celebrate the final victory of getting a bill through a state legislature, only to realize that this is just the beginning and that a planning process must begin. To carry out policy intent, details of the program resulting from a policy have to be thought through. Enacted policies are usually intentionally vague about programmatic details because consensus could never be achieved if every detail were included in the legislation. Thus, it is important that there is a vision of how the policy will be implemented in programmatic form, and that vision may develop prior to, during, or after the policymaking process.

Obviously, not all programs are publicly mandated. When policy mandates are not in place but needs exist, sometimes programs develop in response to unmet community needs, designed by concerned grassroots community groups and/or staff in human service organizations. These are essentially community initiatives and may look very different from traditional mandated plans, given the possibility that the planning may include local groups that are not always highly professionalized but whose members engage in collegial interactions. Many times, this sort of planning is not limited by legal strictures about public services, so they may tend to be either more creative or more idealistic and less detailed. For example, when a local senior citizens center reopened under a new board of directors, local volunteers worked with the Area Agency on Aging (a nonprofit organization) and several elder providers and conducted an informal needs assessment of older persons within a five-mile radius. A task group of several older consumers and various stakeholders agreed to use the needs assessment data to guide their efforts in designing the center's program of services and activities, but without having a clear idea about specific funding sources or other limiting elements. These volunteer and collaborative efforts were not expert-driven but drew from the participants' life experiences and knowledge of the community. This informal program planning seemed to fit well with the needs of the participants, and it contrasted sharply with formalized planning processes in established agencies implementing mandated programs.

Program concepts spring from another place—funding sources. Funders can initiate program planning processes through various initiatives they propose. A foundation might issue a *request for proposals* (RFP) for community organizations to compete for funds to address a community problem, such as teen pregnancy or elder malnutrition. Competing for funding, local organizations will try to design the most innovative and least costly program feasible in their community. For example, one community wanted to address its high rate of teen pregnancy. A local school agreed to be the host organization, and a task force of representatives from various agencies that served teenagers was organized. The school social worker and nurse teamed up to write the grant, paying careful attention to the guidelines provided in the RFP. As the example suggests, by detailing specific demands or highlighting particular issues, foundations have a good deal of control by influencing which problems will receive special attention in local communities and which community groups will have the resources to tackle those problems if they want foundation support.

PLANNING DIFFERENT TYPES OF PROGRAMS

The term "program planning," as used in practice, reflects an assumption that the process most often involves designing direct or personal service interventions, or providing benefits, with and for service recipients. Chambers and Wedel (2005) recognize that "it is easier to set goals and objectives for a 'hard' benefit program (one that delivers goods like housing or food stamps) than it is to set them for personal social service 'soft benefits'" (p. 70). In the current funding environment, with its outcome focus, being skilled in designing direct service programs that document the achievement of personal services and measure specific goal achievement is critically important for practitioners. Practical program planning guides are available for that purpose (see, e.g., Kettner, Martin & Moroney, 1999; Pawlak & Vinter, 2004).

In most cases, funders are interested in supporting direct service interventions, but some have interests in staff development and training and advocacy actions (Netting, O'Connor, & Fauri, 2007). As Chambers & Wedel (2005) point out, if designing soft benefit programs with measurable outcomes was not challenging enough, some program planners also focus on indirect interventions. Staff development and training programs are focused on the needs of the persons who provide the services and not directly on consumers. Sometimes these programs are overlooked or disregarded because it is difficult to see the impact staff development and training have on clients. Philosophically, orientation, training, and continuing education are seen as important by many, but when it comes to taking staff time to engage in these actions (let alone plan and fund them), there may be resistance.

Probably, the difficult type of program planning to convince funders to support is even broader—social change, or cause advocacy, programming that seeks to alter the status quo, reforming the larger system, which may or may not include direct practice interventions. Such efforts are often guided by the more radical or transformative planning theories. Programs that do not offer direct services present complex measurement challenges in terms of program implementation and achievement of goals and objectives. There is also the possibility that funding sources or decision-makers may not want to have their names affiliated with a controversial set of issues or methods (Netting, O'Connor, & Fauri, 2007).

An example comes from a local ACLU that was attempting to develop and fund what it termed a "prisoner advocacy program." It hired a community organizer to systematically collect information on social justice violations against prisoners in the state's correctional facilities, mobilize interested constituencies to take action, and lead a campaign for prison reform. The goal was to promote prisoners' rights as a collective. It did not intend (nor did it have capacity) to address individual prisoners' needs. It was targeting the state correctional system for reform. This transformative change process was seen as controversial by funders because it threatened the status quo of what was a very punitive prison system, which had broad political support from politicians and the public in crime-ridden urban and conservative rural areas. Determining how to define and measure outcomes is very different for this type program than for one in which individual prisoner needs alone are to be addressed. In this example, direct services might have been acceptable and fundable, but this was an organization that considered itself to be an advocacy organization. It was not concerned with providing direct services, although those might have been more "fundable." The language of advocacy organizations that are rooted in "cause" or social change provide clues to understanding what is different about transformative program planning. Prison reform is quite different from helping prisoners one at a time. Beyond this, the question is how this level of change is translated into measurable programming. Clues can be found by investigating the auspices of these advocacy efforts—advocacy organizations themselves (Netting, O'Connor, & Fauri, 2007).

Another example is provided by Brooks (2005) in his case study of the Los Angeles Association of Community Organizations for Reform Now (ACORN). This reveals how one program can engage in both direct service and advocacy types of interventions simultaneously. ACORN's planning and organizational efforts did not originally include direct service provision, and this was the case for much of its history, heeding the advice of many who feared that more focused case advocacy efforts would reduce ACORN's ability to maintain its transformative goals. But in 1998, ACORN began providing individual case advocacy services without redirecting, diminishing, or fundamentally changing its larger-scale change efforts (Brooks, 2005). Similarly, Minkoff (2002) examined the role of hybrid organizational forms in which identity-based services and political action coexist. Thus, programs with different orientations do coexist under the same organizational auspice.

SUMMARY

In this chapter, we examine differences between programs, projects, and services/interventions. Programs are defined as a group of services or action linkages designed to address human need on an ongoing basis. Three types of programs are introduced: direct service, staff development and training, and support programs. Direct service programs, sometimes called human service programs, provide direct client benefits. Indirect benefits are obtained through staff development and training, in which providers become more knowledgeable and skilled in doing their jobs. Support programs also provide indirect benefits, and are designed to engage in fundraising or advocacy efforts. Advocacy planning is discussed as one type of support program, designed with macro-level interventions in mind. Projects, in contrast to programs, are short term (usually a year or less) and are used to discover what services or combinations of interventions might be helpful in addressing more complex human need.

Most programs exist in or are tethered to organizations, particularly if funding is involved. Organizations are defined as "a social unit with some particular purpose" (Shafritz & Ott, 2001). Some programs are nested in huge public agencies, while others reside in nonprofit or for-profit settings. Sometimes, small programs are their own organizations, thus making the program and organization the same entity.

Program planning is initiated as a result of public mandates, local community efforts, or foundation initiatives to meet identified needs. The genesis of a program is important because it will provide clues to what type of planning approach can (and perhaps should) be used. There are challenges in following the guidance of less traditional theoretical approaches, including managing accountability expectations that do not necessarily match the approaches or theories being used. These challenges will be the focus of much of what follows in Chapters 3 through 6.

DISCUSSION QUESTIONS

1. How would you define "program" to allow for maximum flexibility in program planning and design? How does your definition differ from other definitions you have seen in the literature?

2. Identify important differences between programs and projects.
3. In Chapter 2, we list three types of programs (direct service, staff development/training, and support). Come up with another typology of programs and make a case for why your typology is more helpful than the one we use.
4. Services are defined in this chapter. Provide examples of services for each program type you have identified in your typology in question 3.
5. How do organizations differ from programs? How are they the same? Select an example of an organization with which you are very familiar and identify the programs that this organization hosts. Are these programs congruent with the organization's mission and its basic cultural assumptions? How?
6. Can you think of a program that was founded before it found an organizational "home?" What challenges did this impose for the founders? What are the implications of the program being housed in different organizational auspices?
7. Are there advantages and disadvantages of having public mandates? Of being a grassroots program? Of having a program that responds to a foundation initiative?
8. Do you think there is good reason to distinguish between "hard" and "soft" program benefits? What other terms might be used to describe these benefits other than hard and soft?
9. Hybrid programs and organizations contain both direct service programs and advocacy programs. What are the strengths and limitations of having this dual focus in one organization? What are the implications for program planning?

Case Exercise: Chronic Pain

The National Association for Chronic Pain Control (NACPC) developed in 1990 in response to the numbers of people living with chronic pain in the United States. An entire industry had developed to control pain so that employees could work longer and retirees could lead more productive lives, but a major concern had emerged in the process: more and more people were dependent upon high-powered, often addictive prescription drugs. NACPC viewed searching for alternative treatments and interventions as urgently needed.

The mission of this national organization was originally stated as: "To eliminate chronic pain through the advancement of research; to provide and enhance the quality of life and support for all affected; and to educate the public so that no one faces a life of pain." As charitable donations grew, and a major public relations campaign spread, multiple chapters of the NACPC began to spring up all over the country. By the year 2000, there were more than 100 chapters in place and at least 30 more developing.

The NACPC chapter in Arizona was established in 1993, one of the earliest local chapters to come on board. Located in Phoenix, where many people had moved from cold climates to take advantage of hot temperatures that seemed to help their aches and pains, interest had quickly mounted. As the chapter had grown and incorporated as a nonprofit organization, a board of directors composed of 12 members hired a CEO, in 1994. By 2000, this chapter was a thriving organization with three paid full-time program coordinators, in addition to the CEO and an administrative assistant. Each of the three coordinators was responsible for a specific program initiative—advocacy, education, and

(Continued)

service. A policies and procedures manual was developed, along with an organizational chart (see Figure 2.1) to depict the relationships among staff positions.

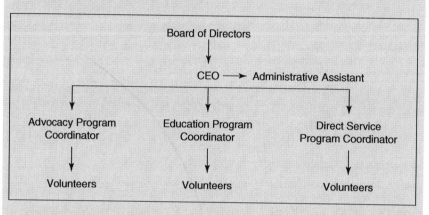

Figure 2.1
Organizational Chart: National Association for Chronic Pain Control (NACPC)

In 2008, the Phoenix NACPC held a strategic planning retreat. There, it became clear that the three programs (advocacy, education, and direct service) were not very integrated with one another. The advocacy program coordinator said that she was not certain how what she did varied from what the education program coordinator did. Both were going out into the local community talking about the NACPC, and telling the public about chronic pain. Sometimes, they found their speaking engagements overlapped. The direct service coordinator had a different problem. He felt that no one really respected what he was trying to do, and that the organization was so advocacy- and research-oriented that actual intervention with victims of pain and their caregivers had all but been forgotten. "And this is the bread of butter of what we *should* be doing," he said. "Without direct intervention through information and referral, care consultation, support groups and counseling with *real* people, we are not addressing community needs."

A very heated dialogue began at this point. The advocacy coordinator explained that her program was most in line with the overall mission of National, that the intent of local chapters was to advocate for research so that pain could eventually be eliminated. She added, somewhat as an afterthought, "Direct service is fine, but it really is only a Band-Aid to meet immediate need. What we need to do is find alternative approaches to drug dependency." This had turned the direct service coordinator's head, but he had held his tongue. The education coordinator was quick to respond that without education of physicians, nurses, social workers, and a host of allied health professionals there was little need to target the general public. "Unless you get health professionals to acknowledge that chronic pain is a problem for their patients, and that drug companies have to be kept in line, it doesn't matter what anyone else thinks or does. They have to be willing to recognize that patients are not just hypochondriacs who are difficult to treat. [The patients] live in hell most of the time and it affects everything they do!" The direct service coordinator, seeing a window of opportunity, quickly added, "My point exactly! If we don't intervene with the people who need us most, how will they ever advocate for themselves within insensitive systems of care?" He sat back, certain that he had countered the previous point about "Band-Aids."

As the dialogue continued, it became obvious that the three programs within this small organization were in competition with one another, rather than connected in a joint collaboration. In addition, each coordinator was a champion for his or her program, but the staff as a whole didn't know what all the programs were doing nor how they worked together. And when concerns about volunteers came up, it was clear that they were competing for the same volunteers. In some cases, and almost by default, volunteers were the only links between programs, such as four retired social

(Continued)

workers who were all engaged in doing advocacy, education, and direct service functions. Ironically, these volunteers seemed to see the linkages between the programs better than did the coordinators of the programs. The volunteers had actually taken the initiative and developed a pilot project with local hospice and palliative care units to share information on pain management.

As the retreat continued, a number of questions were raised: Should we restructure the programs so that they don't have their own identities, and make them into one large program with different component parts? Should we combine the advocacy and education programs into one unit, since there is so much overlap? Should we hire a volunteer coordinator for all volunteers so that assignments can be monitored and overseen, and so that the program coordinators do not compete for volunteers? Should we go back to the drawing board and think through what it is we want to be, and then consider if reorganization of program units and services are in order?

As these questions were raised, the direct service coordinator became increasingly concerned. With a furrowed brow, he said, "This raises the whole question of identity and vision. We are a chapter among many, and we can't be the first chapter that has struggled with these issues. What are other chapters doing? And, more importantly, what guidance can National provide for us? They must have some idea about what they want to see happen."

As the meeting ended, there appeared to be more questions raised than directions set. In the weeks that followed, the CEO met with other chapter directors in the region, hoping to locate an ideal programmatic structure. In fact, more questions came to mind as he talked with others. He made a list:

- What is our relationship to National? If we are branded as a chapter of NACPC, how far can we go in what we do and still maintain our relationship?

- Can we be all things to all people? Do we need to focus on one program; and, if so, which one?
- What exactly do (and should) our programs do? What does advocacy look like as an intervention? What types of educational interventions should we be doing? What are the actual services, and how are they linked, in the direct practice program?
- Is it possible for broad-scale advocacy programs to coexist with education and direct service programs, or is it inevitable that we lose our focus if we do all three?
- How can we go about program planning so that we actualize our mission?
- How do we include consumers in our planning process?
- Is it better to develop a volunteer program and dole out volunteers to various program units, or to have each unit do its own volunteer recruitment?
- Should we think about sequencing programs, perhaps going back to the drawing board and refocusing our efforts?
- What do we do about the project that the volunteers have developed? Will this eventually develop into an established program, and, if so, where might it fit?

As the list grew, the CEO planned for the next strategic planning meeting, concerned that he had more questions than answers. The day before the meeting, he received a phone call from the National office. National's new executive director spoke with excitement.

"New facts and figures about chronic pain were released yesterday at the National Policy Forum in Washington. National media are spreading the word that over 8 million people experience chronic pain, and that the number of persons

(Continued)

is growing. Currently, there are six new drugs in the last stages of development, and each will work somewhat differently. Researchers are more optimistic than in previous years. We've been working with the FDA to push forward any or all of these drugs, if they look promising and are not habit-forming. In the fall, there will be a prevention conference where scientists will present their findings, and the results of the drug trials will be released. Current drugs only work on symptoms, but these drugs get to the source of the problem. In the next two years, these changes will alter the status quo, and we'll have even more demand for what we do as an association. A major thrust must be public education and that will impact where we put our efforts."

There was a pause.

Stunned by the amount of information he had just heard, the CEO hesitated before responding, "Are you saying that advocacy and public education programming will be our priorities over direct service programs?"

"I suppose I am. Of course, this doesn't mean that you can't raise additional local funds to mount direct service programs, but those will be the icing on the cake."

"But we have a very committed program director who is doing good things in the local community and already feels under-appreciated. As a chapter, we have been committed to direct service interventions from the beginning because there are people who are suffering every day."

The voice on the other end of the line replied, "And that is certainly a signature of your chapter. Your direct service program is strong and worthwhile. I'm just saying that some priorities may have to be set and that we are getting ready to break into the public scene in an even bigger way. I didn't want you to be caught off-guard."

Having read this case, consider the following questions:

- If programs are containers for ideas, what different ideas does each of the three programs (advocacy, education, and service) contain? How do they differ in terms of interventions used, and why?
- In the larger national environment, how is "the paradox of engagement" (political, organizational, and evaluative demands) affecting this local organization?
- In the context of the Phoenix chapter of NACPC, what constraints (things they cannot change) and contingencies (things about which they have to compromise and negotiate) are they facing?
- If you were the CEO of the Phoenix chapter of NACPC, how would you plan for the next strategic planning session? Are there priorities you would recommend, given what you learned from other chapters and the call from National's executive director?
- If you were a program coordinator in this organization, how would you approach program planning? What would be your concerns? What else would you want to know?

CHAPTER 3

Rational Planning and Prescriptive Approaches

Service program planning is essentially a rational decision and an activity process carried out in successive stages of work. Planning is *rational* in that it is a means-ends driven process. Planning is also purposeful, just as the program-to-be is intended as a purposeful system of activities.

—Edward J. Pawlak and Robert D. Vinter, Designing and Planning
Programs for Nonprofit and Government Organizations

Chapter Outline

Case: The Mayor and the Street Educators
Introduction
History of Rational Planning and Prescriptive Approaches
Dimensions of Rational Planning and Prescriptive Approaches
    The Logic Model
    Assessing Needs
    Defining and Analyzing Problems
    Selecting Intervention Strategies
    Writing Goals and Objectives
    Program Design and Decision-Making
Accountability in a Prescriptive Approach
    Accountability Challenges

Information Systems
Budgeting
Rational Planning
Mind-sets
Skills
Strengths and Challenges of Rational Planning
Summary
Discussion Questions

Assumptions upon which the chapter is built:

- Linear thinking is useful in producing a logic model that lays out a plan of action to solve a social problem.
- Prescriptive approaches have various identifiable dimensions, all of which relate to one another in ways that result in problem resolution.
- In rational/prescriptive approaches it is important to know where one is going, thus a goal is established toward which one plans.
- Planners who use a prescriptive approach are typically viewed as experts who bring certain personality and skill packages to accomplish the specified tasks; some of these skills and abilities are harder to acquire than others.
- Prescriptive approaches, such as logic or problem-solving models, have limitations that must be understood when making appropriate decisions in the planning process.

We begin this chapter with a case designed to stimulate your thinking about rational planning and *prescriptive approaches*. One important note about this case is that it clearly acknowledges that not even a fully rational process can ignore the political context of decision-making about programming. Some may argue that political influences may ruin professionally and technically based problem-solving, but in fact, responding to the political context may be seen in some cases as highly rational. Immediately following the case, we work through the concepts involved in rational planning, and we will return to the case from time to time. In this way, you should more easily be able to explore some of the details in knowledge or skills that a rational planning process requires.

Case: The Mayor and the Street Educators

In one of the larger metropolitan areas of Brazil, the newly elected mayor used his power to announce that the Street Educators, who had been previously employed in the mayor's office, would change the service direction of the Children's Street Education Program. The new direction would be aimed at getting street children off the streets and into the city's unused and abandoned detention facilities. The new program would be featured as the mayor's initiative to "rescue children" from street life. Until now, the Street Educators met children on the streets and helped them with developing survival skills, including such things as health self-care knowledge, self-defense, reading ability, and identifying means of legitimately acquiring income.

The Street Educators, a team of five college-educated professionals with undergraduate social work degrees, and 10 paraprofessionals, some of whom were themselves "graduates" of the Street Education Program, were extremely dedicated to their work; proud of their successes; and totally surprised by the announcement from their new boss, the mayor. Nothing in what they were currently doing to assist street children included removal of children from the streets; rather, the idea was to provide practical education to help the children survive, if not thrive, in a difficult environment.

(Continued)

All members of the team understood the historical background and sociological roots of street children in Brazil. They recognized that history and culture led to a constant flow of children onto the streets and that, while social reform was an issue constantly discussed in the media, their jobs were to conduct a professionally based program to address the situation faced by children "on the streets" at any given moment. Theories of education drove their work, and it was understandable that they would be surprised by a new political mandate for institutional care, especially in what seemed like unfriendly former detention facilities. Clearly, their professional commitment and current programming were being put into a whole new context.

Within one week of the mayor's announcement, the mayor's wife, who had been placed in charge of all issues related to human services, walked into the Street Education Program office early one day. She declared that she and the mayor wished to know exactly how many street children there were in the city; how many were receiving services; how many children needed services, but were not receiving them; and what services were being provided. The team responded that they had some of the information in their records but that they would need help in providing a reliable and verifiable estimate of the total numbers of street children. They were also unsure as to how they could determine how many children needed services but were not receiving them. When the mayor's wife left, one of the Street Educators contacted her former research professor in the Social Research Institute at the local Federal University to see if the institute might be able to assist.

It turned out that the professor was looking for a hands-on research experience for her research students, so together they decided to undertake a "point in time," or "snapshot survey." The mayor's wife was pleased with such a quick response to the request, so she facilitated a small stipend for the student researchers through the mayor's office. In the meantime, the Street Educator team reviewed their records to provide a service record-based accounting of the numbers of children contacted by the team, and what precisely was delivered to each child by way of service. This was quite an undertaking because each street educator had his or her own way of reporting on his or her daily activities. Some did head counts. Others did service activity counts. Still others wrote a narrative about the day. Sometimes the files contained sweet notes from the kids, either expressing gratitude or recounting particular successes. Other times there were death notices of children from street violence, drug overdoses, or unknown causes.

On one weekend, right after the winter term started in March, about 50 student researchers fanned out across the city to do a person-by-person count of the children, but they also asked a few extra questions to try to understand why the kids were on the street. Forty-eight hours of data collection and weeks of data analysis later, the numbers they came up with were surprising, even to the Street Educators. They had found 3,120 children in ages ranging from about 6 to about 18, with most of the children being in the 10 to 13 age range. There were slightly more boys than girls in all ages, except over 14, for which very few girls were located. After the count, based on the research design, the student researchers could not provide assurance that the figures they provided would be valid during different seasons of the year, from year to year, or during varying economic conditions. However, based on additional questions they asked the street kids, and from discussion with the team members, they were able to develop a typology of street children.

The first type was "on" the street for the purposes of earning money for their families. They maintained strong connections

(Continued)

with families and returned home most nights with whatever money they were able to earn. A second type was children who had fled from their families; they were "of" the street, as they left home due to abuse or neglect and had no inclination to reconnect or maintain family ties, or for that matter, leave the street (unless they died of AIDS or were killed). A third type was composed of children who were on the street and wished to return home but could not do so because they could not find their families. Their families, living in abject poverty, could not afford stable housing and, while the children were on the street, had left the home known to their children without having or providing a forwarding address. These children were essentially abandoned to the streets with a similar life expectancy of the children "of" the street, which was about 6 years total as a street kid.

This information was passed up to the mayor through the mayor's wife, with a very professionally worded request for further exploration as to how the educational component of the team's work might be maintained while bringing children off the streets to the institutions that were located all over the city. In response, the mayor sent back the message that the research findings were very useful. He also stated that education was a wonderful idea, but not if it included street survival instruction, since that would no longer be the direction of the mayor's office program. The mayor also expressed great interest in the three types of street children because that, in connection with the count, would allow for planning the appropriate number and types of beds in "rehabilitated" detention facilities.

This gave the team greater insight as to what was going on, and they pressed the mayor's wife for more information the next time she stopped by to share a coffezinho with them. It was clear that she was not totally comfortable with the discussion, reminding them that being a city employee meant not getting too far into elective politics. Reasoning that just about everything out of the mayor's office tended to be political, the team members continued to press the mayor's wife. She was a well-intentioned, though rather bored, wealthy matron who really wanted to make a difference in the plight of these children. She also really enjoyed the benefits of being the mayor's wife, and it was clear that she felt torn about what was happening.

Nothing was really resolved, and no clarity was achieved even as the team continued to chat with the mayor's wife, until she came one morning with a message that led the team to realize they had better get on board and start planning a new program if they wanted to maintain any educational effort at all for street children. In fact, their city positions might just depend on that! The message was, while nicely and very reasonably put to them, very pragmatic, in a political sense. Essentially, the mayor had been backed in the election by local business interests, which found the presence of street children discouraged business and investment in the city. The children made a mess around popular tourist spots. They tended to beg outside the best stores. Some of the more entrepreneurial kids would stop traffic at major intersections to wash car windows, whether the drivers wanted the service or not. When traffic was heavy, the kids tended to beg in the same spots, creating an added complication to the already challenging traffic patterns. Discussion about these challenges had been appearing in the editorial section of the newspaper on and off for years, but the Street Educators had no idea how strongly the local business leaders felt about "their" children.

The mayor's wife certainly wasn't specific, but in roundabout discussion, she helped the team understand that the business interests had not gone public with this "concern" because they realized that in order to win the election, the mayor also needed votes of poor people. A couple of team members thought these

(Continued)

might be the very families who had children "on" the street during the day. It also became clear that both business leaders and the mayor feared a negative reaction from Church authorities, who had a long history in organizing the street children so that the children could gain their rights as established in the Brazilian Constitution.

However, the mayor, once elected, had to hear the concerns of these supporters, who had added much to the campaign treasury because they trusted that he would act to solve the "street children problem." Immediately it became clear to most of the team that the other issue at play was related to homelessness and the efforts of the homeless advocates in helping those without shelter to "take over" abandoned buildings owned by the city, citing squatters' rights. This created havoc all over the city, which undoubtedly wasn't pleasing to these same business leaders. The deterioration of state and city properties could be corrected, and the invasion of homeless persons could be stopped, if rehabilitation of the facilities for street children were to occur. Now, none of this was ever explicitly stated. What was stated was that the mayor's wife was certain that the team wanted to help "make the new mayor's administration successful," as this was so important to the city and to its children.

Armed with all this information, including the data and the typology from the university researchers, the team held a strategy session to focus on planning for the change in services demanded by the mayor. They knew now that they would have to respond in very different ways than they had previously, as the challenge was now being identified as getting children "off" the streets and into institutions, rather than as helping children "on" the streets in the community.

Based on their experience and the data, it was clear to the team that they had three very different populations in need of service, and to combine them might not only be dangerous to some, but was sure to create mayhem in the institutional settings. So the team divided into three subcommittees. One, composed of one graduate educator and three paraprofessionals, was tasked to develop ideas about how to serve the children on the street during the day. It was felt at that stage the "regular" program might be able to continue with these children; but something else was also needed so that they didn't slip into the last category of street kids, who lose track of their families. A second subcommittee was tasked with developing ideas about how to serve the street kids who wanted off the streets and really wanted to be in a family, but who could not find their families. The last team was tasked with generating ideas about how to deal with the children actually lost to the street. They needed to determine what could be developed to keep these children off the streets altogether.

Each team went to the various university libraries to see what ideas they might discover. Because the libraries had such old holdings, they also asked the mayor's wife if she might make it possible for them to use one of the city computers to access Internet resources. Two team members visited some of the internationally funded foundations in the area to see what helpful publications they might have. They all had to keep reminding themselves that they were actually dealing with three different kinds of street kids, probably with different needs, but all of whom would have to be housed in these new institutions. Interestingly enough, each team seemed to have one member who believed the only acceptable approach was education. These individuals believed that if the children were not educated, they would never be able to enter responsibly into civil society, and that they should not be allowed to simply move from these new institutional settings for youth, when they came of age, to the next institutional setting, which probably would be prison.

(Continued)

As the subcommittees progressed in their efforts, the team as a whole would meet to share what they were learning and finding. It became clearer and clearer that they could propose a unitary intervention based on an orphanage model, with a positive peer culture twist added to it, and figure the total cost of that; but most of the kids needed something else. They began to worry about how much the mayor was willing to spend on all this. They knew, at a minimum, the current budget for the Street Education Program would be available, but that certainly would not cover housing and maintenance for the approximately 1,000 children served last year on that budget. They also knew that this figure was a guesstimate based on what they could pull out of the disorganized files from last year. That also did not account for the other 2,000 or so children the student researchers had located who had never found their way to the Street Education Program; nor did it account for what they thought was the ideal intervention of "differential programming" for each of the three different groups.

Finally, the team decided to plan a program designed to serve at least 3,000 children. They researched some potential funding sources over and above what might be available from city, state, and federal governments; they knew to do it right, some serious money would need to be made available. The plan detailed everything that would be needed. It started with an outreach/ assessment effort designed to first get the kids off the street, and then to triage them for placement into the appropriate program setting. They developed three distinctive interventions depending on the type of street child; these were built upon assumptions about housing, food, and the elements necessary to make the children safe while they were being appropriately educated. They developed a family outreach aspect intended to connect kids with their own families whenever possible, and when that was not possible, to find other families willing to take in the children. And difficult as it was to admit, they were sure some of the institutionalized children would not find families. Thus, they needed to prepare some children to go into the world as responsible citizens without any family support.

All this work took several months, during which time they kept the mayor's wife informed about what they were learning and thinking. Finally, they prepared a fully developed plan that they shared with her first. She liked it so much that she facilitated a quick response from the mayor so that the two most senior Street Educators could present their ideas in a formal session with him.

The two educators were well versed in the literature about street children, along with what worked in other places and what had not; they also thoroughly understood all the numbers, and were well prepared to present their ideas to the mayor. They were certain they could explain clearly all the reasons for the choices the team had made. In short, they believed that the plan had a good chance of success. Then, just before they were to go into the meeting, they got word that one of the wealthiest people in town would also be in attendance. Neither of the Street Educators knew this person, but everybody in town knew the family. The word on the street was that the family was very interested in becoming a major philanthropic force in town. They went into the meeting convinced that they had found the best way to solve the problem of street children in their city, and they were ready for any questions that might come their way . . .

INTRODUCTION

In Chapter 1, we introduced the concept of rationality, on which many decision-making and planning models have been based. To be rational in this sense means to move forward with purpose toward a preidentified goal based on the assumptions that one can know the problem if one analyzes it well enough; that one can solve a problem if a clear direction of how to proceed can be identified; and that there are logical ways in which to move through this *problem-solving process*. In *rational planning*, there is a type of linearity present, in that the plan, when produced, goes from one step to the next until the established goal is achieved. Faludi (1973) refers to this as a "blueprint" mode of planning (p. 131). The linearity is still present even if one starts with a goal and works backwards. This process is called "*reverse-order planning*" (Brody, 2000, pp. 77–78), establishing a goal and then backtracking to fill in the actions that need to occur to arrive at the selected goal. In a way, that is exactly what happened in the case just presented.

We have engaged in many rational, prescriptive, problem-solving processes in our careers. In fact, they have provided some comfort in times of uncertainty in our work, when many unexpected situations would arise and when having a blueprint seemed necessary. Having a predetermined goal and keeping sight of that vision felt good, in the face of so many uncontrollable variables.

For example, Mulroy and Lauber (2004) reported on a three-year demonstration grant from the U.S. Department of Health and Human Services designed to prevent homelessness among public housing residents in Hawaii. The goal was to move these families toward self-sufficiency, requiring stabilizing the families' living situations and addressing barriers to obtaining jobs. As a grantee, they were expected to use a logic model in which the program was graphically represented by a series of components and expected accomplishments that led to predetermined outcomes. They demonstrated how important it was not to lose track of the ultimate goal—that families would be independent of government assistance over a period of time.

In this chapter, we focus on traditional rational program planning, using prescriptive approaches. We begin with a brief historical background. Building on well-known scholars in planning and

Table 3.1
Hierarchy of Key Concepts

Ways of knowing (philosophy)	Positivism
Ways of thinking (thought)	Rational
Ways of doing (approaches)	Prescriptive

administration, we review the dimensions of a typical rational problem-solving process that moves from needs assessment and problem analysis (based on theories, principles, and assumptions) into goals and activities resulting in outcomes and, sometimes, *impacts*. We examine accountability, which takes the form of monitoring and evaluation, and discuss the skills required to develop sound *program designs*, well-conceived information systems, and fundable budgets. The pros and cons of using prescriptive approaches are introduced, as we move toward specifics of how such processes work and in which situations such approaches would likely be most valuable.

Table 3.1 serves as a reminder of the focus we are taking in this chapter. Recall that positivism as a way of knowing leads to rational ways of thinking. Prescriptive approaches are based on rational thinking.

HISTORY OF RATIONAL PLANNING AND PRESCRIPTIVE APPROACHES

Freidmann and Hudson (1974) offer an overview of the tradition of rationalism in planning that is tightly tied to the earliest work of Chester Barnard and Herbert A. Simon. Simon assumed that decisions could be made centrally and would eventually filter down through an administrative hierarchy. Charles Lindblom later referred to this sort of centralized decision-making as *synoptic rationality*. Freidmann and Hudson identified three major problems faced by rational decision theory. First, rational decision-making does not always take into account the uncertainty about conditions that will exist in the future and that cannot always be predicted. Second, if decisions were made democratically—that is, various voices are heard—it would be difficult to calculate the trade-offs among stakeholder preferences because objectives are so different. And, third, decision theorists assumed that once a decision was made, it would be implemented with minimum friction. But beyond these problems, probably the most notable critique of the rationalist school was the "neglect of the human side of planning" (p. 164).

Even though concerns about rational approaches to planning have been articulated for decades, rational program planning/ prescriptive approaches based on outcome-based measurement are part of an era of accountability that has swept through the United States in the last three decades. Kettner, Moroney, and Martin (1999) wrote: "As the decade of the 1990s unfolded, these concerns [about accountability] became part of a national debate, and funding agencies at all levels began to require that service providers develop mechanisms to respond to these issues. Rhetoric gave way to practice" (p. 3). Over a decade ago, Martin and Kettner (1996) named five major forces driving performance measurement: (a) the Government Performance and Results Act (Public Law No. 103-62) in which all levels of government were required to develop performance measures; (b) the National Performance Review, which sought to carry out in practice the movement to reinvent government; (c) the Total Quality Management (TQM) approach, which promoted performance reporting; (d) managed care (with its deep monitoring system); and (e) the Service Efforts and Accomplishment (SFA) reporting initiative of the Government Accounting Standards Board, phasing in mandatory collection and reporting of performance measures by all state and local governments (inclusive of human service providers). Although not without a strong critique (see, e.g., Gray & McDonald, 2006; Witkin & Harrison,

2001), calls for clinical practitioners to engage in *evidenced-based practice (EBP)* tied to the measurement of outcomes have gained momentum (e.g., see Edmond, Megivern, Williams, Rochman, & Howard, 2006; Fraser, 2004; Gilgun, 2005; Gordon, 1991; McNeill, 2006; Pollio, 2006) and spread into planning practice.

It is important to frame a chapter on rational program planning in light of EBP because it has taken on such intense interest. It is no longer a choice but a requirement in professional standards of practice (e.g., see Council on Social Work Education, 2004) for contemporary professional survival. Therefore, it is important to recognize what a driving force the EBP movement is for support of rational program planning. It is also important to be aware of its political antecedents and their intended and unintended consequences (Netting & O'Connor, forthcoming).

For example, just over a decade ago, Lawlor and Raube (1995) analyzed the movement toward outcome-based studies that began with a focus on the physiological aspects of health and their high cost. Looking for ways to deliver health care more efficiently, it was believed that better outcomes would result if the "art" of medicine, in which individual doctors collaborated with patients, could be transitioned into practices with more standardized protocols. Lawlor and Raube examined the inherent complexities in moving medical outcomes into social interventions. Using home health and hospice services as examples, they illustrated just how difficult it is to measure outcomes in highly heterogeneous and complicated patient populations. In the absence of sophisticated tools to adequately measure outcomes in at-risk and vulnerable population groups, their concern was that there would be a rush to develop the instrumentation necessary to measure outcomes without the simultaneous development of complex interventions and practices keeping pace. Critical challenges in choosing outcome measures continue (Moxley and Manela, 2001; Mullen, 2006).

One way to manage those challenges has emerged from the program evaluation field. *Logic models*—also known variously as program logic, logic modeling, program logic models, theory of action, and theory-based evaluation—emerged to help identify the basic elements and the logic behind a program, even the most complex one (see, e.g., Bickman, 1987; Glanz & Rimer, 1995; McLaughlin & Jordan, 1999). Program logic was introduced as a tool for rational planners, program managers, and evaluators to demonstrate why a program should work or why what was being proposed programmatically was a good solution to an identified problem (Funnell, 1997; McCawley, 1997). Logic models became the building blocks in rational planning for demonstrating and describing program effectiveness by showing the logical linkages among program resources; activities; *outputs;* audiences; and short-, intermediate-, and long-term outcomes related to a specifically defined problem or situation. The assumption was that a program logic model could be the road map to show how outcomes would be achieved (W.K. Kellogg Foundation, 2001) and could be used in a step-by-step test of program impacts and outcomes.

Just as Lawlor and Raube acknowledged the push for outcome-based measurement, emanating in health care as the intent to become more effective in containing costs, and Kettner et al. (1991) described a multitude of driving forces in government, Easterling described the push for outcome evaluation increasingly coming from private foundations. "Foundations need to be able to measure what grantees accomplish with their grants to compute the return on their investment. Moreover, foundations operating under the new paradigm are much more impressed with *outcome evaluation* (i.e., an objective assessment of the actual effects of the funded program on the target population) than they are with *process evaluation* (i.e., an assessment of how the program was delivered by the staff and received by the clients)" (p. 482).

As you can see from this brief overview, the synoptic rational planning model is alive and well, even though scholars and practitioners have recognized some of its intrinsic limitations, and others have experienced the challenges in practice arising from the contexts in which rational program planning is carried out. These limitations do not seem to deter devotees, who recognize the usefulness of rational plans for those seeking to understand the work. The desire on the part of funders and others to work toward certainty with the goal of control and *objectivity* is part of contemporary practice. Thus, any program planner must recognize the deep tradition in which the prescriptive approaches, with their linear logic, is invested.

DIMENSIONS OF RATIONAL PLANNING AND PRESCRIPTIVE APPROACHES

To plan for interventions that "work" in solving problems, rational program planners believe that evaluation is part of every step of the process. If one carefully attends to each step, beginning with a well-conceived problem definition and a visionary goal of where one is going, the pieces can be put in place, always keeping that goal in mind. Planning is intended to be an intentional, systematic, and carefully conceived movement, from problem analysis to completion of the plan that results in the measurable resolution of a problem. There is a clarity and precision in the logic of this problem-solving approach.

THE LOGIC MODEL

To understand the important aspects of logic model development in program planning, this section will touch on and define the basic components and connections between a planned intervention and the intended results of problem-solving. The flow of the section follows the general logic needed to move linearly from problem setting to results identification, through program implementation and evaluation planning. Although they will vary somewhat, depending on the source or developer, dimensions in a rational planning process when a logic model is applied include: (1) assessing needs, (2) defining and analyzing the problem, (3) selecting intervention strategies, (4) writing goals and objectives, and (5) program design. These dimensions comprise what is called performance-based, effectiveness-based, or outcome-based programming, and are listed in Table 3.2.

Using this conceptualization of program planning, the program is conceived as a sequence of objectives. The planner begins with some social impact in mind that could be considered the goal and, in effect, works backwards to lay out what must be done to accomplish the desired result. It is recognized that, first, some intermediate outcomes must be reached to attain those final outcomes, and that to do this, first the program must produce some outputs. To produce the outputs, certain activities are required to be accomplished, and to do the activities, inputs or resources are needed. When all that has been determined, the planner has created a program logic model.

The sequence of a logic model in its simplest form would look like this:

Resources/Inputs → Throughputs/Activities → Outputs → Outcomes → Impact/Goal

The planner recognizes that resources will be needed to operate the program. If one gets access to the resources, then those can be utilized to accomplish the planned activities. If the planned activities can be accomplished, then the service to the degree and amount intended will be delivered. If the planned activities are delivered as

Table 3.2

Dimensions of a Rational Planning Process

Dimension	Function
Needs assessment	• Focus scope of needs assessment on a specific group or geographic location; and when not available, extrapolate to the targeted group/area. • Use needs assessment of the targeted population as basis for designing a program to meet client needs.
Problem identification, analysis, and definition	• Identify causes of the problem and focus on conditions that can be reasonably addressed by the organization at the direct service level. • Refine problem definition in the process. • Frame the problem to focus on those alternatives that can change the client's status/situation, acknowledging that it may not be possible or feasible to change root causes at this time.
Intervention strategies (hypotheses)	• Select best strategy that directly intervenes with individual clients or groups. • Intervene based on studies, practice wisdom, best practices, clinical technologies, and so on.
Goals and objectives	• Recognize that broad goals will not be achievable in the short run, but objectives will be very specific and measurable. • Write outcome objectives that focus on measuring quality-of-life changes in individuals and groups. • Base formative evaluation on process objectives. • Base summative evaluation on achievement of outcome objectives.
Program design decision-making	• Make program elements specific and detailed, leaving little room for guesswork. • Focus intervention directly on providing services to clients and improving their quality of life. • Expect criticism of the program based on decisions made that appear to provide "Band-Aids," and as potentially perceived to be a mechanism of social control.

Source: Adapted from Netting, O'Connor, & Fauri, 2007.

intended, then the service recipients will benefit in expected ways. If the benefits are achieved, then expected changes in larger systems will occur. The planned work leads logically and linearly to intended results. To get there, however, first the rational planning process needs to have a well-defined problem to solve.

ASSESSING NEEDS

Success for the logic model of problem-solving rests on clearly defining a need and developing a deep understanding of the problem that a program addresses. Without this, a faulty logic model can result, overlooking important positive and negative influences on the problem, resulting in wasted efforts or off-target results.

In a rational process, it would be ideal to assess what people need, and then translate those needs into problem statements that can be targeted. In actuality, needs are not always fully identified when a problem emerges. Street children in the case study represented a problem to elected officials and businesspeople in a city dependent on tourism. In this case, a *needs assessment* regarding the types of children on the streets was initiated when a problem was already assumed. In another situation, a problem may be so glaring, such as a rapid increase in persons who are homeless, that it becomes a crisis situation in which a program must be rapidly designed without a systematic needs assessment having been conducted. Thus, needs assessment is part of rational planning, but it may take different forms.

Kettner, Moroney, and Martin (1999) identify four types of client needs: (1) normative, (2) expressed, (3) perceived, and (4) relative. Each type requires somewhat different methods of data collection. Each type contributes to an understanding of effects and benefits of the problem situation. *Normative need* is what is already known by persons working in the field, like the Street Educators in our case.

Therefore, it is incumbent upon the planner to access sources such as existing surveys, census data, and resource inventories. *Expressed need* is sometimes called demand. Expressed needs are those that have been presented in some way by current or potential program participants. These needs are demonstrated in service statistics for persons served and in waiting lists of individuals who sought service but for whom services were not available. In the case, this need was difficult to measure due to faulty record-keeping.

Perceived needs are invisible because they have not yet been formally expressed. Capturing these data is particularly relevant to planners eager to address real human need, but can meet with some resistance within overtaxed systems. Identifying needs that have not been expressed means revealing needs not recognized, possibly raising issues that add to already stressed workloads. Perceived needs are the hardest to get to because they require some type of outreach, through such things as a survey of community residents or a public hearing. Also, perceived needs usually need to be translated into expressed needs that can be managed by planners. For the mayor in our case, perceived needs were his greatest fear because it was likely that more children were on the streets than the program was aware of. Raising perceived needs was not something he wanted to do. If anything, he wanted to reduce the visibility of those already expressing needs.

Relative needs are those that involve comparisons between one set of needs and others. For example, one neighborhood may have higher poverty rates than another, causing planners to focus their efforts on the more "needy" neighborhood. One population group may have much higher instances of domestic violence than another, drawing the energies of advocates who want to intervene. In our case, the mayor may decide that one type of street child has a greater need in comparison to the other two types. A number of methods can be used to identify relative needs, including using normative needs data (what is already known) to compare what is known in one location or about one population with another; analyzing expressed needs data to see where the greatest demand is; or holding hearings in numerous communities to determine where the greatest effort should be directed.

If possible, the planner will want to locate all four types of needs assessment data because they reveal different aspects of the problem. As in the Street Educators case, it is often hard to do this in a short period of time when a program has to be designed and submitted to a funding source by a set deadline, or when a public mandate creates pressure on staff to get the program up and running. Unfortunately, it is often the situation that planners rely on what is already known about the needs because they do not have the resources to complete their own needs assessment. Many programs are designed based on normative and expressed needs data without capturing perceived needs. This limits the information to be used in both defining the problem and determining the appropriate alternative for addressing it.

DEFINING AND ANALYZING PROBLEMS

An assumption in rational planning is that if one is planning a program to address an identified problem, then needs assessment data are important sources of information for problem definition and analysis. In direct service programs, client needs are usually taken into consideration because their needs should be central to problem definition. Defining and analyzing a problem is a conceptual process that initiates the causal chain established in the logic model (from inputs to outcomes and impacts). The planner needs to know in detail the situation, conditions, and the problem that the plan is to impact so that it is clear what the future situation will look like when the desired change is achieved. Then appropriate outcome indicators for evaluation can be established.

Every other element of the planning process is affected by this first element of problem definition and analysis. Therefore, program planning books emphasize the importance of a thorough problem analysis process (see, e.g., Kettner, Moroney & Martin, 1999; Pawlak & Vinter, 2004). In problem definition, it is helpful to recognize the difference between a condition (what is; just the facts), such as children living on the streets, and a problem (making a judgment call that something needs to change). In our case, business interests saw street children as an economic threat and, therefore, a problem.

In another example, a planner contacted a local politician. She had analyzed state-level data, finding out that the state was close to the bottom nationally in meeting the mental health needs of its citizens. Her hope was that she could convince the politician to lend his support to a mental health initiative that would result in local communities enhancing their community-based programs. Presented with the data, the politician seemed unmoved. Taken aback, the planner asked, "Doesn't it bother you that we are almost bottom in the nation when it comes to serving the mental health needs of our citizens?" He replied, "No; actually, it makes me satisfied to see that we are containing our costs when other states are obviously not doing that well." The politician clearly saw these data as evidence of a condition that he had not labeled as a problem, but that showed progress on another problem, as defined by the politician. The planner had made an assumption: these data represented meaningful information about mental health needs that she thought were in urgent need of remedy. In a situation like this, it may take some effort on the part of planners to convince persons in power about what the problem is and that a solution is worth pursuing.

Rational planners believe that problem identification must be accompanied by *problem analysis*, in which terms are defined, population demographics are reviewed to determine who is in need and how prevalent the problem is, what forces are driving or restraining the problem (*force field analysis*), who thinks this is (or isn't) a problem, and what is known about the problem in the professional knowledge base and in the field of practice (Kettner, Moroney, & Martin, 1999). What are the causes? What are the symptoms of the problem? What are the likely consequences if nothing is done to resolve the problem? What are the actual costs if the problem stays as it is? What are the costs to eliminate the problem? Who is affected by the problem? How are they important to the community? Who else is interested in the problem? Who are the stakeholders? An evidence-based practice approach, in which any available studies, model projects, or best practices are identified, is part of the problem analysis process, so that the best possible intervention to solving it can be designed.

Once the analysis is complete, or as complete at it can be given time constraints, using what one has learned in the process, a choice is made among possible directions one might take, and a *problem statement* is written. It might look something like the problem statements in Box 3.1. Note that the first statement relates to our case. Note also how each statement includes a general qualitative statement followed by quantitative data about the size of the problem, and ending with a course of action. The problem statement should flow so smoothly and logically from the problem analysis that anyone reading the problem analysis immediately sees its connection with the problem statement and can begin to support the type of intervention strategies that are also logically connected.

SELECTING INTERVENTION STRATEGIES

The intervention strategy in a human service plan is the part of the logic model that defines the necessary *inputs* to successfully enact a

Box 3.1
Sample Problem Statements

Problem Statement 1:
At Risk Population: Street Children
Poverty, domestic violence, substance abuse, child abuse, and neglect are factors related to the existence of street children throughout the area. Approximately 3,000 children in the city spend some time on the streets. The majority of these children, both boys and girls, range in age from 10 to 13, and have a life expectancy of about six years, if they remain on the streets. Efforts must be undertaken to help these children.

Problem Statement 2:
At-Risk Population: Caregivers of Persons
with Alzheimer's Disease
Caregivers of persons with Alzheimer's disease often feel isolated and alone, not knowing how they will manage, both psychologically and financially. In this state, 1 in 10 persons over the age of 65 has Alzheimer's disease, and 75 percent of those who are diagnosed live in the community. Supports must be developed for those often-invisible caregivers who are trying to care for their loved ones with Alzheimer's disease in the community.

Problem Statement 3:
At Risk Population: Persons Who Are Chronically Homeless
Chronic homelessness is defined as being continuously homeless for two or more years, as contrasted with the majority of the homeless population who are transitioning in and out of homelessness, defined as either temporarily or episodically homeless.

(Continued)

Considering that chronically homeless persons make up 25 percent of all homeless people, this group poses unique challenges to service providers. A model, a cost-effective effort to produce housing stability for chronically homeless adults, and lower cost to government agencies, is desperately needed.

program aimed at impacting the defined problem. Inputs include knowledge, skill, and expertise, but more specifically involve human resources, fiscal resources, and other inputs such as facilities and equipment, and the knowledge base for the program. Inputs also include the necessary involvement of collaborators needed for planning, delivery and/or evaluation. In our case at the beginning of the chapter, the inputs include everything necessary to house, feed, and care for the street children, as well as all the human and other resources needed to treat and educate the children and prepare families for them.

The intervention input should be built on a knowledge base regarding the problem, and empirical, evidence-based knowledge about what might be effective. To assure this, the program should be grounded in well-conceived theory. Savaya and Waysman (2005) examine how hard it is to actually incorporate theory when complicated programs use multiple theories. They see the logic model as a way to do this. They refer to the growing number of users' guides that walk planners through the step-by-step "process of articulating the program theory by dividing it up into discrete units (inputs, outputs, outcomes, etc.) that are connected via links that can be readily examined for logic and feasibility" (p. 88).

Chambers and Wedel (2005) say four things about program theory. First, *program theory* is the source from which the program activities are drawn. In other words, program design and specification are directly tied to theory. Second, theory is central to program management in that it is required as a measure in observing the program in order to assess the quality of its implementation. Theory, then, leads to measurable outcome objectives. Third, outcome data showing success are useless unless one knows whether the program was implemented successfully. Based on this, measurable process objectives are also needed. And fourth, a good program theory will contain statements that are essential to high-level planners (like those in foundations) whose role is to decide when and where such a program might be successful.

Another way to understand a program theory, its linkages to a logic model and selected intervention strategies, is through a *program hypothesis*. The program hypothesis is a series of if/then statements that help to solidify what must be undertaken in order to achieve change. The hypothesis is based on selecting what is considered the best intervention strategy identified in the problem analysis process.

Kettner, Moroney, and Martin (1999) advise the planner to consider the preconditions necessary for the construction of a useful program hypothesis. Taking the planner beyond simple descriptions of inputs, they help the planner to lay out necessary elements of the intervention, called factors, which must be in place for change, or multiple levels of consequences, to be possible. See Box 3.2 for an example of a program hypothesis, based on factors and consequences, for one of the three types of street children.

Box 3.2

Example of a Program Hypothesis Using Factors and Consequences

IF children "of" the street are contacted through outreach (FACTOR), and

IF their needs are carefully assessed (FACTOR), and

IF they come to live at the children's center (FACTOR), and

(Continued)

If they participate in educational and support programs designed to meet their needs (FACTOR), and

IF they are given appropriate service referrals for family care (FACTOR), or appropriate preparation for living independently (FACTOR), based on treatment plans,

THEN there will be a decrease in return to the streets by children "of" the street (CONSEQUENCE), and

THEN there will be a decrease in numbers of street children (CONSEQUENCE), and

THEN there will be an increase of ex-street children who are not dependent on government support after their release from the children's center. (CONSEQUENCE).

Looking at the hypothesis in Box 3.2, how complex is the intervention? It seems to have several factors: participants responding to outreach, having their needs assessed, providing alternative living arrangement in the children's center, participating in educational and support programs, and making appropriate referrals for family care or preparation for independence. The logic of the program hypothesis provides the rationale for defending one's program to decision-makers and funding sources. With this program hypothesis it should also be clear that the output from one effort in a program plan becomes an input for the next effort in the logic model. The output from outreach is a child who is an input for assessment.

In human services rational planning, when you are considering intervention strategies, it is helpful to ask yourself these questions to contextualize the logic of your plan within external and environmental situations as well as in related programs:,

- Whose description/definition of the conditions did you select, and why? Were there some sources of information more helpful than others? Are there some sources you feel you couldn't get to or that were left out altogether?

- Did you consider strengths as well as challenges in the problem statement?
- Whose analysis of the problem did you rely on most heavily, and why?
- How did you locate needs data, and do you have a grasp of perceived needs?
- Which theory is guiding what you are planning to do?
- Does the intervention you are selecting flow logically from your problem analysis?
- Can you provide a strong rationale for how you based the intervention on what you learned from best practices, model programs, evaluations of successful programs, and other evidence you have collected?
- What other interventions might have been considered, and why were they not selected?

WRITING GOALS AND OBJECTIVES

Having analyzed problems, assessed needs, and determined a potential intervention, it is time to identify a goal or goals. The intended results in the logic model, including outputs, outcomes, and impacts, require goals and objectives in order to create the details needed to guide the various resources through the selected strategies to the planned-for results. More important, goals provide the broad vision, and objectives become the measurable indicators that those implementing the plan will use for creating a sound, well-targeted evaluation.

Goals are to programs what mission statements are to organizations. They are broad and visionary, setting the stage for measurable objectives. Note that there is inconsistency in the definitions of goals and objectives in the planning literature, and sometimes they are used interchangeably. However, there is an important reason to separate the two. Goals provide a broad-enough direction so that most people can embrace them. A common shared vision may be what ties various constituencies together, even if they disagree about the actual program design.

Program planners have long known that there are different types of outcomes (Mullen, 2006). For example, Kettner, Moroney, and Martin (1999) identify three types: (1) immediate, (2) intermediate, and (3) final, or ultimate. Immediate outcomes are benchmarks moving toward intermediate outcomes, which in turn move toward final or ultimate outcomes. In the same vein, logic model language calls for short-term, medium-term, and long-term outcomes. Those long-term outcomes are sometimes identified as impacts. Whatever the language, the focus is on a series of linked changes that will produce the achievement of the final change goal. Outcomes, then, are based on the assumption that certain objectives must be achieved. Further, to get to outcomes, certain processes, also known as process objectives, must be undertaken.

In developing measurable objectives, specificity matters. Each objective, whether outcome or process, must include at least four elements: (1) time frame; (2) target of the change; (3) results to be achieved; and (4) criteria by which results will be documented, monitored, or measured. Depending on the source, some planners will include those personnel responsible in each objective. This may not be necessary if the planning process includes specified activities under each objective. In this level of planning, specific activities under each objective will include who will do what at what time. These are essential activity lists that identify tasks and actions to be carried out, as well as who is responsible for them.

The program hypothesis can be used to guide the writing of process and outcome objectives. The "if" statements, or factors, seen in the program hypothesis become the process objectives of the plan. The "then" statements, or consequences, become the outcome objectives. The links in the chain of the logic model become stronger in this way. Box 3.3 provides an illustration of how to translate one to the other.

Box 3.3

Translating a Program Hypothesis into Outcome and Process Objectives

Program Hypothesis
IF children "of" the street can be contacted (PROCESS), and

IF their needs can be carefully assessed (PROCESS), and

IF they come to live at the children's center (PROCESS), and

IF they participate in educational and support programs designed to meet their need (PROCESS), and

IF they receive appropriate referral to either family care or independent living (PROCESS),

THEN numbers of street children will decrease (OUTCOME), and

THEN the numbers of ex-street children who are not dependent on government support will increase (OUTCOME).

Process Objectives
- By January 2009, at least 1,000 children "of" the street will be contacted, as documented in field logs kept by Street Educators.
- By March 2009, at least 80 percent of the contacted children "of" the street will be assessed and come to live at the children's center, as documented by a service plan signed by the child and assessor.

(Continued)

- By June 2009, 100 percent of children living at the center will receive educational and support programs designed to meet their needs, as documented by daily service logs.
- By June 2010, 40 percent of the original children will be referred to family care, and 60 percent will be referred to preparation for living independently, as documented by a living plan signed by the appropriate parties.

Outcome Objectives

- By June 2010, at least 75 percent of former children "of" the streets will be ready for community living, as measured by a client life plan report.
- By December 2010, the number of children "of" the streets will decrease by 25 percent, as measured by a "point in time" survey.

The hypothesis guides the development of process and outcome objectives in which time and indicators of the desired outcomes are added. Because measurement is so critical to the usefulness of rational program planning, and will lead to the production of "evidence" for sound evaluation, it is incumbent upon the planner to select the most robust measures possible.

Outcomes can be measured in many ways. Martin and Kettner (1996) focus on four in particular: (1) numerical counts, (2) level of functioning scales, (3) standardized tests, and (4) client satisfaction scores. One may have to be creative in developing measures, as innovative human service, advocacy, staff development and training, and other types of programs may address needs not previously addressed. Due to this, developed scales and tests may not exist. Sometimes, robust tools will not have been "normed" to vulnerable or specific population groups. Methods of measurement may become a barrier, and mixed measurements may be needed. The use of both qualitative and quantitative research skills will be very helpful here. In thinking about measurement, it helps to keep asking yourself: How would I know if this outcome was achieved? What would tell me it worked? What would I look for? What would provide evidence that this outcome occurred? Identifying indicators beforehand is essential.

One might ask these questions about the outcome measures selected:

- Which factors influenced the selection of the outcomes you identified as important for your program?
- How much input did you have from consumers or former consumers?
- Which measurements did you select for your outcome objectives? Why did you select those measures?
- Do you think these are the most sensitive measurements you could have chosen? Why or why not?
- What value conflicts did you encounter as you worked on the development of your hypothesis, goals, and objectives?
- If you are being very honest with yourself, do you think the outcome measures you have selected will truly indicate progress toward the goal(s)?
- Do your outcomes represent the outcomes that consumers would choose?

PROGRAM DESIGN AND DECISION-MAKING

Program design is sometimes called *action planning* because it serves as a guide for decision-making about detailed tasks. This is where the logic model goes deep into specifying what is to be done with whom and to what standard of quality. "The purpose of program design is to put together that service or combination of services that appears to have the best chance of achieving the program's objectives" (Kettner et al., 1999, p. 12). The program design aspect of a logic model for the full street children program is shown in Figure 3.1.

Inputs must be described, including the needed resources—such as type of staff, physical surroundings, supplies, materials, and equipment—to serve a defined client, customer, or participant base. For example, if the program is to be housed in a large organization with existing staff, then "buying out" staff time by shifting them from what they are already doing to the new endeavor, and using the funding for staff to hire new people in the old program, may be logical. In other situations, an assortment of practitioners may need to be recruited, depending on the expertise needed to achieve the objectives. In addition, volunteers frequently work as adjuncts with professionals to implement programs. Chambers and Wedel (pp. 148–169) stress the importance of aligning the host organization and the structures within which one will pursue one's program. This was certainly one of the major challenges in the Street Educators case at the beginning of the chapter.

It is in the program design phase that the multidimensionality of a prescriptive approach is solidified, within the context in which it will be implemented. Thus, program design includes assessing the fit of the program with organizational auspice (Netting & O'Connor, 2003). Selecting a "home" for a program may be predetermined because one is already working in an agency and writing a grant to fund an existing, new, or redesigned program. When an idea has come to fruition outside the boundaries of an organizational auspice, it may be important to link that program with an appropriate organization because the program plan must fit with the context in which it will be implemented. All of this was yet to be worked out with the mayor's office in our case. Would the program stand alone and evolve into an independent organization? Would it

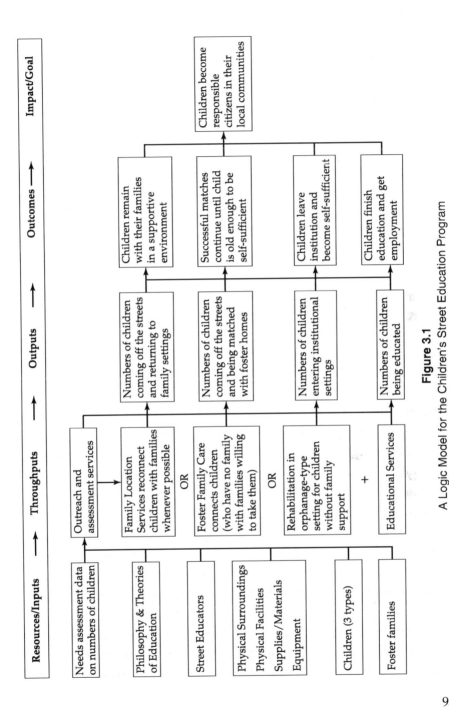

Figure 3.1

A Logic Model for the Children's Street Education Program

93

be attached to an already existing nongovernmental organization (NGO)? Would it remain a political entity connected to the resources of the mayor's office?

Even if a program has enough resources, one cannot know that a practice works, unless one knows what the practitioners, staff, and volunteers actually do (what happens in the intervention). If a workshop is the intervention, what is the precise content and process of the workshop? Who will deliver it, based on what level of experience or capacity, and to whom, how many, and for how long? If a therapeutic intervention is to be undertaken, precisely what will be the knowledge base and actions of the therapists? What is the required expertise to deliver the intervention? Who precisely will receive the intervention? How many of these people will receive the intervention, and for how long? The effort in deep program design means that the service must be defined in detail, including its theoretical foundations, along with all the service tasks that go into the provision of the service. In systems language, the crux of program design is about planning for what needs to happen when a mix of resources is brought together in the *throughput* process. Kettner, Moroney, and Martin (1999) recommend that throughputs be specified in service definitions, tasks, and methods.

Once throughputs are determined, it becomes time to consider outputs, which are documented by the *units of service* provided. Kettner, Moroney, and Martin (1999) identify three types of service units: (1) episode or contact unit, used when the important thing is the client contact, rather than the time spent; (2) material unit, a tangible resource provided to a client; and time unit, measured in minutes, hours, days, and weeks spent. In our Street Educators case example, the initial units of service would be days of care and hours of education or support provided. And even if a service completion is logical, it does not speak to the quality of the services delivered through a program. One must be aware of standards set by key funders or stakeholders (policies, rules, licensing, certification, accreditation, professional codes, etc.) that address the quantity or the quality of the defined service. For example, in the Street Educators case, attention would focus not only on institutional health and safety standards so that children were well cared for, but also on educational and treatment standards. Box 3.4 illustrates the nature of throughputs, units of service, and quality standards, and how they might be articulated in our case example.

Box 3.4
Program Design Decisions about Throughputs

What is the Intervention(s)?
- *Service definition*: One or two sentences of the service to be provided and its theoretical or knowledge base
- *Service tasks*: The actions that go into the provision of service (e.g., intake, screening, assessment, and care planning)
- *Method of intervention*: The ways the service will be delivered
- *Unit of service*: Service identified per unit of delivery (including contact, materials, time, etc.)
- *Standard of quality*: Professional, procedural, and policy criteria

Street Children Program Example
- *Service definition—education and support*: Providing academic knowledge, survival skills, and therapy with attention to specific children's needs
- *Service tasks*: Child identification, child recruitment, child assessment and treatment planning, provision of safe housing, classroom education, therapeutic support, referral to family care or independent living services

(Continued)

- *Methods of intervention*: Traditional education model in classroom setting with focus on preparation for independence, positive peer culture within the institution, cognitive-behavioral therapeutic approaches for children and potential family caregivers
- *Unit of service*: Time/day of care; hours of direct educational or support service
- *Standard of quality*: Health and safety standards; professional codes of ethics; educational quality standards

As you can see, program design gets very specific and technical because rational planning is detail-oriented. Designing the program is assessing fit within the organization in which the program is housed, identifying the resources one needs, and then carefully detailing exactly what will happen in the intervention. The assumption in program design is that if one plans every detail, then someone who was not part of the planning process could pick up the plan and follow it, thus implementing the program.

The program design provides the detail to establish the linkages between the problem as defined and the outcomes intended to solve the problem. Program design creates the bridge between the problem and the impact, highlighting the necessary connections between and among the components of the logic model. Program design is the last necessary stage prior to planning for program evaluation, one of the major elements of program accountability.

ACCOUNTABILITY IN A PRESCRIPTIVE APPROACH

The numerous forces driving outcome-based measurement have created a new awareness about accountability. No longer is it enough to report inputs (money, labor, facilities needed to produce the program) or outputs (what was done and who was reached); it is now necessary to know whether dimensions of the identified problem were changed as a result of the intervention. "Justifying outcome management is the perspective that human service work must become more rational and more amenable to measurement if it is to be managed properly and effectively . . . Today's call for the broad-based use of outcomes in human services comes at a time when the general society is demanding more accountability in a wide range of service sectors" (Moxley & Manela, 2001). All links of the causal chain of the logic model must now be evaluated in a way that is appropriate to each point in the chain. Did the inputs produce the activities? Did the activities produce the output? Did the output produce the outcome? Can impacts be measured?

The logic model used in planning can be central to accountability responsibilities. The logic model is essential in clarifying program theory, demonstrating program progress, and establishing appropriately targeted program evaluation questions and indicators. But in practice there are limits to linear program logic. All aspects of accountability cannot be addressed without some degrees of challenge.

ACCOUNTABILITY CHALLENGES

The definition of evidence-based practice (EBP) is variable, depending on whom one is citing. EBP can be viewed as a decision-making process that involves integrating: (a) the concerns and values of the client, (b) practitioners' experiences and practice wisdom, and (c) best relevant research evidence (Gibbs, 2003, p. 19). The challenge of the approach turns on the definition of what constitutes acceptable evidence. Rational planning and its prescriptive approaches are dependent on locating the best relevant scientific research evidence.

Empirically based, quantitative findings are privileged in prescriptive approaches.

For anyone who is paid for their professional work, it has become incumbent upon them to demonstrate that they are making a difference. To do so requires systematic data collection that can be appraised and synthesized, so assertions of the causal linkages not only can be made, but supported. When human service workers focus on psycho-social aspects of care, the evidence is harder to document than changes in more observable and, therefore, measurable areas such as functional ability or physical health. The pressure to provide evidence of effectiveness and efficiency does not always take into account the complexity of timing, controlling of intervening variables, and the myriad other contextual factors that make EBP a particularly challenging undertaking in human services (Netting & O'Connor, forthcoming).

As Lawlor and Raube (1995) maintained in their work on outcome-based measures, human service professionals design, develop, and coordinate programs that are primarily involved in complicated, multitarget, often multiphase interventions with multiple stakeholders that range from vulnerable individuals to more powerful communities and to society as a whole. These programs are not of interventions in which a precise research design or a hastily constructed instrument can easily determine a response to the question, "Do these interventions work?"—no matter how well the program logic has been constructed (Netting & O'Connor, forthcoming).

Linear program logic has other limitations related to accountability. The potential for unintended consequences, even though most programs have side effects, may be missed. The logic in a linear, prescriptive approach creates a goal hierarchy within a particular time sequence, which has the potential to reduce the effects of feedback or to be embraced in a cookbook fashion. For example, logic models do not address issues/effects of power, control, and participation. These models calls for expert intervention, often using terms like "target population" as if the target is a passive blank slate. In the same vein, linear program logic does not offer suggestions for how to cope with conflict because it primarily captures the program planner's perspective and professional needs. Because the program plan is enacted within a real action environment, what occurs will always have doubtful generalizability, not only because of the uniqueness of individuals in contexts, but also because of the practical inability to demonstrate the connection between outputs, outcomes, and impacts with much certainty. Even with these challenges, prescriptive approaches remain a powerful method for shaping and evaluating complex programs. Proponents assert that many of the limitations can be overcome when the planners involve a wide range of stakeholders in the model-building/planning process.

Attending to multiple stakeholders also adds to a growing array of accountabilities. These are essential to effective rational program planning. First, the planner is accountable to professional standards. Second, the planner is accountable to those entities that sanction the plan. In this aspect of accountability, to respond with integrity means the elements of design must fit with what was learned in the problem analysis, and flow logically from the agreed-upon goals and objectives. Third, the planner is responsible for designing an information system that will capture the data elements necessary to evaluate program effectiveness. Fourth, the planner is accountable to the providers of resources by having a realistic budget that can produce the program at reasonable cost.

Here again, the logic model is very useful in creating an evaluation because each step in the logic model chain can be evaluated using measures for that stage. Creating an information system to track services, and establishing budgeting and accounting procedures, goes a long way toward assuring accountability. Table 3.3 provides an overview of these accountabilities.

Table 3.3

Types of Accountability

Accountability Mechanisms	Functions
Evaluation of the logic model	• Make program inputs (such as staff or volunteers) specific and detailed, leaving little room for guesswork. • Place program under a feasible auspice and assure it "fits." • Focus interventions directly on providing services to clients and improving their quality of life. • Seek program integrity so that rationale for various actions will hold up.
Information systems (IS)	• Use program design to dictate an IS that captures results of both process (formative) and outcome (summative) objectives: work-time logs and financial data evaluate inputs; program data provides link between activities and outputs; surveys and/or experiments document how outputs result in outcomes; official statistics may show extent to which outcomes produce impact. • Design monitoring to be straightforward, tied to specific data elements collected at different points in the process.
Budgeting	• Develop a well-stated line-item budget with justification. • Document resource needs. • Account for expenditure of funds.

INFORMATION SYSTEMS

Data to be collected must be considered throughout the program design process. We have observed often that program staff view data collection as a time-consuming headache that holds little meaning for their daily work. No good data collection and analysis plan can be enacted without staff buy-in. Staff must recognize the need for an information system, and they will do so when it is relevant to their work. This happens when all involved recognize the difference between "data" and "information." *Data* stand alone without meaning; but when data are translated into *information* they tell a story. The information system is intended to tell the program's story.

It may be helpful to put information systems into perspective. Every human service agency has an information system; some are just more organized than others, and some are just more sophisticated than others. That was certainly evident when the Street Educators had to go directly to the case records to find data because that was where their information was found. If an agency has forms on which data are collected, and if results are uniformly used by staff, then data have been turned into information. A well-conceived *information system* provides a systematic approach to data collection so that data can be regularly translated into information that can be *used* by staff. If there are data elements collected that no one in the agency needs or can use, then deleting these items from the forms should be considered. It is important as part of rational planning to carefully think through all the data elements so that critical elements are not missing and, conversely, so that unnecessary data are not collected.

Sometimes powerful sources (e.g., funders, regulators) want certain data collected that do not seem useful to staff. If these data elements are needed to obtain future funding or to comply with funder reporting requirements, then it would be politically wise to continue to collect those data even if staff do not find them useful. In these situations, managers and planners have a responsibility to explain to staff the purpose of collecting certain data and the importance of assuring that accurate data are collected and interpreted. The planner in the problem-solving model and the manager tasked with implementing a plan must balance the data collection needs of various constituencies. What one person may see as essential to collect, another one may find less useful.

Written measurable objectives provide clues to what data need to be collected. The program hypothesis will help to identify the components of the most important aspects of the program. From each portion of the hypothesis, indicators should be identified that will provide the necessary information to communicate the status of the program and its participants. Using the Street Educators case as an example, look at Box 3.5 for an illustration of how to examine one's program hypothesis and actually identify data elements that need to be captured. In this case input data are identified.

Box 3.5

Logic of Identifying Data Elements from Examining a Program Hypothesis

First Line of Hypothesis:

If children "of" the street are contacted through outreach, and . . .

This statement from the hypothesis contains "inputs":

If **children "of" the street** are **contacted** through **outreach**, and . . .

Children "of" the street
- Characteristics (age, gender, race, family situation, etc.)
- Reason for being on the street
- Length of time on the street

Contacts
- Characteristics (when, by whom, length of contact, content of contact)

Outreach
- Auspice (nonprofit, for profit, public)
- Affiliations (chain, national/local, religious group)
- Type (relationship building, information sharing, recruitment to program)

BUDGETING

Once data elements are identified and the program design has been established, the logic model is complete; but the planner's planning responsibilities are not complete until costs are considered. Budgets for most program plans will include *line items* such as personnel, fringe benefits, travel, equipment, and supplies that have been drawn from the inputs and activity sections of the plan. Predicting actual costs can entail a bit of guesswork when the planner is faced with shifts in priorities, adjustments that become necessary to manage power dynamics, and unforeseeable impinging forces that appear on the long-term road to program impact. The Street Educators in our case seemed to understand some of the power issues that might be involved in budgeting.

Kettner, Moroney, and Martin (1999) view budgeting as a combination of political forces influenced by interest groups, incremental processes built on the previous year's work, and rational planning influenced by program information. They remind us that budgeting is a decision-making process, neither magical (Kettner et al., 1999) nor miraculous (Lewis et al., 2001). Budgets imply political choices that affect people's lives, and program planners are responsible for those choices.

Program revenues may come from various sources, such as client fees, third-party payments, contracts, fundraising activities, United

Ways, private grants, public grants, contributions, and endowments. Since programs are usually tethered to organizations, the planner needs to know the sources and percentages of agency funds assigned the program, as well as how those funds might change over the life of the program. It is also helpful to know how the host agency develops line items. Most program plans will be heavily committed to salaries and employee-related expenses (ERE), which are usually at least 20 percent or more of the employees' salaries. Because human service programs are labor-intensive, it is expected that personnel costs will constitute a high percentage of a program's budget. Operating costs, such as rent, utilities, telephones, tutors, supplies, equipment (both purchased and rented), equipment maintenance, professional fees, postage and shipping, and printing and publications, should not be overlooked. Travel costs may include in-state, out-of-state, and conference registrations. The most problematic aspect of program accountability is accurately targeting true costs in advance without under- or overprojecting. An off-target budget can do more to destroy the potential of a well-developed logic model and program plan than any other aspect of the problem-solving process.

RATIONAL PLANNING

There are some very specific skill sets needed to engage in rational planning and when using prescriptive approaches. In addition to skills, there are mind-sets that are "natural" or that can be acquired in order to engage in high-quality rational planning to impact on a social problem.

MIND-SETS

To pursue prescriptive approaches, planners must think rationally. Linear logic must be part of the manner in which the planner encounters situations, thinks about problems, and establishes ideas about ways to address those problems. Although the ability to envision the whole final picture is important, it is the details that are essential.

Details should be the planner's friends. Rational planning welcomes the thought precision needed to construct the logic model and appreciates the prescriptive nature of the process. Precise thoughtfulness is essential to develop the rationale of a program, and this includes the insightfulness to uncover unstated assumptions. Having the patience to face what may feel like the tedium of connecting the links in the logic model chain is necessary. The planner must be willing to spend the time and the thought necessary to connect the program hypotheses to the solution.

Patience is needed to develop the details before moving to action. The planner must embrace the notion that it is important to identify as many as possible of the presumed effects of all aspects of the plan before launching into action. Once action happens, the planner must be willing to learn from the lessons drawn from a program theory-based evaluation, rather than simply relying on his or her own instincts. Then the full power of the logic model can grow through revisions.

In rational planning, the planner must appreciate systems theory. Recognizing that inputs such as clients, staff, equipment, and various materials and supplies come together in an interactive process, and knowing how to measure what happens in that process, are critical. Thus, the planner must be organized in thinking through possible scenarios in advance, and planning for contingencies that could arise along the way. The person who will enjoy this type of planning will have a mind-set that it is important to influence the future by identifying in advance as many potential consequences as possible. The planner whose comfort zone includes order and precision may naturally take to rational planning.

Skills

In using a logic model, it is important to be skilled in thinking through the fit of what one wants to do with what it is possible to do, following the goal as a vision of what can be. For example, the planner must seek integrity between the problem analysis and the intervention hypothesis, because if both are strong, then the logic will hold. And since the hypothesis literally fits hand in glove with the measurable objectives, there is consistency between the two. Box 3.6 provides the planner with questions necessary to engage in this hypothesis assessment.

Box 3.6

Assessing a Hypothesis for Logic and Fit with Objectives

- Who is the primary target population? Is there a secondary target? How specific do you need to be about the target population (or subgroup of the population) so that you do not set yourself up to do more than you can?
- What is the problem statement this program hypothesis addresses? Is there more than one problem here?
- What theoretical, empirical, or practice knowledge guides this hypothesis?
- What values does this hypothesis reflect?
- What is the organizational or interorganizational context in which this hypothesis fits? What does this mean in terms of the feasibility of achieving the hypothesis?
- Does this hypothesis address a public mandate, or does the hypothesis come from another source?
- Who are the stakeholders who have an interest in this hypothesis? How are consumers' interests represented here?

- What is the final (ultimate) outcome? Is this a direct service or personal service, staff development and training, and/or an advocacy (transformative change) program outcome?
- How might you measure this final (ultimate) outcome?
- Are there intermediate and immediate outcomes? If yes, what are they and how might you measure them?
- Are the intermediate and immediate outcomes direct service, staff development and training, and/or advocacy outcomes?
- What are the inputs (processes) in this hypothesis?
- Could you write process and outcome objectives for this hypothesis?
- Based on this analysis, how feasible is this hypothesis in guiding program planning?

Another skill in rational planning must be the ability to translate program needs into a resource plan. Budgets are composed of numbers, but the skilled planner will understand the decision-making process in which the budget is developed. The planner will make choices that fit with acceptable values, will appeal to decision-makers, and will best position the program for funding. Thus, budgeting is critically important and political; and the planner constructs and defends it. Examples of questions needed to fully comprehend the nuances of budgeting are provided in Box 3.7.

Finally, in the current human service environment, the planner must be able to define evidence-based practice, use evidence in the construction of the plan, and explain to decision-makers how the program will contribute to the next wave of evidence about impacting the specific problem. It is also necessary to explain exactly why the proposed outcome measures are the best means of evaluating

Box 3.7
Questions about the Context of Budgeting

1. How have decisions about the budget been made in the past?
   - New leadership may shape things differently
   - Source of authority may have shifted (from national to state)
   - Cultural norms surrounding the budget

2. Who will be included in the process?
   - The board (as rubberstamp or as experts)
   - The advisory council
   - Staff (Is the budget viewed as something magical/ untouchable by staff?)
   - Consumers

3. What assumptions will those persons bring to the budgeting process?
   - May assume that budgets are easy to change
   - May assume that their input will assure that their voices are heard
   - May assume that budgets can always be manipulated

4. What funding sources will be approached?
   - In order to preserve autonomy?
   - How much control will they assert?
   - What interests do these sources represent?

5. How do we frame what we want to do?
   - To please a funding source by covering up our real goal
   - To stay consistent with agency's mission
   - To appeal to certain interests

6. What constraints will be imposed by those who control the revenues?
   - Regulations/standards
   - Political ideologies

7. How much will we pay/reward personnel? Pay determined by:
   - Choices to hire professional, credentialed staff
   - Choices to provide adequate fringe benefits
   - Possibilities of Cost of Living Allowance (COLA)/merit

8. Will we use volunteers, paraprofessionals, and so on, and will their efforts be calculated?
   - Into the cost per output, per outcome?
   - In trying to use volunteers when we truly need paid staff
   - By investing in a volunteer coordinator

9. Will in-kind contributions be considered and recorded? Will they be calculated into the cost per output, per outcome?
   - If yes, we will know what the real cost is.
   - If no, then decision-makers will never really know what it costs.

10. What corners will we cut? How will cutting those corners affect staff, clients, others?

for program effectiveness. To do this, rational planning is conducted by persons capable of evaluating research results and able to translate those results into decisions in the program logic or design. This also means that the planner must be capable of engaging in program evaluation, or at least have the necessary program or organizational expertise needed to facilitate the collection and analysis of data in program evaluation.

STRENGTHS AND CHALLENGES
OF RATIONAL PLANNING

There is an identifiable logic and progression in rational planning that provides a sense of predictability, comfort, and security in a world that is anything but certain. Being able to employ a formula and talk the same language as others who understand basic systems concepts and the nature of prescriptive approaches, such as the logic model, provides a sense of competence. This is particularly true when demonstrating to decision-makers that there is integrity in how everything fits together, from problem definition through program design. Programs based on this logic allow evaluation to be integrated into every step of the implementation process. This provides a competitive edge for funding, which can add to a program planner's reputation. Also, programs based on prescriptive models stand the chance of contributing to the growing need for evidence that interventions work (or not), because the planning details document how those interventions were carried out, and with what results. Evaluations continue to reverberate because they can be used to plan other programs and establish further need for funding.

The logic model, as a prescriptive approach, provides a visual representation of a project, which allows all stakeholders to understand the connections among all the components described. The model can serve as the basis of collaborative work because it makes explicit assumptions and expectations for each step of the program. It adds to transparency because of the discussions it engenders among various constituencies. When designed appropriately and used consistently, it creates more than a static picture. It furthers problem-solving because it provides structure and language for conversations and decision-making in moving toward an envisioned result.

However, there are times when one is not absolutely sure that the result was due to the intervention provided. For example, a number of years ago in a pet-facilitated therapy program for older people, we found that well-being was increased for those persons who received companion animals. But there was a nagging question about whether the rise in subjective well-being was a matter of the animal as an intervention or because a very affable male veterinarian made house calls. The older women were delighted to have this "visitor," who monitored the animals, and they entertained him with various stories and assorted goodies whenever he visited. We are still not sure the older women would have taken animals (or even desired them) had this veterinarian not been part of the package. Without the presence of the veterinarian, we are unsure that the same positive effects would have occurred. What seemed like a highly rational process based on a logic model produced uncertainty in the interpretation of evaluation data.

Rational planning can also lead to highly unexpected results that can call into question the original theory used. Unfortunately, this tends to lead to questioning of the integrity of every step in the process. Sometimes one does not see the expected result, but instead sees an unanticipated result when an intervention works beyond expectations. For example, hospice programs require a physician's referral to be based on the patient having six months or less to live. When multiple patients in hospice programs start living way beyond the six-month limit, it is possible that for the first time in their lives they are getting the attention of a full-fledged interdisciplinary team and so have discovered a reason to live. Although the team is supposed to document that the person is getting worse (otherwise, he or she would not be in hospice care), they discover that the patient is getting better (and has to be discharged from hospice care). There is a paradox in this situation that raises questions about using a rational approach. For that reason, in

Chapter 4, we will focus on interpretive planning and compare it to rational planning discussed here.

Prescriptive approaches can sometimes give participants a false sense of security. Sometimes one sees very satisfied practitioners, but it is unclear if the intervention worked. The practitioners may enjoy one another's company so much that turnover is low, morale is high, and a feeling of "doing good" prevails in the culture. They may have a logical set of activities in which they are engaging, leading toward a predetermined set of outcomes. However, these positives do not always create results in systems. The logic model based on a specific program hypothesis for this situation simply does not hold. Sometimes, in real life, linear reasoning, program logic with a problem-solving focus, and a clear program design do not move efforts to expected results. The next chapter will explore in detail an alternative way to plan, based on different assumptions about what should go into the planning process.

SUMMARY

Prescriptive approaches such as using problem-solving or logic models are based on assumptions of rational planning. To be rational means identifying a goal and then doing reverse-order planning—determining what needs to happen in light of the goal rather than moving forward without an end in sight. This type of planning has deep roots in decision-making theory and is within the synoptic tradition. Numerous forces make this type of planning in high demand today as public and private interests are requiring that programs have measurable outcomes.

Rational planning follows a general logic, moving linearly from problem setting to results identification, through program implementation and evaluation planning. The logic model is used as an exemplar of rational planning because it is based on a series of steps: assessing needs, identifying and analyzing problems, selecting intervention strategies, writing goals and objectives, decision-making about the details of program design, and evaluation. Each step builds on the others.

Prescriptive approaches can be made to be accountable, but there are challenges. In situations in which outcomes are difficult to measure or in programs with diverse clientele, various constituencies may not be able to agree on what data need to be collected. In the process, the planner is accountable to the organizational context in which s/he is placing the program, as well as to decision-makers who approve and fund the program.

Rational planning occurs in a linear way, so that the planner is attentive to detail, is patient, and has a solid understanding of systems theory and its relationship to planning. The planner must be organized with a capacity to think through costs and benefits of potential scenarios in advance. The planner must be able to envision the future.

To those who embrace rational planning, it can bring a sense of security amid uncertainty because one does the best one can to think ahead and anticipate consequences. Because evaluation is integrated throughout the process, a strong case can be made for the use of a prescriptive approach such as the logic model in positioning a program for funding. There are, however, times when the rational, reductionistic processes mask what may really be happening. In these cases, sticking rigidly to preconceived steps may cause failure to see unexpected (but important) results, or even create a culture of success among staff when clients are not benefiting. Therefore, knowing when (and when not) to use rational planning is an important skill.

DISCUSSION QUESTIONS

1. Can you give an example of how program theory is incorporated into planning a rational program with which you are familiar? What are the process and outcome objectives of this program?

2. Analyze the Street Educators case at the beginning of this chapter using the logic model. What were the resources/inputs, throughputs/activities; outputs, outcomes, and impact/goal? How is the logic model useful (or not) in analyzing this case? What would you have done differently if you had been asked by the mayor to redesign this program?

3. What are the four parts of an objective in rational planning? If all objectives have four parts, then how do process and outcome objectives differ?

4. Are these outcome or process objectives? (Fill in the blanks.)

   • By September 1, 2005, to have established a program office within the Department of Human Services and the Department of Vital Records that will help people find their birth parents. _____

   • By April 30, 2005, to reduce the involvement of Amerasian youth at risk of delinquent behavior by 50 percent, as documented by the decreasing number of cases reported to the Amerasian youth worker in charge of court/policy contact. _____

   • By December 31, 2004, to have approved a treatment program for sexual trauma victims at the rape crisis center, which will alleviate acute symptoms, as measured by approval of the program by the administrator. _____

5. Examine each of the objectives listed in Question 6 and determine whether they are complete, according to the following list:

   • Time frame

- Target of the change
- Results to be achieved
- Criteria by which results will be documented, monitored, or measured
- Responsibility for who will carry it out

6. Consider whether each of the following objectives is a process or an outcome objective? Why or why not? Could the objective be more clearly stated? If yes, how would you reword it?

   - By January 15, to develop a sense of community among residents of Farmington as measured by their meeting together on a regular basis.
   - By one year after the youth enters the support program, 90 percent of the youth will have his or her G.E.D. or will be enrolled in and regularly attending a local high school. This will be documented by his or her caseworker in the form of G.E.D. test scores, registration forms, attendance records, and continual contact with the school.
   - By the end of their first year in the program, 70 percent of stroke survivors will have maintained or enhanced their levels of rehabilitation as measured by an increase of at least 50 percent in their pre- and posttest scores on the Barthel Index, which measures activities of daily living and mobility and by pre- and posttest scores on the PULSES profile, which provides a global assessment of functional status. These assessment instruments will be administered by the social work coordinator of this program.
   - By January, all home care recipients over the age of 85 will be assessed by the social work and nursing case management team, using the multidimensional OARS assessment tool developed by Duke University.

- Within a month of program start, provide the community with a central meeting place that offers educational, recreational, and spiritual programming seven days a week, as demonstrated by written daily schedules documented by program staff.
- One year after the program has begun, 75 percent of the families who participated will not have had to interrupt employment to care for their sick child. This shall be documented by the existing employment records kept by the current child care case managers.
- By January, racial oppression for low-income families of minority children will be reduced by 50 percent, as measured by self report.

7. Can you identify some ethical dilemmas you might encounter in using a prescriptive approach to designing a human service program?

8. Come up with a problem you would like to address. If you were going to design a program to address this problem, how would you select a theory or theories to guide the problem analysis? How will the organization in which you place the program affect your program design? What theory, research, practice models, literature, and experience can be used to guide your program design? Which theories (whether explicit or not) and models (both empirically and nonempirically tested) led to your intervention hypothesis? What is the rationale (or set of rationales) behind your intervention? Will your intervention hypothesis lead you to a creative program design?

CHAPTER 4

Interpretive Planning and Emergent Approaches

An emergent world asks us to stand in a different place. We can no longer stand at the end of something we visualize in detail and plan backwards from that future. Instead, we must stand at the beginning, clear in our intent, with a willingness to be involved in a discovery. The world asks that we focus less on how we can coerce something to make it conform to our designs and focus more on how we can engage with one another, how we can enter into the experience and then notice what comes forth. It asks that we participate more than plan.

—Margaret J. Wheatley and Myron Kellner-Rogers, *A Simpler Way*

Chapter Outline

Case: The Invisible People and the Area Agency on Aging
Introduction
History of Interpretive Planning and Emergent Approaches
Dimensions of Interpretive Planning and Emergent Approaches
   The Logic of Emergence
   Engagement
   Discovery
   Sense-making
   Unfolding
Accountability in an Emergent Approach

Accountability Challenges
Accountability Options
Interpretive Planning
  Mind-sets
  Skills
Strengths and Challenges of Interpretive Planning
Summary
Discussion Questions

Assumptions upon which the chapter is built:

- Interpretive planning and the emergent approaches create a viable framework for competent program planning, even though planning will be different from rational, prescriptive approaches.
- Interpretive planning focuses on understanding stakeholders' perspectives as a means of continual information gathering and analysis.
- Interpretive planning is nonlinear, in that engagement, sense-making, and discovery interact continually as a program design unfolds.
- Data collection in this type of planning tends to be both formal and informal, with whatever structure that is applied being tentative and open to reformulation, depending on what is being learned.
- The planning process is continually emergent by being attentive to time and context.

We begin this chapter with another case, this time placed in the United States. Again, our purpose is to stimulate thinking so that you may see how an emergent approach to planning might be useful. Throughout the chapter, we will refer back to this case, illustrating some of the major points to be made.

Case: The Invisible People and the Area Agency on Aging

A social worker in an Area Agency on Aging in a large U.S. city took on an agency project that no one had really wanted to tackle. The project was originally framed by a supervisor as "something we've not been able to get our minds around." It dealt with the observation that older mentally ill clients were being "dumped" on the doorsteps of various facilities when no one knew what to do with them. The supervisor explained that these people were "invisible" to the larger population; and unless a specific situation received press coverage, the practice of dumping seemed to be a last-resort measure, with no firm information on how widespread it might be. The task was to create a program intervention plan for this vulnerable population in a community setting. But the challenge was that no one, not even the supervisor, knew where to begin.

Older, mentally ill persons appeared to be at extreme risks of alcohol use, homelessness, and a host of other problems, all of them quite dangerous and potentially life-threatening. The local shelter that had focused on mentally ill adults' needs had recently closed. Other shelters were open to taking in selected older adults with mental illness, but they had to be referred through a professional source and had to be willing to continue taking their medications. Ironically, staying on medications meant having some ability to manage meds, as well as the resources for obtaining them, abilities these older adults did not have. In addition, the severely mentally ill and the oldest of the old had typically been abandoned by any remaining family members (if they had family at all), who had given up trying to provide care; and due to chronic risk-taking behaviors, the physical health of these two groups was often impaired.

(Continued)

The social worker's assumption, in the beginning, was that the problem of these abandoned, older, mentally ill adults was becoming even worse since the one shelter specifically serving them had closed. The practice of discouraging walk-ins and self-referrals by the remaining shelters did not help, either.

Immediately upon taking on the project, the social worker encountered a puzzle. Early one morning, as she sat over a cup of hot coffee, reviewing field notes and beginning to create a work plan for the project, it dawned on her that while the conditions of these adults was apparent to those close to them, helping uninvolved parties to understand the social issue would not be so easy. One difficulty was that there was no effective way to gather needs assessment data in a traditional manner. The traditional planning process, used for years at the Area Agency on Aging, called for assessment data to be gathered about conditions so that each issue could be defined to show its extent and severity. This was needed to enable the setting of change goals within a formal intervention plan.

However, in this situation, mentally ill adults were not "visible"—that is, they were not easy to find or find out about in any typical way by social agencies. They occasionally appeared in gero-psychiatric units of the three major medical facilities in town; but by the time they were admitted there, their lives were in peril. If they were released, usually there was no place for them to go, and no one to oversee continuing care. Thus, they occasionally ended up in emergency rooms soon after leaving an acute care setting, creating a nightmare of recidivism for hospitals—not to mention that they rarely had insurance to cover mental health care.

As to who gave them taxi fare and sent them to the emergency rooms or long-term care facilities that would not take them, it was anyone's guess. No one openly admitted to this practice, but occasionally it happened. When the problem caught the attention of the city's newspaper, a bit of attention was paid, but interest soon waned as other news items took precedence. And without numbers to show the size of this population and potential of harm to mentally ill persons, or the community in general, how could it be demonstrated that there was a social issue at all? Further, without this information, how would support for changing the situation be generated?

A puzzle, indeed. Fortunately, this social worker was not easily deterred from challenges. The social worker began by considering how to locate and/or gather information about this vulnerable population, knowing that the agency, potential funders, and the supervisor would need these data to support any intervention plan that might be developed. Of course, one might walk the streets looking for homeless persons who appeared old; but it was difficult enough to figure how many persons of any age were homeless in this city, much less identify their ages. Nevertheless, the social worker believed a way could be found to learn significant information about this population, and that this was a critically important concern for the Area Agency on Aging to tackle. The social worker decided to start with the shelter that had closed, as it had provided service to a steady stream of older adults who had presented themselves for overnight stays. But where had they gone? The social worker knew they were still out there, somewhere.

Rational planning used to construct the agency's four-year plan required by the Administration on Aging was linear—hold public hearings to gather needs assessment data; write goals, measurable objectives, and action steps based on what was learned; and submit a formal plan to the state agency on aging. In this case, however, the social worker reasoned that without needs assessment data, movement to the next step in the linear

(Continued)

process was not possible. Essentially, the invisibility of the population group facilitated doing nothing. Perhaps, reasoned the social worker, it would be necessary just to start somewhere, and trust that doing so would lead to unpredictable next steps. Although this tactic was somewhat disconcerting, it appeared to be the only logical choice. After having a long talk with her supervisor about this approach, the social worker was given the go-ahead. At the very least she felt she had support.

The social worker began contacting professionals at the gero-psych units of all the major hospitals, staff at long-term care facilities that accepted indigent clients, and shelter staff experienced with older adults. Though valuable to pool this information, it still provided no data of the actual experiences of mentally ill elders. Would it be possible, the social worker wondered, to interview older adults who had made their way to gero-psych units, given the strict privacy laws? The social worker decided to investigate this possibility. To contact older adults within the community, the cooperation of at least one shelter would be necessary. Fortunately, the Area Agency on Aging and a local shelter had an established relationship. Permission was gained from that shelter to allow the agency to use up to two beds per night for self-referrals by mentally ill elders. (The shelter agreed to modify its policies as a trial because evidence might come from the effort that would lead the facility to serve an additional population in need of services.) The idea was for a community worker employed by the shelter to spread word on the streets that walk-ins were acceptable at this shelter. This was the way to determine whether there was, in fact, a problem.

The possibility existed that no elders would show up, perhaps because they were distrustful or did not want to be "pursued." Still, a great deal could be learned from the effort, even if it was that older persons were reluctant to accept the offer from the shelter. The social worker remembered what she had learned by fishing with her beloved grandfather—that one should always be willing to try out or test a fishing spot, as you would at the least learn where not to fish that day. He told her, "Just let the bait lie awhile, and if there are no takers, move on." Thus, if no elders came to the shelter, that, too was useful information. On the other hand, if there were some bites, if even one or two people did appear, they would be a source of information for planning. They could help further the assessment, as they were participants who had essential knowledge and "expertise": they knew about their own lives and, probably, the lives of other elders on the streets, and about their needs and what it might take to engage them. This test would be an opportunity to build on the information and allow the shelter staff to adjust its efforts, even while a fuller plan for larger-scale intervention was being created.

The social worker thought, "We'll see what emerges when we try this out. Then we'll incorporate what we learn into our thinking and revise our planning as we move ahead." Thus the process would become part of generating results. What seemed to be important was that the next step was dependent on the process continuing, rather than everything being dependent on fully completing the needs assessment before moving to the next step. This was a flexible approach, one that allowed for adjustments along the way. And although it was a bit unsettling, it felt right. The information necessary and the form it would take really needed to emerge from the process. This way, if the initial effort met significant barriers, adaptations could be tried. For example, staff had ideas about offering free telephone calls, hot showers, morning coffee on a walk-in basis, and hot meals, to help bring in the elders and to identify some basic services they might need beyond survival and safety issues.

(Continued)

The social worker jumped into the process with conviction, determined to establish a committed relationship with the various parties from whom information could be gathered; at the same time, she remained open to adding new stakeholders as they were identified. Within three weeks, in addition to service people with interest in the issue, five mentally ill older persons had taken advantage of the shelter's offer, three of whom agreed to be interviewed by the social worker from the Area Agency. Their stories revealed that they all had adult children who lived in the city, an unanticipated fact. Thus, the expectation that mentally ill elders probably did not have family (at least locally) was proven wrong, raising the possibility that other key stakeholders might be family members who had spent years trying—and, ultimately, failing—to deal with an untenable care-giving situation. It addition, it was learned that two of the three had houses that had been condemned by the city but that were still standing. This raised the question, was substandard housing better than no housing at all? And what was the city's role and responsibility when residents were evicted but had no place to go?

Additional information was gained by talking to hospital staff at gero-psych units in the city's hospitals (permission to talk with patients at these facilities was not granted). These professionals agreed to talk with Area Agency staff about their experiences, under the condition that patient names not be revealed. The social worker found these dialogues to be eye-opening, for she learned that these patients had such complex situations that even the experienced, trained staff in the units often found themselves at a loss as to how to help them. One psychiatric nurse explained, "We have an older patient on the unit who has a long history of severe mental illness, is likely suffering from cognitive impairment, and who is in emotional trauma most of the time. She came to us through an emergency room admittance from the local nursing home, and they are refusing to take her back. She has a daughter who is at her wit's end, who had tried to provide for her mother, and who is now in danger of complete burnout. The patient repeats over and over again that she wants to go home, but there is really no place for her to go. We can't find any facility that will take her, and her daughter is on the verge of an emotional breakdown. What do we do?"

The social worker asked, somewhat tentatively, "Is this what you would call a typical situation?"

The nurse replied, "Nothing is typical in this patient population . . . . But all our situations are equally complicated."

The social worker returned to the Area Agency and reported this information to her supervisor saying, "It seems that the key stakeholders who need to be part of our planning process have increased. We need to include family members, because it is becoming obvious that, at least in some situations, they are part of the picture. We also need to consider the input of organizations like the Alzheimer's Association and the Mental Health Association, because we are seeing histories of mental illness, as well as organic impairments."

The social worker continued, "In addition, we need to consider that what we are discovering is not commonly known—even we are surprised at the complications involved with attempting to find out about (much less intervene with) this population. I had hoped to be able to tell you that we could start focusing in on a specific problem, but in all honesty I think we need to keep asking questions and gathering more information, because this story just keeps unfolding and it is far more complicated than we thought."

INTRODUCTION

In Chapter 3, we focused on rational planning and often used prescriptive approaches such as logic and problem-solving models. We noted that effectiveness-based models with measurable objectives in all their versions have become increasingly popular. Yet other approaches have also existed, flying under the radar screen, subjugated due to the predominance of both positivism and Western thought. This chapter is devoted to *interpretive planning* and *emergent approaches,* which developed when rational or synoptic planning did not provide for inclusion of diverse groups or intense relationships in the process. In this chapter, we elaborate on what Brody calls "forward-sequence planning," as opposed to "reverse-order planning." *Forward-sequence planning* begins by asking where can one start rather than what does one want as the final result, which is the focus of rational planning (Brody, 2000, pp. 77–78). Durant and Carr (2003) elaborate on emergent strategy development "with its acknowledgment that uncertainty is here to stay" (p. 1).

We have participated in interpretive planning and emergent approaches many times, and we have initiated an emergent approach when we had no idea where to begin and had to trust the process as a guide. We are not alone, and responding in this way is not without challenges (Christie, Montosse, & Klein, 2005; Morrison & Salipante, 2007). For example, Jewell, Davidson, and Rowe (2006) conducted a study of the Connecticut Peer Engagement Specialist Initiative in which peer mentors (persons with mental illness) worked on community mental health teams to engage persons with serious mental illness and a history of violence. Using their own personal experiences with mental illness, peer mentors offered an alternative program to the mandated or involuntary outpatient commitment process typically used with these hard-to-reach clients. Mentors needed to be flexible, with the ability to change their tactics midcourse because each client was unique. The evaluation suggested that peer mentors had a positive effect on many clients, yet state policymakers were unconvinced and deemed the program a failure. Strapped by the very policies that allowed the mentors to work with clients, an "institutional paradox" occurred in which "peer specialists were not able to help their clients in ways directly relevant to policymakers" (p. 3). The evaluators concluded that decision-makers were not willing to allow the process to unfold as needed, and when it did not conform to rational expectations, they were quick to pass judgment. Why did the program "work" from the perspective of clients and staff but fail on a grander scale? The evaluators acknowledged that the program initiative had been compromised because policymakers wanted a quick resolution "to solve intractable social problems in a short period of time with incremental funding and staff increases," and the program design that emerged in process diverged "from strongly held initial expectations" (pp. 20–21). In short, decision-makers expected a rational planning process to lead to an expected set of outcomes, when in reality the program had to emerge and change, based on *unfolding* experiences.

To prepare you for professional responses in similar situations, we build on the discussion in Chapter 1 about alternative ways of knowing and approaching planning, introducing interpretive program planning based on an emergent approach. Following a nonrational, nonlinear view of planning, and guided by *social constructivist, social learning,* and *sense-making theories,* in program planning you may see a more collaborative, less reductionistic approach to decision-making. This is an approach you might use when you have an opportunity in which you learn along the way, letting what happens guide where you go. Sometimes, there are what appear to be intractable challenges that are beyond one-size-fits-all remedies offering predictable, measurable results. Simple or complicated tasks, such as baking a cake, replacing a flat tire, or sending a rocket into space can be accomplished in a step-by-step way—and typically need to be done in a particular, sequential manner. These sorts of "recipes" (in rational planning, called "program theories") are helpful in many situations, but they are not sufficient in the face of the complexity of some social problems. Sometimes, sequential, stand-alone tasks do not serve the purpose of solving a problem. Instead, tasks that all interact with one another are necessary to produce desired results, allowing simultaneous attention to the simple, complicated, and complex.

Many of the more modern planning theories have suggested both the need for and the actual form of planning processes that, in one way or another, have been developed and tested for their capacity to guide problem-solving that is anything but straightforward. Earlier we talked about incremental, advocacy, transactive, and radical theories of planning. Each grew in reaction to the limits of the traditional model. However, most of these theories or the more recent planning approaches such as scenario planning, search conferencing, participatory planning, or feminist planning, also discussed earlier, did not totally depart from the assumptions and hopes of positivistic thought. Each identified with some aspect of the challenges planners face when expected to produce prescient, reductive work prior to enacting a plan. Each recognized challenges in the planning process, but none specifically identified the fundamental differences that can emerge when planning starts from a completely different standpoint, with a different set of assumptions. It is a story of reflectivity, of astute thinking coupled with acting deliberately and intentionally in settings containing complexity and uncertainty. What follows is a discussion of just that. It covers the landscape of questions, tensions, uncertainties, relationships, and mind-sets necessary to enact interpretive planning.

Table 4.1
Hierarchy of Key Concepts

Ways of knowing (philosophy)	Interpretivism
Ways of thinking (thought)	Interpretive (nonrational)
Ways of doing (approaches)	Emergent

Table 4.1 serves as a reminder of the focus we are taking in this chapter and how it compares with that of Chapter 3. Recall that interpretivism as a way of knowing leads to interpretive (nonrational) ways of thinking. Emergent approaches are based on interpretive thinking.

HISTORY OF INTERPRETIVE PLANNING AND EMERGENT APPROACHES

Miller, Hickson, and Wilson (1996) provide a historical perspective on theories and studies about decision-making in organizations. They recognize that "the rational model of decision-making begins to break down when faced with [pluralist visions] of multiple, competing interest groups vying for supremacy" (p. 297). They suggest that "empirical studies of decision-making have added weight to the criticisms of rational choice models as being idealized prescriptions, depicting an unreality" (p. 298), and they credit Lindblom (1959) with his insights related to incrementalism and the *science of mudding through* as dispelling "the myth that decision-making, in public institutions at least, was a linear, sequential process. Decisions here were made in a halting 'incremental' way with periods of recycling, iteration, and reformulation. The process was a nonlinear one" (p. 299).

Lindblom argued for a normative approach to decision-making because context was inherently unpredictable. In incremental decision-making, each step is not radically different from previous steps so that stakeholders are not unduly overwhelmed with rapid change or threatened. If steps taken are upsetting to participants, then one can easily retrace one's steps because a great deal of change has not occurred; in essence, each step is reversible. Lindblom contended that steps being retraced allowed decision-makers to resolve differences and maintain relationships with various stakeholders in the process. This was seen as an interpretive process of planning that is nonrational, or certainly different from the process used in rational thinking.

Hudson (1979) contends that some organizations thrive on what he calls future studies or troubleshooting, "where neither the problem nor the solution is well defined, and the client is more likely to be open-minded about surprise findings and unorthodox recommendations for action. Some planners feel that the really interesting problems are those being encountered for the first time and those which are too 'wicked' to be reduced to standard [rational approaches]" (p. 260). This represents an emergent approach closely aligned with Weick's (1995) work on *sense-making*. Weick raises the possibility that when one is lost and does not know what to do next, any old plan will do because plans are similar to maps in orienting people.

> Once people begin to act (enactment), they generate tangible outcomes (cues) in some context (social), and this helps them discover (retrospect) what is occurring (ongoing), what needs to be explained (plausibility), and what should be done next (identity enhancement). Managers keep forgetting that it is what they do, not what they plan, that explains their success. They keep giving credit to the wrong thing—namely, the plan—and having made this error, they then spend more time planning and less time acting . . . when more planning improves nothing (Weick, 1995, p. 55).

Theorists like Lindblom, who was doing his work right after World War II, and Weick's more recent work, suggest decision-making processes totally different from linear ways of deciding, and lend scholarly respectability to an emergent approach. In addition, in the concept of the learning organization as identified by Peter M. Senge (1990), one finds a very interpretive orientation to organizing. All of these writers provide clues for how planning and program implementation can be conceptualized not just reductionistically, but also as a continual, ongoing process of learning.

There are even earlier indications of the presence of interpretive planning. Several years ago, we discovered *Lady Boards of Managers*, all-female governing boards, whose members were founding, chartering, governing, administering, and managing beneficent organizations in the United States and Britain as early as the early 1800s, and continuing through the turn of the twentieth century (Netting & O'Connor, 2005). In our historical research on organizational planning, we were not surprised to find socially constructed, distinctive roles in organizations stratified by gender, race, and religion. What was surprising was witnessing the heyday of Lady Boards of Managers, which oversaw many health and human service organizations up through the Progressive era, only to be replaced by their male counterparts and returned to subservient roles in the early part of the twentieth century. What surprised us was that the concepts of partnership, collaboration, cooperation and other behaviors of connection in organizations seen to be "new" in the management literature in the last decades were present in the "old" Lady Board of Managers. What we found when we "exhumed" Lady Boards of Managers for the purposes of understanding interpretive planning and programming was a time when there were no organizational theories and no management textbooks to teach those interested how to plan programs. Handwritten records survive to document a quiet revolution that included emerging plans for service delivery, organizational designs, staffing patterns, and decisions about difficult issues. Their work has never been officially codified as a way of planning, but plan they did, in an emergent manner.

These boards were unabashedly engaged in micromanaging, discovering as they worked. There were no rules about keeping board members and staff separate, about roles distinctive from service provision, or even about not having board members involved with service delivery. Their approach was one of loose boundaries and semipermeability, with a good deal of multitasking. They demonstrated collaboration, partnering, and consensus building. They were attuned to their sociopolitical context and engaged board members in the community and the life of the organization in whatever way was necessary to achieve their goals. They offer a historical precedent for a context-embedded planning that emerged relationally and flexibly when there existed no certain guidance about how to proceed.

Much more recently, perhaps one of the most fanciful views of decision-making is seen in Cohen, March, and Simon's (1972) work on the "garbage can model," in which decisions appear to occur in an anarchical way, with ideas being "dumped into the can," only to occasionally interact with seemingly unrelated ideas that move the process along. This is an example of efforts to address the challenges of managing complex decisions in conditions of uncertainty. For some, interpretive thinking has been an invisible force all along in creative planning, in the face of complexity and uncertainly (i.e. Faludi, 1973). For others, interpretive work has been a type of planning used as a secret weapon of most innovative change agents (Wheatley & Kellner-Rogers, 1996; Zimmerman, & Patton, 2006). However, most program planning textbooks have focused on prescriptive approaches, stopping there as if those were the only tools available.

DIMENSIONS OF INTERPRETIVE PLANNING AND EMERGENT APPROACHES

Capturing exactly what constitutes an emergent approach for planning sometimes resembles efforts to herd cats. There is no predetermined order, but there is directionality, and it includes nonlinear dynamics that allow the unexpected to present itself. Planning does get from one point to another, but not in the clear, predictable steps expected in prescriptive approaches. Instead, it proceeds from one point to the next in responsive fits and starts, stopping where someone thinks it is important or interesting to do so, sometimes backing up or starting over again, and then continuing in an approximate (and perhaps different) direction.

An emergent approach to planning usually takes the form of a Slinky, rather than a nice, clean line. Remember the Slinky toy we used to illustrate *nonrational planning*? Planning will not unfold smoothly or linearly because barriers, threats, resistance, doubts, hope, and timing, coupled with luck, play important parts in the process. What actually occurs in the planning process is most likely describable only *after* the process has produced a product, because in the doing of the planning, unexpected learning happens along the way that influences all the next steps in the process. This retrospective approach is what Weick (1995) called sense-making. It resembles what occurred in the case of the Invisible People and the Area Agency on Aging case. There, and with other emergent plans, prediction beforehand is not possible.

THE LOGIC OF EMERGENCE

There is logic to interpretive planning, but it is a different logic than used in rational planning. It is a logic in which *engagement* with others leads to a process in which *discovery* occurs and a tentative understanding of the problem evolves. Things begin to make sense;

but this sense is tentative because through continual engagement with others and ongoing learning, new discoveries emerge that redefine the problem, requiring subsequent adjustments in order to be responsive to what has been learned. The logic assumes that interactions, behaviors, attitudes, and a multitude of other factors must be taken into consideration because they are cues to what happens next. Logic is developed from attention to context, and since no two contexts are exactly alike, each planning process will unfold differently and responsively to the stakeholders involved. This contextual embeddedness is central to interpretive planning and assures appropriate emergence in the approach.

Wheatley and Kellner-Rogers (1996) call this type of logic a "logic of play" or a "logic of life," and they identify seven elements that form this logic:

- Everything is in a constant process of discovery and creating. There is constant change. Even change changes.
- Life uses messes to get to well-ordered solutions. It is often through inefficiencies, redundancies, and uncertainties that new possibilities emerge.
- Life is intent on finding what works, not what's "right." Solutions are temporary, but it is the ability to do what works now in a certain situation that keeps people engaged.
- Life creates more possibilities as it engages in opportunities. Rather than assuming that there are only windows of opportunity, there are infinite possibilities if one can only recognize them.
- Life is attracted to order. Human beings are committed to discovering ways to make things come together in order to benefit themselves and others, to buffer themselves from being overwhelmed by the constancy of change.
- Life organizes around identity. Every living thing finds an identity in order to make sense of the larger world.

- Everything participates in the creation and evolution of its neighbors. There is an inherent interdependency among all living things (pp. 13–14).

This logic, upon which interpretive planning is built, attempts to remove barriers to innovation through intense interactions, networking, and information exchange among those with a stake in change. The assumption is that they should be empowered to create and re-create as new discoveries occur. There will be patterns of interactions, but specific content cannot be determined in advance. There will be benchmarks of data collection, analysis, communication, consensus building for the purpose of decision-making, all based on responses to the probing questions of those engaged in the evolution of the plan; but the timing and content of those benchmarks will emerge with the plan. Planners are involved in finding opportunities in the resources at hand, detecting emerging patterns, and helping a plan to take shape. The precise order and content of all of these junctures and the numbers of times each occurs depends on the problem, the situation, and those involved in the process.

According to Westley, Zimmerman, and Patton (2006), it is necessary to think about the planning process as movement on a rugged landscape as the planner tries to move across it, making adjustments to fit the demands of the landscape; the plan is responsive to a continuously shifting "fitness landscape" (p. 203). "Fitness landscape" is a term developed by complexity scientist Stuart Kauffman (1996), who recognized that neither external (large systems) nor internal (individuals) aspects capture the full view of what is necessary for social innovation. Interpretive planning with its emergent approaches responds to shifting landscapes that are influenced by, and are influencing, external forces, such as changing attitudes and policies, structures, and power resources.

Table 4.2

Dimensions of an Interpretive Planning Process

Dimension	Function
Engagement	• Assures that multiple perspectives are heard, and reinforces their validity. • Provides a mutual respect and relational focus. • Assures understanding of and attention to context. • Assures a complexity focus.
Discovery	• Draws from multiple data sources. • Assures validity and complexity of information.
Sense-making	• Uses compromise and consensus-based decision-making. • Assures complexity, sophistication, and validity in decision-making. • Respects context by assuring that decisions fit and work for particulars of the situation.
Unfolding	• Assures options and possibilities for the particulars of the situation. • Builds on what was learned and attends to continual learning. • Privileges complexity rather than reductionism. • Assumes continual revisioning.

Precision about how to plan may be impossible, but capturing the feeling of the emerging process is possible. A variety of dimensions of the emergent approach to interpretive planning are essential to assuring emergence *and* successful planning and implementation (see Table 4.2).

Using this conceptualization of program planning, then, means that the program is thought of as an ongoing process of engagement with others, discovery through ongoing participation, sense-making of what is discovered in process, and continual unfolding within the context. Unfolding is both the process and product of program design. This unfolding occurs within the context, as engagement, new discoveries, and sense-making continually emerge throughout the planning and implementation process. Rather than steps being determined in advance, as in prescriptive approaches, or even leaving steps behind as they are achieved, all dimensions of interpretive planning work in tandem and in continual interaction. This is the difference between a line and a circle. "Reality is made up of circles but we see straight lines" (Senge, 1990, p. 71). Let us illustrate.

It is possible to draw a linear depiction of the dimensions of an emergent plan that would look very much like the logic model in Chapter 3, only with different language. It would look like this:

Engagement → Discovery → Sense-making → Unfolding

However, this characterization fails to capture the altogether different feel and intent of this planning process. In interpretive planning, using an emergent approach, these dimensions are continually happening and are always in interaction. Engagement informs discovery and sense-making, but sense-making can serve to enhance engagement. This sort of mutual influence of the process on its parts continues even in the unfolding process. The planning product that unfolds will continue to be shaped as the process continues to reverberate and to unfold in reaction to and interaction with the context during implementation. It is difficult to capture the true form of an emergent approach to planning without the capacity to show a holographic form. We chose the Slinky as the metaphorical form. It is important to think of an emergent approach in terms of multiple dimensions with many embedded circles spiraling toward a planning product, which itself may remain in continual motion in the process. Notice also that there is an aspect of retrospection here, in that, for example, the planner may only know that engagement has occurred by looking back to see that the various aspects of gaining entry have been attended to. Therefore, the parts of engagement, namely multiple stakeholding perspectives, mutual respect, relationship building, understanding the context and understanding complexity, are shown prior to engagement. The same is true with the other dimensions. It may only be possible to articulate discovery and sense-making in retrospect. In addition, the planning product, itself, may never be fully stabilized due to its continual responsive unfolding. See Figure 4.1.

In the following sections, we discuss each dimension, the details of which are necessary to assure quality in an emergent approach to planning.

Engagement

Engagement requires inclusion and inclusiveness and is essential to interpretive planning. The elements of engagement assure that multiple perspectives are heard; engagement also reinforces the validity of multiple truths. It provides for attention to importance of context, while providing a framework for mutual respect and relational focus.

Multiple Perspectives

An emergent approach to planning is based on hearing from multiple persons. Thus, the process opens the possibility of revealing competing ways of viewing the situation. For example, in the Invisible People case, the social worker had to rely on the knowledge and experience of local professionals, any older adults who would talk about their situations, and others who cared enough to help out. There were no statistics to document need or traditional needs assessment data available. Since the goal of an emergent approach is less of an assessment of a problem in need of attention and more of an understanding of the problem in its complexity, multiple perspectives are valued, to assure that complexity is the focus. Because complex systems cannot be totally explained by their parts,

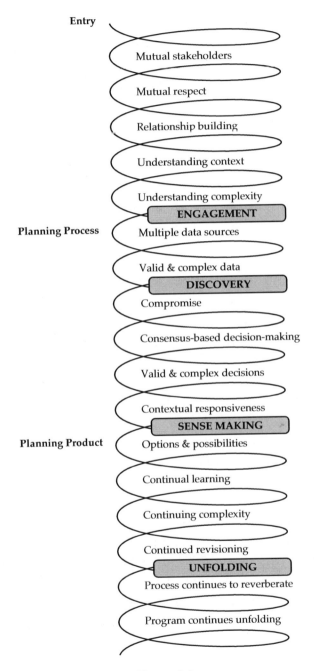

Figure 4.1
Form of an Emergent Approach to Planning

it is important to see the relationship among all the elements. Planning participants hear all ideas from multiple standpoints to gain insights about how to approach the change process. Perceptions, regardless of their "truth" quality, are crucial to understanding not only what the problem is, but also how to create solutions to the social problem(s) of interest.

With the acceptance of multiple, unpredictable, emergent, evolving, and adaptable sources of information, what constitutes a problem means that both subjective and objective dimensions of the problem description are important. Analysis is viewed as a broadening, not as a reducing, process. Premature narrowing of the articulation of the problem of interest is to be avoided. The problem is defined when the participants in the discovery process say it is, and it may change as new information emerges as the plan itself unfolds.

Decisions, then, on all levels of the planning process include understandings or multiple perspectives, bringing a respect for subjectivity to the planning culture that values inclusion and attending to process. Managing this level of complexity requires other relational elements such as mutual respect and relationship building.

Mutual Respect and Relationship Building

Process is emphasized in emergence because relationships are essential to planning. In complexity, connections or relationships define how systems work. It is the quality and content of relationships, not a linear flowchart, that guides the work and is essential to success. The norm is that there is no one best way to proceed. With no best way, there really can be no single expert because all of those involved in the context and in the decisions are experts in their own part of the reality. In the Invisible People case, the social worker is as much an expert as any other professional in the field;

the real experts concerning what is going on are the elders (and perhaps the newly discovered families) themselves. Everyone is needed because it is assumed all have something to add. Therefore, ongoing negotiation based on respect and trust must be the standard.

This sort of planning does not evolve from top-down provider/ client relationships; rather, it is one of mutual learning based on the premise that there is no one right answer, and that those involved in the planning process continue to ask questions. The process, then, is one of mutual shaping, not control. All are part of a planning process, and share responsibility for it. This is a hermeneutic process that epitomizes and provokes new patterns of interaction. Because the process evokes identification with, empathy for, and confrontation with all elements in the process, there are often changes in the power relationships.

Context

Like other programs that grow from a planning process, emergent program plans tend to have organizational, community, or group tethers to aid in the enactment or implementation of plans. What should be noted is that an emergent approach to planning requires leadership that one might call relational, in that it attends to perceived and expressed needs and projects a deep respect for the positive power of relationships. Power is at issue. A relational mind-set of management and supervision will support the thoughtful and reflective roles participants take in matters of power dynamics. That could be seen in the support provided to the social worker in the Invisible People case. As was true there, a relational administrative style will help planners to engage in continual assessment of self and others in order to know when to resist and when to foment change.

Complexity

An emergent approach to planning at its core is collaborative in decision-making about problem definition, program design, and implementation. Collaboration includes all stakeholders in the enterprise as a means of information gathering and consensus building, ensuring trust that complexity is recognized. Agendas, priorities, needs, and biases are included to be tested and critiqued so that all participants become more informed and sophisticated (Rodwell, 1998).

In fact, the collaborative process is meaningful unto itself, regardless of the planning that ensues. Participants become knowledgeable, and get smarter, which is a result. In our Invisible People case, it was clear that the early stakeholders were beginning to think differently about what was going on, which enhanced collaboration and eventual consensus.

Collaboration generally does not occur based only on good intentions. It requires skilled interpersonal work on the part of the planner. There will likely be confrontation and conflict, but from the conflict can come bridge building through identification and empathy. The planner helps to bring people along, and in doing so, power issues change from maintaining the status quo to establishing the power to change. This is accomplished with shifts in time, energy, money, talent, and connections. Congruence in values and focus emerge from the process, and the service activities that are derived from the plan will encounter fewer barriers to goal achievement.

Box 4.1 lists a few of the methods one might use to achieve engagement. Note that these methods, attentive to relationships, context, and complexity, may be useful in any type of planning, but are particularly salient in interpretive planning, where the intent is to gather more, rather than less, information.

Box 4.1
Methods to Achieve Engagement

- Using ethnographic strategies, gaining a sense of what constitutes the context of planning.
- Talking informally with people in the community and/ or organization in which planning will occur to understand who has a stake in the issue and to begin a mutual process.
- Reaching out to all identified stakeholding groups to build relationships.
- Using multiple information sources, including the media, to understand the history and politics of the context.
- Conducting community forums or organizational meetings in ways that assure multiple voices and perspectives are present and heard.
- Using formal data collection techniques, such as nominal group, Delphi, or focus groups, while sampling for maximum variation.
- Getting the word out about the planner and the process through popular media.
- Setting up a Web site, list serve, chat room, or other appropriate systems to facilitate communication.

In the Invisible People case, an *ethnographic approach* is taken that immerses the social worker in the community to establish a foundational understanding of who are the various players. Talking informally with older people who do access shelter services reveals new information—that they have family members in the city and that two of them have homes (although they have been boarded up by the city). Talking with the psychiatric nurse opens additional avenues of exploration about family members, as well as about additional stakeholders who might have more information. The process of engagement is ongoing as the social worker reaches out to others in the process of discovery.

DISCOVERY

Initial discovery occurs in the process of engagement and results in part from planning participants hearing from one another. Discovery requires openness to multiple data sources. The validity of information in the context is essential to discovery, as is continuing recognition of complexity of data.

Multiple Data Sources

Recall that nonrational/interpretive planning assures that a plan comes through no fixed sequence of analytic steps. It is nonlinear but very attentive to power and politics. It is reactive to the context regarding the data that are collected and considered as important. Data collection must be congruent with the general attitudes already presented: that of multiple perspectives and respectful relationship building. If multiple perspectives are important and to be honored, then engaging multiple sources of data is important. If mutual respect and relationships are important to achieve a shared vision, then multiple data sources must be sought and utilized for the purpose of creating a shared vision of what is and what should be.

Different ways of seeing a problem, neither exclusively from a top-down or a bottom-up perspective, creates a fuller understanding of the situation or the system. This certainly was beginning to emerge in the Invisible People case; many data sources including the media were used, though most of the data collection first was undertaken by the lone social worker. Through open observation and data collection, thinking, analyzing, and discovering, consensus can be achieved about the problem and about the planning product.

Validity and Complexity of Information

To achieve shared vision, attention is given to all sources of information, including intuition, word and numeric data from formal (systematic quantitative and qualitative research), and informal (casual conversations and observations) sources. Further, the plan must be open to reformulation as information is acquired and evaluated for its relevance. Both the problem definition and the plan are fluid, with the problem being defined when participants say it is, but allowed to change when new information emerges. The same is true for the plan itself. No information is rejected, because at some stage it might be of use as the plan moves forward in unexpected, unpredictable, and, perhaps, unimaginable ways. This, of course, requires complex mechanisms to keep information in play until the full plan has unfolded. Instead of only systematic data gathering, data are collected wherever possible, many times utilizing ethnographic methods enacted by planners steeped in the culture of the context. Findings are tentative and open to reformulation, depending on what is being learned as data are collected. Data collection is as emergent as the rest of the process, being attentive to the time and the context of the plan.

The Invisible People case is an exercise in discovery, as the social worker moves from site to site and person to person. Once the social worker remembers what her grandfather taught her about fishing, she recognizes that this process of discovery has an element of trial and error to it and that it is okay for this to occur. Being comfortable with discovery becomes part of the case, as illustrated in how the social worker reports back to the supervisor. This reporting back is a validity check. Supervisory validity checks are part of their relationship; and, later, it will be necessary to bring in other stakeholders in validity checking.

Sense-making

Sense-making is a retrospective process in which participants, individually and as a collective, determine what their discoveries mean. Sense-making occurs through compromise and consensus-based decision-making; assuring complexity, sophistication, and validating those decisions; and respecting context by assuring that decisions about the problem and the desired response fit and work for particulars of the situation.

Compromise and Consensus-Based Decision-making

In an emergent approach, there is no expert; instead, there are collaborators whose views are encouraged and critically examined for usefulness. This requires more expansive consensus building than in rational planning. Acceptance of a direction is reached through compromise and consensus. Planners plan by finding allies and expressing vision. Emergence thrives in the interdependencies of every contribution, but no one can claim responsibility or earn credit alone.

Consensus building includes reaching consensus about the problem and the solution because both are set in a particular context (time, place, culture), so decision-making generally requires attention to all stakeholding groups and all agendas. This is, in effect, a political process wherein all stakeholders, regardless of their degree or level of power, are called on to take part in the dialogue that must result in compromise-based decisions particular to the situation. This process results in a complex and sophisticated picture of not only the problem but also of the possibilities for resolution. In the Invisible People case, this part of the story had just begun, and you might want to consider where it will lead.

Validity and Complexity in Decision-making

The problem definition and the solution design are results of a collaborative process. Karl Weick (1998) provided insight into this type of collaboration through his understanding of jazz. Jazz is improvisation, where the unexpected is the rule. In other words, the unexpected is expected. Improvisation is successful when there is deep understanding of patterns; and when players listen and respond to other players, good jazz happens. No one and everyone leads at different times in the musical conversation. The decisions are of the collective. In the planning conversation, listening, responding, and questioning leads to experimentation, learning, adaptation, and connections that allow a course to be set. The problem and the acceptable solution are what are agreed upon—perhaps not as gracefully as jazz musicians might do it, but the improvisation does lead to consensus. Consensus-reaching itself is interventive due to the mutual education that is produces. In looking back at the Invisible People case, the possibility for conversation, listening, responding, and questioning occurred, to allow for experimentation, learning, and adaptations. In the case, and in emergent approaches in general, consensus building about the problem and the solution is the goal of the process; and because the process is steeped in an understanding of the multiple dimensions of power and politics, naiveté is avoided.

Contextual Responsiveness, or Context and "Fit"

The context of decision-making frames the decisions to be made. In emergent approaches to planning, these decisions are based on influence. The planner understands and respects local rules and then leverages them to increase their potential for use in bringing about change. What is identified as important data, what is accepted as the problem, and what appears to be an acceptable solution for which a plan emerges fits the particulars of the time and place, leaving no prescribed, standardized form of problem description or goal statement. Those engaged in the process are attentive to the political and contextual idiosyncrasies that influence the viability of a plan. Attention to the will of the polity (Stone, 1997) is essential to sense-making about what becomes constituted as acceptable problem definition and solution. There is attention to the context-bound nature of language and cognition. It protects the cultural nuances that influence what is seen to be an acceptable problem and what is seen as a viable solution to that problem. Planners accomplish this by being as much process-oriented as product-oriented.

Box 4.2 demonstrates how the problem statement in the Invisible People example changed over time as new information was gathered. None are "wrong," but each becomes more complex and sophisticated. Note that the beginning problem statement is based on professional assumptions, a way of using the familiar to address the problem about the elders and what was needed in order to plan. As the problem statement emerges, new information becomes evident in the process. Watch how the stated problem and the potential "intervention" changes accordingly, revealing how the framing of the problem will alter subsequent decisions in the unfolding of the process.

UNFOLDING

Like the rest of the emergent approach, unfolding represents a continual process, and it is not an end in itself. Unfolding includes assuring that options for the particulars of the situation have been

Box 4.2

Problem Statement as It Emerges

November

Recently, there have been reported incidents in which older adults with severe and chronic mental illness were put in taxis and sent to long-term care facilities for admittance, which was subsequently denied. We have no idea how many times this happens or where these older adults go.

December

In addition, to the older adults identified in November as having no place to go, last year, there were at least 15 older adults with mental illness who accessed shelter services on a nightly basis. These older adults would have been on the street without resources, subject to the risks of drug use, muggings, and a host of other potential situations. The shelter needs to reopen.

January

The one shelter in the city that was open to homeless, older adults closed in December. Practitioners report that they occasionally see older adults on the streets; but without a shelter for them to check into, there is no way to estimate how large or small this problem is. There needs to be a way to determine if there is still a problem of homeless older adults with mental illness in the city. Since they are not presenting at other shelters, it is impossible to tell how many there are on the streets. A project needs to be established with the intent of finding out how many older, mentally ill elders there are.

February

Having opened a few beds in a nearby shelter to older, mentally ill adults, it appears that some of these elders actually have

(Continued)

homes, but have been evicted from them by the city. It also appears that they may have families who live in the city but from whom they are estranged.

March

Mental health professionals report that they see highly complicated situations in which mental illness and chronic physical conditions are exacerbating the problems faced by mentally ill elders. Gero-psych units in all city hospitals are full to capacity, and discharge planning is next to impossible because neither long-term care facilities nor families are equipped to handle care.

and continue to be recognized, building on what was learned and attending to continual learning. Unfolding privileges complexity, rather than reductionism, to assure that the planning product continues to reverberate as the program continues to unfold over time.

Options and Possibilities

In unfolding the planning product, planners do not know exactly what to expect, even though they are opening the way for something to happen. It is like opening a package when the shape of the container could mean that a number of possible items are inside, but not knowing which one to expect. Sometimes one guesses correctly; but if one is not correct when the item emerges, one must be prepared to be surprised and to alter one's expectations accordingly. The interpretive planner is probably more involved in the process than simply opening a package, but the lack of control about content is similar. Openness to possibilities adds to the wonder of receiving a surprise.

Being open to options or alternatives is central to community organizing and to policy analysis. Standard practice is to examine options based on what is discovered in encountering a community, or the possibilities that emerge when competing interests debate policy alternatives. These are political engagements in which multiple participants interact and in which many points of view and many power positions must be taken into consideration if buy-in to the change is to take place. The options that emerge are not always what any one person might have expected to have happen. The same is true for interpretive planning. For example, have you ever been in a meeting with a group of people you know fairly well, yet the final decision about what you are going to do completely surprises you? The engagement of viewpoints and the synergy of thoughts and ideas actually resulted in something you could not have possibly predicted. Nevertheless, you left the meeting feeling good about the direction the group selected because you recognized strength in the process and commitment of the group to the joint decision.

Of course, in a program planning process, the complexities and multiplicities that must remain at play are complicated, and the inclinations of all may be to move to closure for the sake of simplicity. Keeping everything in consideration is hard work. In addition, being open to unexpected options is also part of the unfolding process. The "right" time to select among options actually depends on the other aspects of the unfolding. Learning, understanding, and managing complexity, along with continual revisioning based on compromise and consensus-based decisions, establishes which program option to choose.

This, however, does not mean that the decision will be final and that the plan will move forward without a glitch or that it will always be in the best possible direction. It merely means that for the point in time, it is the best alternative or option the participants could establish that fit the situation at hand. Later, another alternative may be better, as determined in the continual learning process. The evolution of possible changes in the Invisible People case gives some idea of how options and possibilities should be lively parts of an emergent approach to planning.

Continual Learning

Senge (1990) says that, "The organizations that will truly excel in the future will be [those] that discover how to tap people's commitment and capacity to learn at *all* levels of the organization [emphasis added]" (p. 4). Senge identifies five disciplines of a learning organization: (1) being able to think systematically; (2) engaging individuals who are committed to their own lifelong learning; (3) recognizing one's mental models, the basic assumptions one brings to the world, and sharing them with others; (4) building shared visions; and (5) being able to learn as a team, to think together, to dialogue.

Senge focused on organizations, but the principles of a learning organization pertain to interpretive program planning. To engage in interpretive planning, participants must be willing to risk sharing their assumptions, recognizing that the process might contradict or be in conflict with some of the assumptions they hold dear. Commitment to thinking critically is essential. Also, through critical thinking, being willing to engage in mutual learning while having meaningful dialogue (thinking together), the process emerges and the planning product unfolds.

For example, in the Invisible People case, for many community people, the problems faced by homeless mentally ill elders were not visible because they were out of sight and, therefore, out of mind. But invisibility may have lulled them into ignoring real needs of vulnerable individuals in their community. This is often the case with population groups that are invisible to powerful people in a community. The social worker at the Area Agency on Aging sought participants in the planning process who were willing to entertain the possibility that things were not what they appeared to be. In such cases, there may be great resistance because opening the package reveals surprises that no one really wants to address; yet once the box is opened, the participants' eyes may also be opened to seeing things differently. In continual learning, a new process of discovery will have begun as they make sense of what they have discovered together. In this case, the complexity involves community providers, distanced family members, and elders with multiple presenting conditions.

Continuing Complexity

Political reasoning is central to an emergent approach. To attend to all constituencies with a stake in the problem, acceptable planning for change is expected to be acceptable to all stakeholding groups. For a plan to emerge appropriately, a win/win rather than a win/lose scenario must be envisioned, because without that perspective the desired collaborative nature of the process will be impossible.

It should be clear that the goal of an emergent plan is less assessment of a problem and more an understanding of the problem in its complexity. Quinn (1998) describes this as requiring "a kind of thinking that is complex, holistic, and fluid" (p. 9). Following more interpretive theoretical frameworks, emergent approaches are more congruent with social constructivist theoretical perspectives (Rodwell, 1998). Interpretive plans, based on the emergent approach, are less reductionistic and more collaborative. This planning process rejects the notions of linear constructions of the world in favor of recognizing complexity and the need for the capacity to analyze complex systems.

This analysis requires a complex system of integrated information tracking. Information and effects must be tracked as the process unfolds, including adaptations to what is learned. Planning in this sense is like charting a path with rapid feedback, acting, getting feedback, learning, and then acting again. Those involved are always adapting to what is seen and learned instead of following a carefully laid out plan guided by a program theory. This is a process of uncovering, discovering, and creating such that a plan grows organically through strategic thinking. One could see this beginning to take place in the Invisible People story.

In discussing the road to innovations, Westley et al. (2006, p. 21) provide excellent advice that we have adapted to share with those who embark on this road to complexity:

- Questions are central.
- In complex situations, there are no final, exacting answers; but key questions help illuminate the issues as planning emerges.
- Tensions and ambiguities surface as a result of questioning. Interpretive planning reveals and creates tension. This tension can be a creative impetus for planning, if it is understood and engaged in, not simply managed.
- Relationships are key to understanding and engaging with the complex dynamics of emergence. For planning success, everyone with a stake must play a real role. As the process emerges, shifts occur that impact all stakeholders. What happens between people when these shifts occur will affect the quality of the planning process and the product and, ultimately, the program.
- A certain mind-set is crucial. Interpretive planning is framed by curiosity and inquiry, not certitude (Westley et al., 2006, p. 21).

From a practice perspective, Westley et al. suggest the impor-tance of living the paradox of action as reflection, and reflection as action. The planner sets a course, moves to action, and relinquishes the idea that the outcome can be controlled. The planner also realizes that plans are adapted, they change and develop as they emerge. Success with interpretive planning results because the process is attuned to and aligned with the context of complexity.

Before moving on from this section, we ask you to return to Figure 4.1. Notice in the figure that the planning product is unfolding, but notice also that unfolding is not the end of the planning story. The process continues to reverberate as the plan moves into implementation, and the program evolves in its context over time. Information is continually fed into the process, to be used for further program shaping. This honors learning as primary in being accountable. The next section will highlight the realities of accountability when engaged in interpretive planning using an emergent approach.

ACCOUNTABILITY IN AN EMERGENT APPROACH

Once gained, compromise and consensus become the basis for mutual accountability regarding the emerging plan. This is not the at-a-distance, fiduciary accountability usually ascribed to outside funding or mandating sources. This is usually an internal, intense, almost intimate accountability to all those with whom a relationship has been forged in the planning process. Accountability, or more appropriately, "social responsibility," is central to interpretive planning. But in a litigious society, this sort of internally directed accountability is not sufficient to meet the needs of external funding sources or outside regulators. Being satisfied that everything is alright because all the stakeholders say it is alright will not be satisfactory for purposes of acquiring, maintaining, or increasing support.

Interpretive planning has a problem with evaluation, put bluntly, because its shape and form are different, precisely due to the fact that the shape and form of the planning process is different from that of traditional rational planning. Because of this, many will assume that accountability is either not present or impossible to achieve. Emergent approaches cannot compete with the traditional, prescriptive models of planning with positivistic outcome expectations because assumptions of linear problem-solving are present. Emergent approaches are based on assumptions about how one comes to know, which means different accountability assumptions should also be present (Netting & O'Connor, 2007).

Accountability Challenges

The structure and measurement of traditional prescriptive approaches are built on an ideology of generalizable truth, while emergent approaches look for multiple truths, accepting alternative opinions and practices and valuing multiple values and perspectives. The control required to assert causal connection between inputs and program outcomes is not possible in an uncontrolled, emergent approach to the planning process; but other types of assertions about program responsibility and quality are possible. Most funders want accountability defined in traditional ways that are about achieving results. Traditional evaluation processes produce structured, precise responses, but emergent approaches cannot utilize those structures and remain true to the goals of emergence. So, without alternative articulation of what is possible in accountability, interpretive planning will face intense scrutiny and demands for structured evaluations that will only serve to squelch the possibilities presented by an alternative approach to problem solution (Netting, O'Connor & Fauri, 2007).

Interpretive planning and implementation focuses on continuous learning and changing. Emergence focuses not on compliance with prescribed and approved procedures but on attaining results and learning about how to attain desired outcomes. It emphasizes broad learning about not only emergent possibilities but also what turns out to be inappropriate or less important outcomes. Interest is on learning from failures, as well as gaining feedback about the complexity of the problem, the context, and the resources in the process. The way to assure accountability in emergent approaches is to move evaluation from compliance to structured learning that demonstrates mechanisms for informing future appropriate action. Accountability and evaluation then become both developmental and emergent.

With emergent plans, the program implementation remains flexible to assure responsiveness. With this comes ambiguity in operations that is distinctly different from rational planning principles, as emergent plans do not have clearly defined objectives and preconceived tasks. It is important to avoid premature measurement and outcome demands, which can be disincentives for continuous learning. Even though interpretive planning and emergent approaches seek accountability through learning, to remain viable in the current accountability culture, planners and programs must somehow respond to these demands. Emergent planners must be intentional in their commitment to accountability, but they must also assure alternative ways of seeing and using data for ethical, accountable, and effective emergent practices.

ACCOUNTABILITY OPTIONS

Emergent accountability tracks the effects of efforts as they unfold. Documentation of both what is learned and adaptation to this learning reflects the changing planning path and provides rapid feedback into the process. Clearly, emergent designs require broad and nonrestrictive approaches to accountability. Box 4.3 shows how the planners in the Invisible People case established documentation elements that

Box 4.3
Establishing Documentation Elements

Approach 1: Formative Evaluation

Worker (planner) maintains a *contact log* that documents who was seen, when, and for how long, with notes regarding content of conversation, new ideas, and possible new contacts. Stakeholding group creation and maintenance are also documented here (*engagement documentation*).

Worker (planner) maintains a *methods journal* that documents data collected, interpretations provided by stakeholders, decisions made (by whom, when, and based on what), and results that occurred, so that changes are justified and emergence is demonstrated (*engagement, discovery, and sense-making documentation*).

All stakeholders to emergent plan participate in the creation of a *lessons learned chronology* that connects to each formal decision made and its consequence throughout the planning process, up to and including the unfolding plan and beyond implementation (*engagement, discovery and sense-making documentation*).

An *intervention design document* created and ratified by all stakeholders explicitly details all dimensions of the intervention, initially including who will do what, when, and at what cost. Changes in the design are tracked by and linked to the methods journal and the lessons learned chronology, thus allowing for outside audit of the ongoing process (*unfolding documentation*).

Approach 2: Emergent Evaluation

Worker (planner) maintains a *contact log* that documents who was seen, when, and for how long, with notes regarding content of conversation, new ideas, and possible new contacts. Stakeholding group creation and maintenance are also documented here (*engagement documentation*).

Worker (planner) maintains a *reflexive journal* that reports on the planner's progressive bounding of personal subjectivity, in which reflections are made regarding inner biases and conflicts, and the strategies devised that are used to cope with or resolve these barriers to understanding. The journal chronicles the development of different or deeper insights and understandings of the context. It also includes perspectives of the planning participants, documenting multiple views, power dynamics, and insights about needed changes (*engagement, discovery, and sense-making documentation*).

Worker (planner) maintains a *methods journal* that documents data collected, interpretations provided by stakeholders, decisions made (by whom, when and based on what), and results that occurred, so that changes are justified and emergence is demonstrated (*engagement, discovery, and sense-making documentation*).

Worker (planner) maintains a *process log* that documents the process of consensus building by recording issues, concerns, and concepts brought up by stakeholders; the analysis undertaken; decisions made; and adaptations that resulted, and showing the connection between the reflexive journal, the methods journal, and this process log (*discovery and sense-making documentation*).

An *intervention design document* created and ratified by all stakeholders explicitly details all dimensions of the intervention, initially including who will do what, when, and at what cost. Changes in the design are then tracked by and linked to the methods journal and the process log, thus allowing for outside audit of the ongoing process (*unfolding documentation*).

rigorously tracked both the emerging process and the unfolding product.

It was so unclear what was needed or what would be undertaken, that the worker set up two evaluation systems for accountability. The attentive reader will see that some of the efforts at rigorous documentation could be applied in both systems, though each system actually has different accountability purposes.

The first approach, which is somewhat consistent with positivistic assumptions, and thus requires less translation for traditional funders, would be to avoid *summative evaluation* in favor of *formative evaluation*. In interpretive planning, there is no real place for summative evaluation that judges overall merit or worth based on whether goals were achieved, because emergence cannot create goals and objectives in the same way as traditional, rational approaches. The best that can be expected is the creation of benchmarks to watch how emergence is occurring. Information targets based on what should be known in order to move from one stage to the next in the plan, rather than performance targets, are possible and consistent with positivistic formative evaluation assumptions. But by focusing on the formative process over the summative product, short-term, bottom-line measures are avoided. Whatever emerges becomes a goal retrospectively. (For detailed information about the exact structure and design of formative evaluation research, see Posavac & Carey, 1985).

Instead of focusing on goals, emergence documentation in a formative evaluation focuses on improving the chances for effective change. The accountability design gets at weaknesses and strengths when questions and concerns emerge. It documents the trial-and-error aspects that are analyzed for learning and for changing goals based on new understandings of what is needed and possible in a particular context. This formative process provides evaluation of short-term desired outcomes (how and where progress is happening), looking for unanticipated consequences, unpredicted effects, ripples beyond the hoped-for results, including opportunities for critical learning, and to make corrections or take new directions. In interpretive planning, accountability is part of the planning intervention. The challenge remains to help outsiders see this as a sufficiently robust accountability structure.

A second approach, consistent with interpretive meaning-making, is to engage in emergent accountability. Following some of the guidance of *constructivist research* (see Guba & Lincoln, 1989; Lincoln & Guba, 1985; Rodwell, 1998), the hermeneutic process of consensus building and the iterative process of surfacing issues, concerns, and concepts are documented and tracked to demonstrate the critical thinking and analysis that is undertaken at each important juncture in the emergent process. Establishing an ongoing documentation of the process allows accounting for unanticipated occurrences and consequences. Effects and understandings are tracked as they unfold. This design establishes accountability as including documentation of the plan's adaptation to what is learned.

Regardless of the evaluation design, a major measure of quality should be rapid feedback. Process documentation allows the planner to stay with the emergent vision while adapting to day-to-day realities. Documentation done in a transparent way involving stakeholders or stakeholding groups shows and engenders systematic knowledge building. It enhances engagement, discovery, sense-making, and unfolding. Many qualitative research texts now on the market provide details about how to assure emergence, while also demonstrating systematic sampling, data collection, and analysis (see Denzin & Lincoln, 1998; Strauss & Corbin, 1998; Rodwell, 1998). These can be very helpful in guiding the accountability process. However, it is important to assess the underlying assumptions of the texts before applying the methods, since only texts built on interpretive rather than positivistic assumptions will assure appropriate emergence of an evaluation design congruent with an emergent plan.

Emergent approaches to accountability must attend to both the process and product of planning, documenting both learning and what is produced by that learning. Authentic accountability (Rodwell, 1998) looks at the process for fairness, respect for alternative positions, consciousness-raising, and readiness for change. Though success or failure may be important for some at the outset, interpretive planning emphasizes the importance of what is understood and learned. This has important consequences not only for the particular planning process, but also for others in similar situations. In this way, social experiments, much like the experiences of venture capitalists, can inform others. The expectations held for venture capitalists is to risk the implementation of a good idea with the recognition that failure possibility is high and success is rare; but each failure is a learning experience that sets up a better chance of success the next time. This should also be the expectation for emergent accountability—assessment of meaning and relevance for current and future efforts.

INTERPRETIVE PLANNING

Being able to engage in interpretive as well as rational planning means that the planner may have to be adaptive. Interpretive planning allows the planner to gain experience initially in a locality and develop locality sensitivity and good instincts about what works. Interpretive planning requires the innate skills of the local leader, without the ego need to always "have it my way." The planner who uses interpretive planning may be trained to engender and manage emergence. Regardless of the training or the instinct, we think that there are certain personal qualities and skills that assure that a planner can pursue emergence when it is appropriate. A planner may be born to interpretive planning, just as the highly organized and logical person may innately have skills in rational planning. Still others can learn to engage in skillful, appropriate interpretive planning.

Mind-sets

To pursue emergent approaches sometimes requires bravery. This courage will usually be the product of personal awareness, consciousness about self and others, and a confidence born from a belief in his or her skills and abilities. It is coupled with resilience and a capability of living with uncertainty and ambiguity. The planner who flourishes with the challenges of complexity also tries to keep perspective. The perspective needed for emergence involves the ability to maintain peripheral vision while also keeping a focus on the vision for change, which will be a moving target.

The competent interpretive planner is a social creature, building relationships and risking engagement throughout the process. Ability to stay the course requires a deep trust of the "other" while also trusting possibilities for change. This trust is layered with flexibility and responsiveness to the unpredictable and unfolding in events. Adaptability is the key as the planner welcomes challenges, not needing the one best way, not hanging on to what she or he does best when it is no longer working. There is an openness to seeing change as opportunity rather than loss of the familiar or the safe. In short, trusting emergence is critical.

All this requires acting with consciousness and intentionality and living in paradox with profound uncertainty and deep understanding; self-protection and vulnerability; changing others by changing self; balancing change and stability. One cannot expect perfection in the people, the process, or the plan. There is an expectation of unexpected consequences that may shake up the status quo. Failure and less than complete success can be elements of emergence. In the interpretive planning process, planners cannot take things overly personally—either successes or failures; criticism is not avoided, but embraced as a way to engage in critical analysis of assumptions and visions so that everyone gets better at what they are doing. In the end, self-comfort allows avoidance of a traditional "expert" role, replacing it with the roles of facilitator/teacher/learner.

Skills

It may appear that competent planners who use an emergent approach primarily work by instinct and intuition. Planning involves trusting intuition, but also requires having a prepared mind, being able to intentionally engage and to learn through action, ongoing reflection, and careful observation. Attention to details and their relationships, as well as sensitivity to timing are helpful. Consciousness and critical questioning and carefully considered feedback to determine what to do next in a particular situation are necessary. There is little place for denial, delusions, and despair when things do not go as expected. It is important to pick oneself up and engage with others in figuring out what might work next.

Interpretive planning requires emotion and passion. Boundaries that maintain a sense of perspective fit with the nature of the emergent process, matching the nature of the need, not just the planner's personal/professional preferences. The planner seeks support from appropriate sources, recognizing when support is needed to face stresses, doubts, burnout, despair, isolation, loss of perspective, feelings of abandonment, or any of the other challenging feelings that come with ambiguity. Conversely, it is important when things do work well to take time to celebrate the success and to recognize the contributions of everyone who has participated in the process.

Never knowing for sure does not mean that the emergent planner is happy living in a clueless state. It means that the planner stands in a tentative circle, rather than in the certainty of the straight line, knowing how to interpret information and convert it to knowledge. The planner is able to see and feel the human consequences of decisions. In analysis, the planner sees things in complex ways with attention to what is left out as well as what is put forward. Interpretive planning and emergent approaches depend on the planner working in concert with others to surface counter truths, or disconfirming data, to be certain that the uncomfortable aspects of complex reality are addressed.

STRENGTHS AND CHALLENGES OF INTERPRETIVE PLANNING

Interpretive planning is very time-intensive throughout the planning process. What time is saved will be in well-targeted implementation. The planning is neither controlled nor objective, making ongoing accountability monitoring a challenge, especially when precision that can be achieved only through control may be required by an outside evaluative or funding source.

Interpretive planning is overtly political and attentive to ideologies. The beliefs and preferences in the context are driving forces, regardless of empirical evidence to the contrary. In some cases, it might be suggested that it supports best "possible" practices instead of best practices because of its extreme attention to the political will of those involved. In the problem-setting and problem-solving processes, what occurs is dependent on the wishes and choices of all stakeholders. Decisions are consensus-based, and feasibility in all its aspects is at the core of decision-making.

With the attention to process as much as product, it is inevitable that efficiency will be brought into question. Emergent approaches may have to sacrifice efficiencies in service of situational effectiveness. Their strengths lie in the inclusion of multiple perspectives and the willingness to make changes as situations change. Whereas this stance wreaks havoc when outcomes are predetermined, as in traditional program evaluation, the expectation of interpretive planning may be more realistic in complex programs that are attempting to be sensitive to unique service needs of individuals.

Uncertainty is present in any planning process, but more so in interpretive planning. The level of engagement needed provides support when facing uncertainty because engagement will continue even during the rough spots. One should not be naïve about the challenges that uncertainty presents. Order is an expectation held by many, so managing the tension between that expectation and what emerges represents a great challenge.

For planners trained in a rational problem-solving model, a major challenge with the emergent approach is that control is replaced with the need to tolerate ambiguity. A second challenge is to recognize that expertise is shared. This relieves the planner of failing alone, but it also removes the potential for taking major credit. Thus, the planner must be comfortable with never knowing with certainty until the process is unfolded, and not being thanked for his or her brilliance.

Comfort with ambiguity may be the necessary bridge for the greatest challenge of all. Funders want concrete, clear, specific goals with measurable objectives that demonstrate that the planner knows step by step in advance how to attain goals. The planner must respond sufficiently, while simultaneously encouraging formative evaluation and the benefits of attending to complexity and rapidity of change in the planning context.

SUMMARY

Interpretive planning and emergent approaches open the possibility of unique responses to diverse needs, adding alternative ways of considering worth of service, including sociocultural aspects. Interpretive planning allows articulation of quality change that includes intimate aspects of relationship. Because of the enhanced attention to process in planning, it can take longer to accomplish. It requires that the planner and participants deal with complexity and respond with critical thinking. Competent interpretive planning requires both an appropriate mind-set and requisite skills to assure that emergence and quality program planning happen.

In addition, interpretive planning requires extending the language and the framework of service accountability. Documenting process instead of responding to expectations will present a challenge to planners who are using emergent approaches and seeking funding from traditional sources. However, both traditional formative evaluation and an interpretive approach to evaluation help to bridge the gap between emergence and outcome measurement because both are evidence-based and attentive to the varying demands of accountability.

Interpretive planning rests on ambiguity, uncertainty, and emerging ideas. It establishes the value of hearing all perspectives to overcome the values of the status quo in creating together a "new normal." A new sense of security is created out of mutual trust that allows an appreciation of diversity and tolerance for differing opinions. Interpretive planning allows for playing with ideas. This can be refreshing and rewarding. There is enjoyment of what can be learned in a creative process that preserves respect for people and their strengths and insights. Tapping into those strengths allows new ideas to accrue, which will probably be needed as we move into a more fully realized global community.

DISCUSSION QUESTIONS

1. Think about the mind-sets necessary to engage in interpretive planning. Which aspect of the mind-sets concerns you the most? What would help you to overcome that concern?

2. Analyze the case at the beginning of this chapter using an emergent approach. What would you have done the same? Differently? Where do you think the social worker might go next in the process?

3. Now look at the skills necessary to engage in interpretive planning. How many of them are the same or similar to the skills necessary in traditional, rational planning? Of those that are similar, discuss in detail how the skills would need to be enacted differently in emergent approaches.

4. The emergent planning approach is more holistic than reductionistic. After reading this chapter, how would you describe how holism works in this approach? What are the particular challenges you see in the emergent approach? For example, how might you overcome the possibilities of data overload as a plan emerges?

5. The collaboration necessary in interpretive planning to move to real consensus requires a good deal of time. What strategies could be used to deal with the impatience that is bound to accompany the process? What might be undertaken to slow the push toward premature closure, especially when that pressure might be coming from outside regulators or funders?

6. How might you defend interpretive planning in an effectiveness versus efficiency debate?

7. After reading this chapter, what are your unanswered questions about the emergent approach? How might you go about answering those questions?

8. How would you determine if an emergent approach is appropriate for a planning process? What would prevent you from considering using it?

9. What about this approach might be attractive to practitioners in emerging nations? What might be challenging to them?

CHAPTER 5

Knowing When to Use Which Planning Approach

As you begin to experiment with new strategies, remember that leaving the status quo usually involves risk. It sometimes means moving into a situation that requires assumptions very different from those with which you are familiar. Instead of trying to avoid failure, you may need to embrace failure and to see it as an indispensable part of the learning process.

—Robert E. Quinn, Sue R. Faerman, Michael P. Thompson,
and Michael R. McGrath, *Becoming a Master Manager*

Chapter Outline

Case: AIDS Orphans and the Pig Intervention
Similarities in Planning Approach Challenges
    Gaining Entry
    Becoming Oriented
    Engaging in Critical Thinking
    Making Ethical Decisions
Comparing Program Planning Approaches
    Comparing Dimensions
    Examining Accountability
    Thinking about Mind-sets and Skills

Decision Issues for Approach Selection
Summary
Discussion Questions
Appendix

Assumptions upon which this chapter is based:

- Ethical considerations are at the heart of decisions about planning.
- Ethics guide appropriate actions on the part of the planner and choices about the appropriate vehicle for developing the plan.
- Useful to ethical decision-making is critical thinking, to determine whether ethical absolutism or ethical relativism is called for in the situation.
- Planners may prefer one approach over another or be more skilled in one program planning approach; thus, using different approaches may require professional growth and development.
- Both prescriptive and emergent planning approaches represent strengths and challenges, depending on the context for planning.

You, the reader, are likely a practitioner (or soon to be practitioner) wishing to be an effective program planner. You may be a clinician who implements programs and wants them to "work." You may have experienced the unfortunate situation in which you have been tasked with carrying out programs that were poorly designed or so rigidly prescribed that they restricted the work you were trying to accomplish. Perhaps you need the skills to do sound rational planning for the purpose of accessing funding for a program to which you are very committed. You may be the program coordinator in a human service agency, forced to carry out initiatives that use approaches insensitive to cultural needs. Whatever your circumstance, chances are you want to be a professional whose work has integrity and who has the capacity to use appropriate tools for problem-solving, decision-making, and planning.

In Chapters 3 and 4, we examined two approaches to planning based on different sets of assumptions. In Chapter 3, we focused on the logic of rational planning in which prescriptive approaches are linear layouts of plans of action to solve a social problem based on the assumptions that when planning, one knows where one is going. Planners who use these approaches generally do so as experts with predetermined goals developed from an expert perspective. This approach has been termed "reverse-order planning" (Brody, 2000, pp. 77–78) where the results to be achieved are identified early and the planner pursues a logic model or a problem-solving model to bring them about.

In Chapter 4, we examined interpretive planning, an emergent approach, focused on understanding stakeholders' perspectives as a means of continual information gathering and analysis for problem-solving. The logic of this planning process is a nonlinear process of engagement, sense-making, and discovery, interacting continually as a program design unfolds. In this approach, goals emerge in process, and may change, revealing "forward-sequence planning," which begins wherever one can start (Brody, 2000, pp. 77–78).

We believe that there are places for both rational program planning and interpretive planning. When to use which approach is distinguished by context and by what one is trying to achieve, based on what it takes to articulate and develop solutions. Sometimes the selection of an approach is straightforward and clear. Other times, as Quinn (1988) says in *Beyond Rational Management*, it requires the "complex, holistic, and fluid—a kind of thinking that distinguishes the master from the novice" (p. 7). This is when critical thinking steeped in solid ethical decision-making is needed—when what is necessary for competent, appropriate planning is less clear. This chapter has been designed to help you not only distinguish the differences between the approaches, but also to engage in the complex thinking necessary to determine which should work best in a given situation.

Persons skilled in dealing with complexity and critical thinking, who can live with paradox and ambiguity, are likely candidates for designing and developing emergent human service programs; but those without those natural and acquired skills must also be able to use this sort of planning when appropriate. Cultures in which interpretive or nonrational thinking occurs as a matter of course may be particularly receptive to interpretive planning, and even helpful in educating those needing the skills to face these challenges of emergent approaches. Other cultures steeped in rationality may be receptive to rational planning and helpful in incubating planners competent to enact prescriptive approaches. In either case, an alternative way of planning may be necessary to reach needed goals. Both approaches are important and necessary for planning. Sometimes, one approach should be preferred over another. Other times, a strategic combination is appropriate. Determining the appropriate approach requires a consciousness and criticality about contextual constraints and opportunities that is only possible if the planner brings ethics and critical thinking to the decision-making process.

In this chapter, we begin with another case example. Now that you are familiar with both prescriptive and emergent approaches to planning, we will also do a brief analysis of a case to demonstrate how the approaches are used. We then explore program planning approaches in terms of their similarities regarding gaining entry and becoming oriented. Next in that section, we investigate the importance of critical thinking and ethical decision-making in the planning process as guides to all planning practice, with emphasis on nuanced differences between the approaches. This is followed by a section comparing the dimensions of planning necessary for competent work from both rational and interpretive approaches, with clues to the critical thinking and ethical challenges that might accompany an approach. Comparative examination continues as accountability is also explored, recognizing that insider and outsider demands, expectations, and needs must be considered, as do politics and unintended consequences of either approach—representing more critical thinking and ethics challenges. Finally, within the subtext of critical thinking and ethical decision-making, questions are presented to help the reader develop skills in determining when and under what circumstances each approach works best.

Case: AIDS Orphans and the Pig Intervention

Staff in a faith-based nongovernmental organization (NGO) were witnessing a rise in child-headed households (CHHs) in an African country where many adults were being felled by AIDS. Because there were so few facilities to care for these "AIDS orphans," many of the children, especially those of sibling groups with slightly older children in addition to younger ones, were choosing to remain in their villages in their family homes, rather than become street children or go to the few overpopulated orphanages. A European farming concern wanted to donate 2,500 especially resilient baby pigs (3 to 5 months old) to the agency over a three-year period, assuming that the CHHs, helped by the agency, would raise the pigs, butcher them, and then use all aspects of the butchered hogs for their own consumption. The thinking was that the pigs could eventually be a good source of food and would provide manure to enrich depleted land, thus enhancing households' abilities to grow some of their own food.

(Continued)

The first round of CHHs was selected and trained in the care and feeding of pigs and seemed ready to raise the pigs. However, shortly after the first 500 pigs arrived, it became clear that most of the CHHs had other ideas. They wanted to take the pigs to market quickly to "liberate capital," to use as they saw fit. Because of the breed of pig being imported, there was already concern about the competitive edge these pigs represented. If all 2,500 pigs went to market, it would destroy the hog market in the area. It was determined that the first best action would be to curtail pig distribution from Europe. With the direct financial help of the European pig concern, the pig program would continue in a modified way by having the remaining cycles of pig distribution come from the offspring of the pigs initially distributed. The NGO would purchase the pigs, putting funds in the hands of the participants while also extending the program to the planned number of CHHs by distributing the purchased pigs to the new CHH participants (O'Connor & Netting, 2007).

In this example, well-intentioned, competent planners responded to an opportunity that had unexpected results. The initial program grew from the generosity of an unsolicited donor. The CHHs' need was clear, so the plan was conceptualized by planners in a rational way without sensing that it could be viewed differently by the child-headed households. Program planners assumed that a pig given to a household would be used for consumption. This assumption is very rational, in that a donation of a food source is given and a need is met—the projected outcome for this program plan was a child-headed household having adequate food. However, the children wanted to participate in the local economy, not simply be passive recipients of food supplies, which was also a very rational position. This decision on the part of CHHs had implications for the larger community and its economy. In the process of discovery about what the children wanted and how the fears of existing pig farmers related to what might happen, rational planning rightly switched to an emergent approach in which persons in authority began to realize the implications of the program design and the need to change the plan. If a rational process had been maintained, the probable design would have resulted in CHHs being determined eligible for the program only if they agreed to use the pigs for their own consumption and also agreed not to sell the pigs to others except for slaughter (O'Connor & Netting, 2007).

Rational planning might label this example a failure because the original plan was off-target and could have resulted in a national disaster. A one-size-fits-all programming could not respond to the complexities of the context. From a nonrational perspective, however, what was learned was invaluable in thinking through what might actually work better if individual CHHs' needs and preferences were considered, rather than having the various professional experts, without consultation with CHHs, determine what was best.

This example is one in which a combination of rational and interpretive planning was needed and eventually utilized. One cannot mobilize the distribution of large numbers of pigs without a rational approach to detail. On the other hand, the reaction of the children to the pigs (what they decided to do with them) could not be usefully subject to this assumption. The children saw pigs as a source of income, and this perspective conflicted with the assumption held by planners. The economic complexity also became an issue. So for this context, a far better approach required rethinking and adjusting the intervention as it emerged. The planners were prepared to redesign the program as information was gathered through experience. That redesign resulted in a self-sustaining effort with positive outcomes for all stakeholders (O'Connor & Netting, 2007).

(Continued)

It is important to point out that the planners in this case engaged in appropriate sequencing in which they began using a prescriptive approach, then learned in the course of implementation that certain assumptions were no longer valid. In process, they shifted to an emergent approach in which assumptions of rationality were suspended. The emergent process netted a new design from lessons learned about how the CHHs used the pigs. In this process, a different conceptualization (pig-as-income versus pig-as-food) emerged. In doing so, the planners reversed the process, discontinuing the importing of pigs. Using rational planning, this decision would have been seen as a failure in light of the original goal, but it was perfectly appropriate in a nonrational interpretive planning design. This sequencing, or phasing, of rational and interpretive planning over the course of the program required culturally competent critical thinking on the part of planners. They possessed a willingness to learn from experience, rather than holding a dogged determination to implement the original plan. In doing so, they were able to reach the original goal of the rational, prescriptive plan and go beyond what was hoped for in the beginning. These planners were competent in using two different planning approaches. By thinking critically and nonreactively, they produced a highly responsive, culturally competent, and, therefore, ethical program response to the need.

SIMILARITIES IN PLANNING APPROACH CHALLENGES

This section contains important and challenging aspects of successful program planning, regardless of the approach used. We begin with gaining entry and becoming oriented, which are very similar in the two approaches. We then move to critical thinking and ethical decision-making, in which there will be some nuanced differences to consider.

GAINING ENTRY

Generally, gaining access is understood symbolically as having doors or gates opened to allow one to enter. Many program planners don't think of access because they are in the employ of an organization and see the program planning process as an agency assignment. However, there are rules of engagement, an identified culture, and multiple stakeholders to a change process. Some of the stakeholders may have agendas that will not be served by a proposed change. Gaining entry into a group, a coalition, or a community brings credibility. If one is hired to develop a community-based program, then gaining the trust of community stakeholders is necessary. For example, for a social worker, it happened this way on being hired to develop a new senior center program. The county Council of Elders interviewed her, asking if she could read a map, because this was a rural county and a lot of outreach to seniors would be required. Hired for the position, she was anxious to establish credibility. Her supervisor, in a supervisory meeting, told her that his parents were retired and living in the rural area of the county. More importantly, she discovered that his father was a retired minister who had performed the wedding ceremony for her aunt and uncle many years ago. Once the word spread that she was related to Stella and Dale, she had gained entry because she "belonged." The importance of relationships and reputation by association cannot be underestimated. Being able to read a map was important, only after she was well-enough accepted to be asked to go somewhere.

Very little has been written about the beginning stages of planning in general, much less program planning. It is almost as if planning begins once the planner has been given the charge, is in the community or organization, and the human resources have been identified. Clear instructions about practice are built on assumptions that the professional already knows the context. But what if the context is new to the planner? It doesn't matter which approach to planning is used, you cannot begin competent, ethical practice until you have gained access (Brown, de Monthoux, & McCullough, 1976).

Gaining access requires attention to the status and power of those who can give access (Hardcastle, Powers, & Wencour, 2004). Gaining entry leads to agreements to participate in the program planning process at least at the level of the gatekeepers to the project. It is the gatekeepers who will, for the most part, facilitate access to the stakeholders. In short, it is with the gatekeepers that the future of the plans rise or fall.

Finding the people who can open doors or gates is just the beginning. It may not get the planner started in the right direction, because how one gets in can determine the information that is made available. The process is relational because access is not entirely in the hands of either the planner or the ones granting access. It is a mutual process in which rapport must be established. In the community organizing literature are a series of tips that include reminders to understand the motivations, issues, and concerns of those with whom one speaks (Mondros & Wilson, 1994). Talking to everyone who is willing to talk to you is important because anyone might be a source of access or a part of a network that leads to those who can provide access.

Using the guidance developed for qualitative researchers (Feldman, Bell, & Berger, 2003), there are some important aspects about building productive relationships that help to avoid rude surprises. There is nothing worse than to be faced with disinterest, indifference, or rejection. Critical thinking about initial contacts to gain access includes identifying who might help with access. Finding the people with whom one wants to have a relationship requires preparation. This includes some thought about who might have the power of access and how to appeal to them. It also requires having strong interpersonal skills and being self-aware in order to gather the information needed and follow through on it. Access, once given, must be continually earned or renegotiated by nurturing the relationship, as access is not gained once and for all but developed and enriched over time. Creating and maintaining trust is the key and is acquired through the establishment of strong, respectful ties with the organization or community. Fenno (1978) reminds us that trust is "less a special talent than a special willingness to work hard—a special commitment" (p. 264).

Becoming Oriented

One cannot know the power dynamics or other important aspects of the planning context without coming to know the environment. Determining the various access and power points in a community (whether that community is an organization, a geographical entity, or identity group) requires good skills in using an *ethnographic approach* (Hammersley & Atkinson, 1983). Usually the planner may acquire this information through what Spradley (1979) calls *grand tour activities*, whereby information is collected by hanging out and observing, walking around, touring the agency or community, and chatting with people in the agency or neighborhood. These activities help in the initial exploration of the environment and determining what it will take not only to gain entry but also to move in the appropriate directions in relationship building.

The art of self-presentation is central, recognizing who you are and how you present yourself. Your identity and their identity and cultures impact the ways and degrees in which people connect with others. Language skills, prior experience, affiliations, ideology, and interests are all important when positive connection is the goal.

Access for an outsider is eased when an insider thinks the outsider can be trusted. Age, gender, culture, or ethnicity may present barriers to garnering trust, but these barriers can be overcome with extra efforts to demonstrate competence. Persistence, flexibility, and luck also are important. Luck should be understood as being prepared to take advantage of an opportunity. This involves being conscious about what is initially noticed and gradually becoming more informed about the problem for which the program plan is going to be designed. Taking into account the physical and psychological dynamics of the context aids in determining the appropriateness of the context for the planning that is about to be undertaken and the human and political feasibility of the project.

Orientation allows discovery of what is salient in the environment, who might be the important stakeholders or stakeholding groups, and important aspects of the political environments. Box 5.1 offers tips for gaining access and becoming oriented.

Throughout the entry and orientation process, whether in a new program or coming into an existing program that requires redesigning, the planner must be engaged in a constant process of critical thinking and ethical decision-making. In the following sections, we emphasize the importance of critical thinking and ethical decision-making processes, also illustrating how some aspects might look different in a prescriptive or in an emergent approach. Both critical thinking and ethical decision-making are important to all planning processes, because in the conceptualization of what needs to happen the framework is established for creativity that can lead to innovation. The appropriateness and usefulness of the innovation is dependent on the depth of the planner's ability to think critically and act ethically.

Box 5.1

Tips for Gaining Access and Becoming Oriented

- Respect what has happened before; know the history.
- Figure out who the key stakeholders and major players are.
- Observe interactions through grand touring activities.
- Establish credibility by having the endorsement of a respected source (hired by an agency, affiliated with a coalition, associated with a powerful group).
- Remember that access is about relationship building, and work to build relationships.
- Surround yourself with local people who fully know the organization or community in which the program will be developed.
- Never underestimate the power of who one knows.
- Understand the motivations, issues, and concerns of the persons with whom one interacts.
- Listen carefully.
- Attend to the status and power dimensions of the situation.

ENGAGING IN CRITICAL THINKING

Critical thinking is a conscious, complex approach to thinking that takes into account factors, including sociopolitical forces, that influence what one can do. Kroeger and Thuesen (1988) identify five levels of complex thinking, all of which may be used in critical thinking in program planning. They are provided here with examples:

- *Copying*: Writing down what is observed or heard, verbatim, as one learns about the situation.

- *Comparing*: Looking at what occurred alongside what has happened in another situation, such as evaluations of model or pilot programs or lessons learned from similar situations in other locations.
- *Computing*: tabulating data (words and numbers) from the comparison, such as comparing demographic data sets;
- *Analyzing*: Drawing conclusions about the differences or similarities in the comparisons, such as linking conditions to problems.
- *Coordinating*: Sharing information from the analysis process with stakeholders, such as demographic comparisons.
- *Synthesizing*: Moving from data and information to examining the implications of what has been compared, such as developing intervention strategies.

Synthesizing is the area in which critical thinking is most demanding, but all levels in complex thinking are necessary to create a useful basis of synthesis. Critical thinking, as deep, thorough thinking, results in examination of assumptions, goals, questions, and the various elements of evidence. It involves the use of reflection focused on what to believe or what not to believe. Critical thinking is part of problem-solving, not just an effort in appraisal of claims or arguments. Critical thinking critiques mistakes in one's thinking and strives for a deeper understanding of issues. No matter the planning approach, the planner thinks critically. What differs may be the focus of the critical thinking.

The AIDS Orphans and Pig Intervention example reveals critical thinking. The staff in a faith-based NGO were immersed in copying as they took note of the rising numbers of child-headed households. They were immediately faced with comparing two situations: the distribution of pigs as food for the household compared with the marketing of pigs to liberate capital. They began to compute the potential impact of the marketing of pigs on the local economy. They analyzed the situation and adjusted the intervention by coordinating with various stakeholders to adjust what they were doing, thus responding to the implications of what would happen if the pig distribution from Europe continued. In the process, the planners probably did not name what they were doing as copying, comparing, computing, analyzing, coordinating, and synthesizing; but they engaged in all of these processes. It was part of a critical focus on problem-solving. The interesting aspect was that the problem changed. With that change, the critical thinking moved from a linear to a more circular method. In the process, they were thinking critically about what was happening while moving to action that altered the original program design. Had they not analyzed, coordinated, and synthesized what was happening, what seemed like a wonderful intervention could have had disastrous consequences.

Though Kroeger and Thuesen describe levels of thinking in a rather hierarchical manner, indicating that one stage is completed prior to moving to another, our example shows that the process might not be either sequential or linear. In the example, what began as a highly rational process sequenced into an interpretive process, and then sequenced back into a rational process in the course of the program. Thus, for us, the levels of complex thinking do not belong to one type of program planning, but are necessary ingredients in any successful program planning process.

Critical thinking is a dialogic process comprising reflective/analytic listening, active pursuit of clarity of expression, evidence, and reason, as necessary. What is considered appropriate evidence and the reason employed may differ, depending on the planning approach. These must be combined with an evenhanded consideration of alternative points of view. The required evenhandedness is possible through fair-mindedness. The critical thinker sees the interplay between various beliefs and is willing to test these beliefs, including his or her own. Testing closely held beliefs requires intellectual courage and security that comes more easily when the critical thinker possesses self-knowledge about personal strengths and limitations. However, the critical thinker also must be able to question what others accept.

Critical thinking includes critical reading and critical writing, to surface and deal with differing perspectives of experts and others who may or may not have a stake in the process. If multiple perspectives are not easily expressed, they must be generated so comparative analysis can occur.

Finally, the critical thinker is a conscious thinker. Rehner (1994) has developed some strategies to demystify critical thinking. We provide adaptations from that work to fit the experiences of the program planner. To become a critically conscious planner, the following are useful basic questions to ask and answer in the thinking process:

- What is the *purpose* of my thinking?
- What precise *question* (problem) am I trying to answer?
- Within what *point of view* (positivist/interpretivist ideology) am I thinking?
- What *concepts* or ideas are central to my thinking?
- What *assumptions* am I making? What am I taking for granted?
- What *information* (data, facts, observations) am I using? What might I be overlooking?
- How am I *interpreting* the information? Are there alternative interpretations?
- What *conclusions* am I coming to? If there are alternative conclusions, why do I prefer these?

- If I accept the conclusions, what are the *implications*? What would be the consequence (positive and negative) if I were to put my thoughts into action?

In short, program planners must be critical thinkers in order to determine which planning approach is needed in a particular situation and to competently carry out that approach.

How, then, is critical thinking different for rational and interpretive planning? The answer probably depends on where the planning process begins. If a program is being designed "from scratch" and is totally new, then both rational and interpretive planning will likely begin at a similar place. Each will begin with general observations and move toward synthesizing thinking in order to determine which approach is appropriate and move from there. However, if redesigning an existing program, then the process will look different. Rational planning would probably respect predetermined goals of the existing program and think critically with others about how the program needs to be modified to reach the goals. Interpretive planning, coming from a different perspective will likely begin by questioning the goals because goals are useful only as long as they function, the need for program redesign would be seen as an indication that everything might need to change; even the idea of having a program might be questioned. The direction that is chosen may well have an ethical component.

For example, in a large school system, the number of children who lacked consistent medical attention and had incomplete immunizations histories was increasing. Local officials contacted the public health department to see if it could develop an immunization program, along with providing opportunities for school physicals. Public health nurses worked with family physicians who donated their time to do monthly clinics at the schools. Yet school officials were having tremendous trouble getting parental permissions for their children to participate in this program. They decided to do outreach to parents through home visits to explain the importance of the program and to get buy-in from the parents. Volunteers who were doing outreach discovered new information: a surprising percentage of the children did not live in a home but "lived" in shelters with their mothers. The majority of the women using shelter services lacked medical assistance and had to rely largely on hospital emergency rooms, and certainly did not have health insurance for themselves or their children. Without adequate resources, these women had no routine health care. This was in addition to the health needs of their children, who maintained a nomadic existence in the school system.

A goal of their program was to provide preventive health care for school children. Rational planning would work from this goal by going backward, putting in place each step needed to provide physicals and immunizations for school children. Faced with new information, the rational planning process would likely continue, but creative ways would be instituted to capture parental signatures from mothers who did not have a home address and whose children moved from school to school within the system. Adjustments in outreach activities and direct service would be made so that the lack of permission slips would not remain a barrier to program implementation.

The interpretive planning process, in contrast, would look at this situation and ask whether this program was even workable, given the new information. Rather than reducing the problem to one of removing barriers to program implementation, an emergent approach would broaden the process by posing questions about whether the problem needed to be redefined and subsequent planning altered. Deeper interrogation of the situation might begin by raising issues about what was known about women who live with abuse and the impact of that on children's well-being. The planner might wonder if shelter workers and community health providers were working in isolation from the school system. In an effort to expand what was known, along with expanding the stakeholding groups involved in problem identification, the planner could contact local shelters to determine if anyone was working with families on health care issues. This information would lead to further discussion with the school system and the health care volunteers. As the process began to unfold, the planner and other stakeholders would likely be designing a very different program, and the program's original goals would likely change in process.

In either approach, the planner's purpose was clear, but the problem being addressed differed because the assumptions changed, causing the choices about what constituted relevant information to change as well. Because of this, the conclusions of each approach differed. What remained to be accomplished in both planning processes was to consider possible implications of alternative conclusions. This then brings things to the point of consciously making ethical decisions.

MAKING ETHICAL DECISIONS

Ethics, a word of Greek derivation from the root *ethos* meaning habit or custom, is a topic as large as philosophy of science (Loewenberg & Dolgoff, 1992). To cover it thoroughly is impossible here, but some basic elements are important for planning. General questions of ethics tend to focus on what should be considered a morally right action and the articulation of how things ought to be. Much work has gone into the thorny issues of what creates and impacts the determination of obligations one owes to another and what one owes to the greater society, and visa versa (Fishkin, 1982). Issues of social obligation have been extended to include pursuit of professional responsibilities; there is general agreement that professionals hold special obligations in professional practice.

Professionalism rests upon responsibility to the public, making professionals stewards of the public trust. Professionals "have held such positions of honor on the basis of a social contract with the public they serve" (Sullivan, 2005, p. 2). Codes of ethics are typically clear in this regard—the practitioner should strive to become and remain proficient in professional practice and the performance of professional functions. Unfortunately, proficiency or the intention to acquire the necessary proficiency may be hard to determine.

Sullivan (2005) talks about the gestalts of professional ethics that often collide in professional life—the ethics of principles (*ethical absolutism*) and the ethics of character (*ethical relativism*). In ethics based on principles, the planner learns to apply rules to situations, to deduce what to do, to assume that these principles are universal, and to order the principles so that any conflict of principles or quandary can be resolved. Thus the principle is more critical than the context. The major principles of a code of conduct are usually clear, but what constitutes *ethical conduct* when those principles are in conflict is less clear. Conversely, "ethics of character is understood as practical wisdom, the *phronesis* Aristotle wrote about, meaning the ability to act well in context. Practical wisdom . . . demands the ability to balance the complexity of situations while maintaining consistent moral aims" (Sullivan, p. 266). In the ethics focused on character, there is a respect for interdependence in which meaning arises through relationship, and there is a dependence on the social capital of the community.

The planning professional engaged in critical thinking will likely be confronted with *ethical quandaries or dilemmas* in which equally important principles conflict or strongly held values compete. Thus, critical thinking and ethical decision-making are part of any planning process. Codification of professional ethics and articulation of special responsibilities have become an important aspect of most professional associations. Codification of what is morally right might seem like a good idea, except that in a global society with a multiplicity of perspectives about what is "right," the challenge of determining ethical conduct can be almost insurmountable. Neither science nor religion can provide total certainty about adequacy of decisions regarding ethical conduct.

Once one recognizes that there is more than one way to plan, Pandora's box is open. Once opened, one is forced to consider which technology, tools, and procedures are appropriate in a specific situation. Otherwise, one has failed to use the technology that fits with the needs of the client (whether the client is an individual, group, or community). A premise of ethical conduct is to "engage in paradoxical thinking . . . and challenge yourself to see the value in areas that are not your strengths, to seek out that which is outside of your comfort zone" (Quinn et al., 2003, p. 349). It is the versatile planner who can be sensitive to the situation, and can respond by being proficient in different planning approaches.

Over time, two major approaches to ethical decision-making have evolved. Both will be present in planning, and each is more closely aligned with one planning approach than the other. The two major approaches to ethical decision- making are deeply rooted in differing value systems or perspectives. Because of this, each takes a quite different view on what constitutes the boundaries of ethics and ethical conduct. Each has had a variety of different names, but for the purposes of our linking these two approaches to planning (Loewenberg & Dolgoff, 1992), we refer to them as ethical absolutism and ethical relativism.

Ethical absolutists stress the importance of fixed moral rules to guide behavior. This comes from a belief that action is inherently right or wrong regardless of the consequence. From this standpoint, ethical rules can be formulated, and once formulated should hold under all circumstances. It is in the source of these rules that one finds some variation in ethical absolutism. One perspective, called *autonomous ethics*, holds that humans can and should determine the moral rules. The alternative perspective, *heteronomous ethical systems* hold that the moral rules are derived from sources outside of humans such as through divine origins. Religious philosophers who teach that moral rules are divinely inspired would fit in this last category of ethical absolutism.

Ethical relativists reject a system of fixed moral codes, believing that ethical decisions can only be justified based on the context of a decision or the consequences created as a result of the decision. Basically, from this position, ethics are determined uniquely: decisions are based on getting what is desired or rejecting an unwanted result. The goal of ethical decision-making for the ethical relativist is achieving good and avoiding evil, or at least gaining more good or assuring the balance of good over evil. This leaves no absolute standard for decision-making or for determining what is good or evil. For ethical relativists, results, not motivation, matters most. Ethical relativism is the basis for *situational ethics*. Some of the challenges from this perspective are seen with the *ethical egoist*, who maximizes the good for oneself without regard to the consequences, and the *ethical utilitarian*, who seeks the greatest good for the largest numbers regardless of what happens to those left behind.

Some philosophers have made efforts to combine these two approaches at the theoretical level (see, e.g., Fletcher, 1966; Frankena, 1980); but even though the two approaches may intersect in practice, we think it does make a difference for planning, if the planner principally follows one approach over the other. For starters, it would seem that the ethical absolutist would have an automatic affinity to prescriptive approaches to planning, while the ethical relativist would be more drawn to emergent approaches to planning. In both cases, however, rigid adherence to a preferred approach might not automatically serve the needs of clients, the organization or the larger system.

Given different ways of viewing ethics, it is important for the planner to consider an ethical framework built on critical thinking to aid in determining what constitutes ethical conduct. It should help to identify minimum proficiencies and conduct, as well as mechanisms for managing competing priorities whichever planning approach is undertaken. Many times, a professional does not see a practice challenge as an ethical dilemma; but these can become ethical dilemmas. We have developed elsewhere some critical questions to both surface ethical issues and guide ethical decision-making (Fauri, Netting, & O'Connor, 2005, p. 23). We have adapted them to fit the role of the professional planner, as follows:

- Are there ethical issues present? (Are there competing values? Loyalties? Systems?)
- At what level are the issues present (personal, professional, societal, or other)?
- What criteria should be used to resolve the ethical dilemma?
- Who should resolve the issue, and why?
- Who benefits from resolution of the issue, and where are the potential conflicts (with clients, other stakeholders, personal, professional, other)?
- What are the consequences of options considered? Does the proposed resolution assure least harm?
- Are there other issues that should be considered, given your understanding of the ethics of your profession?

As you proceed through the rest of this chapter you may wish to utilize this material about critical thinking and ethical decision-making to delve into a comparison of planning approaches and their costs and benefits. Each approach to planning engages the planner and stakeholders in a critical thinking process that reveals choices among values and poses ethical dilemmas.

COMPARING PROGRAM PLANNING APPROACHES

In this section, we compare rational planning and prescriptive approaches with interpretive planning and emergent approaches (See Appendix pp. 210–212). We consider important issues in the full planning cycle. This section ends with a comparison of dimensions, accountability, and skills in program planning approaches that should enter into any planner's critical thinking about the ethics in choice of approach when engaging in the planning process.

Comparing Dimensions

In Chapters 3 and 4, we followed similar outlines. Each chapter addressed the following: (1) dimensions of that type of planning, (2) accountability considerations, and (3) necessary skills. When it comes to dimensions, accountability, and skills, each approach to planning engages the planner and other stakeholders differentially.

For this to become clear, perhaps a bit of review is in order. The dimensions of rational (prescriptive) program planning as elaborated in Chapter 3 were: (1) assessing needs, (2) defining and analyzing problems, (3) developing intervention strategies, (4) writing goals and objectives (with monitoring and evaluation criteria), and (5) designing/decision-making. Table 5.1 provides a reminder.

For comparison, we offer Table 5.2, a reiteration of the dimensions of interpretive planning and emergent approaches to program planning, as elaborated in Chapter 4. These dimensions are: (1) engaging, (2) discovering, (3) sense-making, and (4) unfolding.

Table 5.1
Dimensions of a Rational Planning Process

Dimension	Function
Needs assessment	• Focus scope of needs assessment on a specific group or geographic location, and when not available, extrapolate to the targeted group/area. • Use needs assessment of the targeted population as basis for designing a program to meet client needs.
Problem identification, analysis, and definition	• Identify causes of the problem and focus on conditions that can be reasonably addressed by the organization at the direct service level. • Refine problem definition in the process. • Frame the problem to focus on which alternatives can change the client's status/situation, acknowledging that it may not be possible or feasible to change root causes at this time.
Intervention strategies (hypotheses)	• Select best strategy that directly intervenes with individual clients or groups. • Intervene based on studies, practice wisdom, best practices, clinical technologies, and so on.
Goals and objectives	• Recognize that broad goals will not be achievable in the short run, but objectives will be very specific and measurable. • Write outcome objectives that focus on measuring quality-of-life changes in individuals and groups. • Base formative evaluation on process objectives. • Base summative evaluation on achievement of outcome objectives.
Program design decision-making	• Make program elements specific and detailed, leaving little room for guesswork. • Focus intervention directly on providing services to clients and improving their quality of life. • Expect criticism of the program based on decisions made that appear to provide "Band-Aids" and as potentially perceived to be a mechanism of social control.

Source: Adapted from Netting, O'Connor, and Fauri, 2007.

Table 5.2

Dimensions of an Interpretive Planning Process

Dimension	Function
Engagement	• Assures that multiple perspectives are heard, and reinforces their validity. • Provides a mutual respect and relational focus. • Assures understanding of and attention to context. • Assures a complexity focus.
Discovery	• Draws from multiple data sources. • Assures validity and complexity of information.
Sense-making	• Uses compromises and consensus-based decision-making. • Assures complexity, sophistication, and validity in decision-making. • Respects context by assuring that decisions fit and work for particulars of the situation.
Unfolding	• Assures options and possibilities for the particulars of the situation. • Builds on what was learned and attends to continual learning. • Privileges complexity rather than reductionism. • Assures continual revisioning.

As you can see, the dimensions are not parallel because the processes are different. There is overlap in the initial stages. Although the rational planning process does not generally stress engagement, it still must occur, and engagement has usually been seen in prescriptive approaches as an instrumental process, necessary to move things forward. Engagement in an interpretive way of planning may be an end in itself, causing some to point their fingers and say that they are long on process (relationship) but short on outcome. Therefore, the emphasis placed on engagement differs greatly. In prescriptive approaches, once the instrumental need for engagement is complete, the plan moves forward and may even be taken over by the professional planner, with occasional input from stakeholding groups. Alternatively, an emergent approach to planning will see engagement as ongoing, seeking to maintain a continual connection and consensus as new discoveries are made.

Here are two examples by way of illustration. A planner was hired to design the programs for a senior citizens center in a large urban area. The center was located in a historical section of the city in a former mansion, which had been donated to the city when the owner had died. The planner was told that the board was struggling because there were about a thousand members on the rolls of the center, but only about 50 people participated in activities on an ongoing basis. In fact, the rolls had not been purged for years, making the planner suspect that a large number of the persons on the list may have developed health conditions restricting their independence and that many members had died. Those members attending activities were reasonably pleased with the center's programs because they received a good deal of individual attention and came to view the mansion as a "home away from home."

The planner quickly realized that the more the board talked about purging the rolls and conducting outreach to identify needs of elders in the local community, the more nervous current participants were becoming about how things might change. One member remarked very candidly, "We like it just the way it is. This is our home away from home, and if you mess that up, we lose the very thing that is keeping us going!" Another member commented that, "Sometimes it doesn't make sense to fix something that isn't broken. We all know one another, and the program works well for us." The dynamics among staff, participants, and board members were strained, at best.

The planner initiated a needs assessment of elders living within a mile radius of the center. Volunteers from a local service agency went door to door. Access and health problems were documented. The planner worked with the board to develop a plan of action in which a goal would be to bring additional older people into the center. The plan included purchase of a van to pick up those persons who did not have transportation, and an outreach effort was designed for homebound members. Goals and objectives clearly outlined each step needed, and new program initiative funding was obtained from the local United Way. The center was praised for a well-articulated logic model that laid out how the improved activities program would be monitored and evaluated.

In this case, critical thinking was guided by the presence of a precise question to be answered within a rather positivisitic, rational point of view. The assumptions about the approach to problem-solving were made within that point of view, so the guiding concepts for data collection served to shape the information that was collected. Interpretations were made from that standpoint as well, so that conclusions about what was necessary were logical derivatives. Few alternatives were considered because the "right" answer had been found, in keeping with an ethical absolutist position. Implications were clearly positive for all stakeholders.

In another part of the city, in a similar, but less grand house, another newly hired program planner started work; outside, a lovely, donated van sat empty in the parking lot because no one called for a ride to senior center activities. Usually, about 50 participants came to daily activities and seemed very happy with what was going on. The problem was, though, that only a small portion of the home was ever used, and it was expensive to maintain. Faced with pressures from the funding source (the United Way) to serve more of the aging population in the catchment area, a crisis occurred when the participant numbers dwindled further; one by one, the participants suffered health crises, and the number in the programs decreased to 35.

This agency's outreach program, however, worked overtime. Workers were stressed to the max trying to get around to people's homes, and feeling that no matter what they did, something new always needed to be addressed. The planner began talking with the outreach workers and was amazed at their stories. They were finding that the appeal of coming to a center seemed to be a thing of the past. The current cohort of elders, though in need of services, and pleased with being visited by the outreach workers, did not see themselves as "seniors." Further, even if they could have used the van, they did not want to associate with "the old people who go to the center." The planner realized that there was a process of discovery going on and began to make sense out of what was happening. She had been studying the demographics of the area and hit on an idea: the satisfaction of the current center participants might be an indication that the center's programs had been designed for an older cohort, not the younger feeling cohort of elders currently predominant in the catchment area. In addition, the neighborhood composition had changed over the last 10 years, becoming much more diverse than it had been previously. This made the planner wonder if persons from different backgrounds would be welcomed or comfortable at the center, and what kind of programming might be of interest to them. This planner realized that she needed an emergent process for planning. Going along with the current plan could be the death knell of the center. Additional stakeholders could help make sense of and shape the process so that an acceptable, effective program plan could unfold.

In this case, critical thinking revealed less clear directions about the question, so that a more interpretive and emergent response was viewed as ethically appropriate. The point of view, the important concepts and assumptions, as well as the needed information moved as interpretations became more sophisticated. To remain authentically connected to the emergent process, a stance of ethical relativism became necessary, as the "right" answer about most of the process was entirely dependent on the particulars of the context.

In each of these situations, engagement led to different processes with differing results. Each was attentive to context. Each was responsive to needed changes. Each reached acceptable ethical results. But what happens when a plan does not work? We suggest that when a plan seems to go off-track, it may not be due to a lack of skills on the planner's part or lack of implementation effort. Critical thinking may lead to the conclusion that the wrong approach has been selected for the context, and an alternative approach is the most ethical one to pursue. Sometimes, the hardest part of using any approach to program planning is accepting the possibility that it simply might not work in a specific situation. Changes might be needed and might need to be translated for, and accepted by, a sanctioning or funding body.

Examining Accountability

Earlier, we examined accountability in light of different approaches to planning. Table 5.3 compares what we said about accountability.

As you can see, both rational and interpretive planning are concerned with causal connections, but for different reasons. In rational planning, one is concerned with identifying appropriate measurement tools to evaluate designated outcomes. A program hypothesis, much like a research hypothesis, guides the planner's work in a controlled, logical manner. In interpretive planning, there is concern with causal connections in that it is impossible to assert those connections when one can not predetermine the outcome. Thus, even if measurement tools are readily available in interpretive planning, one does not know which tools to select because the desired outcome could change in process. A concern is to avoid prematurely determining what should be measured.

Table 5.3

Comparison of Accountability Challenges

Rational Planning/Prescriptive Approaches	Interpretive Planning/Emergent Approaches
Differing definitions of EBP	Impossibility of asserting causal connection in an emergent process
Dependency on quantitative findings	Nontraditional methods often not accepted by others
Assertions of causal links must be supported	Inability to conduct longitudinal evaluation, given that everything can change in process
Measurement difficulties	
Complexity of timing	Focuses on broader learning, even learning from failures
Controlling for intervening variables	
Evaluating complicated, multiphased interventions	Need for the program to remain flexible and to change in process leads to ambiguity
Limitations of evaluation design	
Potential for unintended consequences	Need to avoid premature measurement
Inability to change the model in process	

From a rational planning perspective, evidence-based practice (EBP) is defined in a very traditional manner, which might even be called an ethical absolutist position. The "best" way to plan programs is to base them on studies that are rigorously controlled enough (experimental or quasiexperimental quantitative designs) to assert that findings can be generalized to other programs. Although other program evaluation designs might be useful, their findings will be less respected because their science does not conform to the standards of generalizable knowledge. Traditional funding sources and relatively conservative or positivistic stakeholders will seek outcome-based results congruent with their assumptions and the assumptions of rational planning. The role of the planner regarding accountability is traditional, as an expert who is accountable for planning the intervention using the best knowledge available, reducing complexity rather than adding complexity. The planner is responsible for assuring that the program design will net the expected results. Ideally, in rational planning, clients' voices will be heard at least in a representative way. If client values and preferences are at odds with those of practitioners, the tendency will be to respect the opinion of the experts, the practitioners. The same is true for empirical research. If there are empirical research data available that contradict both practitioners' and clients' perspectives, these data will usually be the most privileged information in rational program planning decision-making.

In interpretive planning, evidence that reveals deep underlying meanings will be most valued, and studies that provoke new insights will be most helpful. Context-based quantitative research will not be disregarded, but the richness of qualitative methods, allowing for in-depth knowing and understanding of the problem, will be highly valued. Qualitative evidence (word data) will assure that the decision-making process is emergent, recognizing tentatively held insights as practice unfolds. This stance can be seen to be more congruent with an ethical relativist position. Funders and other constituencies appreciative of more consensus-based models of intervention will understand and prefer the way interpretive evidence influences program planning. Practitioners and clients will join in a decision-making process in which their joint experiences and values are treated as important elements in moving toward a consensus on what intervention needs to occur. Evaluating the process itself (formative evaluation) will be as important as results or outcome-oriented evaluation (summative evaluation). From the ethical relativist position, then, making clear the consequences of overlooking formative evaluation in preference to summative evaluation will become an ethical responsibility, even when facing the more ethical absolutist demands of EBP. It is within this ethical challenge that critical thinking becomes an essential tool.

In addition, an important ethical question in either type of planning is: to whom are the planners accountable? The answer characteristically reveals multiple sources of accountability. In the case of the planner who was hired at the first senior citizens center, there was accountability to the organization (supervisor and the board of the agency). There was also accountability to the older participants and the potential participants, as well as to funding sources to which the board would be ultimately accountable.

The second scenario, interpretive planning, had the same initial constituencies: the agency, supervisor, the board, participants in the center and in their homes, and funding sources. As the plan emerged, new stakeholders to the problem and the solution also emerged: the home visitors and aging community residents. In this case, having a van to transport local residents to the center was not a solution to the low usage at the center. In fact, access was only one aspect of a multifaceted problem particular to that neighborhood. When the planner listened to outreach workers, it was learned that being accountable included being accountable to community residents, and this required much more than transportation to a center.

Similarly, the AIDS Orphans and Pig Intervention example reveals a situation in which there are multiple accountabilities. The NGO was committed to the betterment of the child-headed households, and recognized their accountability to the pig donor; but when the children took their pigs to market, the agency's accountability to the local community (and its economy) became obvious as well. In all these cases, program planners balanced multiple accountabilities with critical thinking embedded in ethical principles. They were prepared to confront the challenges of program planning.

Thinking about Mind-sets and Skills

The challenges of program planning are managed through mind-sets and skills. Both planning approaches require their own orientation. As you will recall, mind-sets and skills were introduced in Chapters 3 and 4. They are compared in Table 5.4.

When reading the lists, what stands out is that rational planning requires working in a linear way, attending to details in moving toward a preestablished goal, always keeping that goal in mind. As the process moves forward, the planner focuses on details linked to the goal. Conversely, interpretive planning remains conscious of context, engaging people throughout the process, embracing complexity, and flexibly moving in unanticipated directions as new information arises.

Each approach has its own set of assumptions and requires some specific and potentially contradictory skills. This does not mean program planners cannot do both types of planning, but it does mean planners cannot engage in both at the same time because then they would be asking themselves to operate under competing, sometimes opposite assumptions. While the rational plan requires order, direction, and finality in the planning, the interpretive plan requires ambiguity and change as constants. A planner simply cannot hold and give up control at the same time. That creates a paradox beyond what is reasonably possible. With knowledge of and abilities relating to each mind-set, a planner should be able to employ either approach, depending on what the situation calls for. We think this is an ethical requirement for program planning.

Here is an example showing how that might work. An experienced MSW is hired to develop a program serving children aging out of the foster care system who are not being served through Independent Living Services. These youth are on the street without resources, subject to the risks of drug and alcohol use, prostitution, and a host of other potential situations, some of them quite dangerous. The local shelter that had focused on homeless youth needs recently closed. Other shelters are open to taking in youth, but they have to be referred through a professional source. It is all but

Table 5.4

Comparison of Mind-sets and Skills

	Rational Planning	Interpretive Planning
Planners' mind-sets	• Thinks rationally. • Embraces linear logic. • Sees whole picture. • Is detail-oriented. • Is patient. • Connects problem and hypothesis. • Appreciates systems theory. • Is organized. • Thinks about possible scenarios in advance. • Identifies as many potential consequences in advance as possible. • Believes in predetermined goals. • Sees self as expert.	• Is committed to change. • Is conscious about self and others. • Works well with uncertainty and ambiguity. • Recognizes that goals are moving targets. • Builds meaningful relationships. • Engages people throughout the process. • Is adaptable. • Welcomes challenges. • Is open to change. • Trusts emergence. • Lives with paradox. • Expects unanticipated consequences. • Expects criticism. • Does not see self as expert.
Planners' skill sets	• Conceives plan from beginning to end. • Sees goal as a vision and reaches for it. • Crafts causal program hypotheses. • Identifies appropriate measurements. • Translates program needs into resource plan. • Understands budgeting; can construct and defend it. • Knows EBP and can explain how it's being used. • Has strong research skills. • Can develop an information system.	• Trusts instinct and intuition. • Engages with intentionality. • Learns through action, ongoing reflection, careful observation, and attention to details and timing. • Asks hard questions. • Works well with others. • Maintains boundaries. • Sees things in complex ways, with attention to what is left out. • Works in concert with others to surface countertruths or disconfirming data. • Recognizes others.

impossible to know how many of these youth fit into the category the program is intended to serve, nor is it exactly clear what they need. Given the situation, there is no effective way to gather needs assessment data in the traditional manner; therefore traditional, rational planning is probably impossible. An approach to the planning effort is needed to create a program based on evidence that could emerge from actual experiences of youth, shelter staff, and planner.

To pursue this course of action, the cooperation of at least one shelter is necessary. First, the planner develops a network of contacts among those professionals in the city concerned with services for the homeless. Then she seeks and obtains permission from an existing shelter to allow her to try an alternative, and convinces the shelter to modify its policies to accept a few youth on a trial basis. In addition, a community worker spends time on the streets, gets the word out that, for now, walk-ins are acceptable at this shelter.

One-by-one youth begin to appear, and they become sources for providing essential information about other youth on the streets, their needs, and what it might take to engage them. This gives both the planner's agency and the shelter an opportunity to build on the information. The shelter staff adjust their service pattern when the youth appear to help identify some of the basic services they might seek. They spend more time chatting with the youth, rather than offering the traditional shelter services. The responses of the youth are incorporated into everyone's thinking, and planning is revised as they move ahead. The process itself is part of creating results. In less than six months, those participating in the planning process have collected sufficient assessment data so that the scope and depth of the problems of these youth can be precisely defined. Those results point to additional needs that require different programming, such as education, job readiness, and mental health interventions that stimulate creation of a plan on a larger scale.

From this, the setting of change goals within a formal intervention plan becomes possible.

Critical thinking reveals that a flexible approach is necessary early on to allow for adjustments along the way, responding to new information or unexpected barriers. Not responding would have been professionally unethical, but responding without sufficient information could have been just as unethical. Once the full picture of needs and resources has been constructed, it becomes possible to move in more traditional planning directions. In this case, the planner performs emergent planning well but is able to shift to a more prescriptive planning role when needed. The planner consciously moves from one set of assumptions to another, and helps constituencies move as well.

DECISION ISSUES FOR APPROACH SELECTION

By now it should be clear that we are not suggesting that one model of planning is correct and the other is incorrect. There are situations for both, but deep thinking and a clear ethical lens are essential to make the determination of appropriateness. We think that, depending on the agency or larger cultural context of planning, one approach may be more appropriate for the need and the resources than the other. Cultural congruence is an important ethical factor, which will be discussed in greater detail in the next chapter; here, it is important to note that culture is an ethical factor because competent program planning cannot be separated from organizational, community, and societal contexts. For example, currently, it would be foolish for any program planner in the United States to discount outcome-based measurement and its importance in obtaining funding from government and United Way sources; but that should not occur without clear attention to planning consequences. These important sources of funding have embraced (even mandated) a rational, problem-solving or logic model; but an uninterrogated or uncritical acceptance of this may have unintended ethical consequences.

The social worker in the Area Agency on Aging in the Invisible People case in Chapter 4 faced this dilemma when planning services did not conform to a rational planning process for older mentally ill elders in a United States city. In fact, if rational planning principles had been used, there would have been no documented need. In that case, use of empirical evidence to convince funding sources or decision-makers that something needed to happen was next to impossible. Yet the social worker was convinced that if an appropriate means of finding these older persons could be devised they would "come out of the woodwork"—they would emerge. She was also convinced that if she projected too far ahead and attempted to write outcomes that such outcomes would be based on *her* reality, not the reality of the elders. In fact, until she located a few older persons to tell their stories, needs and future directions could only be fantasized. She persisted because the worst-case scenario for the program (but not for the elders) was that there really would be few older people being dumped on the doorsteps of emergency room and long-term care facilities. The best-case scenario for the program would be that these invisible people become visible; and with that, where to go next would become clear. Prematurely assuming outcomes for this program would doom it before it began, and hurt people in the process. Unfortunately, trusting an emergent process is a lot to ask local providers or funding sources that have rational program planning standards in mind. Thus, for them, the "program" will likely have to begin as a temporary, short-term "project" designed to identify what happens next. Translated in this way, an emergent approach to planning is appropriate. The question remains, will traditional, rational planning at some later point be useful in this program?

In other parts of the world, some of the same assumptions may hold based on political or accountability reasons. When stability is required for survival, it may be important for programs to begin to perform in highly rational ways in order to neutralize political pressures that have forced a more emergent approach. Sometimes this emergence is not the emergence we have spoken of but a way of responding to graft and corruption pressures. A more rational way may be needed to assure program survival, even when the more emergent approach has been historically compatible with the larger cultural approach to planning. Critical thinking will help the planner determine what is best in the situation.

On the other hand, application of a rational approach to problem-solving may extinguish that which is powerful and unique in an emergent program. Some programs just cannot be measured and planned for by traditional means, if the program is to be sensitive to the needs of the clients or the development of the service technology. Further, the usefulness of transporting Western, rational planning processes and products into other sociocultural contexts may be limited. Many situations mitigate against attempting a solution based on the application of empirically based models created elsewhere. For us, this is an ethical question.

In addition, we recognize that the predominance of rational planning can force an essentially interpretive, meaning-making process between planners and clients into positivistic measurement in service of accountability. Such forcing may be ignoring the very elements of humane helping and quality change desired because intimate aspects of relationship are not always easy to quantify. Creativity and intimacy can be articulated when words are considered as data and when an emergent approach to planning is recognized. To accomplish this, accountability may need to be reconceptualized away from a bottom-line business model, or what Freire (1994) criticized as the banking model where only deposits and profits count. Cost/benefit efficiencies may not be needed to prove the worth of a program if the meaning of the service process can be articulated through benchmarking the process, for example. Formative evaluation may become as central to an interpretive planning as summative evaluation is to rational planning. The gold standard of quality can be expanded to include emergent approaches, and a full spectrum of processes can become available.

SUMMARY

We close by advocating for an expanded perspective on the program planning process that recognizes that interpretive (nonrational) planning is a good and effective addition to the program planning repertoire. We do so based on the sociopolitical consequences of acceptance of only one planning approach, regardless of the cultural context or organizational tradition. More than one approach creates the potential for more fully responding to human service needs and responding to (and even preventing) signs that something needs to happen differently. Our goal is to open the possibility for different ways of thinking about and engaging in program planning. Our hope is that increasing ways of program planning and accountability will expand the possibilities of creative responses to human needs, all the while respecting cultural context.

DISCUSSION QUESTIONS

1. The Aids Orphans and the Pig Intervention is set in a faith-based NGO. What advantages and disadvantages might this setting offer for the sequencing of rational and interpretive planning? Do you think the scenario would be different had the program been located in a government agency? Why or why not?

2. Think of a situation in which you have entered a new setting. How did you gain entry and become oriented? What lessons did you learn about beginnings from that experience that you might take to a new position in which you are hired as a program planner? Given the lessons learned, what tips would you add to Box 5.1: Tips for Gaining Access and Becoming Oriented?

3. How do you think critical thinking is different in rational and in interpretive planning processes? Do the levels of complex thinking (copying, comparing, computing, analyzing, coordinating, synthesizing) fit both types of processes, or would you alter them in some way? If so, how?

4. In the example in which schoolchildren needed immunizations, are there ethical issues that arise once the planner is aware of the mothers' situations? Who is the primary client for which the program is being planned—the school, the children, the mothers, the family? How does your answer affect the direction that you would recommend for this planning process?

5. We are suggesting that planners have a responsibility to carefully assess situations, then determine which type of planning is most appropriate at that time. Does this pose a dilemma for the ethical absolutist when he or she is being asked to think like an ethical relativist, and vice versa? Can you move between ethical types without losing integrity? Why or why not?

6. Look at the code of ethics for your profession. Does this code help you in answering the questions we pose for the professional planner on page 191.

7. Review the situation in which two planners were hired in an urban center to plan programs for two senior citizens' centers. How do these two centers differ, and why is it appropriate for one planner to use a prescriptive approach and the other to use an emergent approach?

8. Most planners are accountable to multiple constituents. How would you go about determining which constituencies get priority when they do not agree? To whom are the planners in the AIDS Orphans and Pig Intervention example primarily responsible, and why?

9. Can you think of a situation in which you planned in a sequential manner, moving from one planning approach to another? If you do not have a personal example, interview a program planner and ask him or her about his or her planning process. Can you find examples of situations in which the planning was not sequential, but the planner tried to engage in both types at the same time? If not, imagine what the consequences of this might be for the planner and the plan.

APPENDIX: COMPARING PLANNING APPROACHES

Approach Comparisons

	Rational Planning	Interpretive Planning
Planning dimensions	• Needs assessment • Problem identification, analysis, and definition • Intervention strategies • Goals and objectives • Program design and decision-making	• Engagement • Discovery • Sense-making • Unfolding
Accountability concerns	• Differing definitions of EBP • Dependency on quantitative findings • Assertions of causal links must be supported • Measurement difficulties	• Impossibility of asserting causal connection in an emergent process • Nontraditional methods often not accepted by others • Inability to conduct

Rational Planning	Interpretive Planning
• Complexity of timing • Controlling for intervening variables • Evaluating complicated, multiphased interventions • Limitations of evaluation design • Potential for unintended consequences • Inability to change the model in process	• Inability to conduct longitudinal evaluation, given that everything can change in process • Focuses on broader learning, even learning from failures • Need for the program to remain flexible and to change in process leads to ambiguity • Need to avoid premature measurement

	Rational Planning	Interpretive Planning
Planners' mind-sets	• Thinks rationally. • Embraces linear logic. • Sees whole picture. • Is detail-oriented. • Is patient. • Must connect problem and hypothesis. • Appreciates systems theory. • Is organized. • Thinks about possible scenarios in advance. • Identifies as many potential consequences in advance as possible. • Believes in predetermined goals. • Sees self as an expert.	• Is brave and committed to change. • Is conscious about self and others. • Works well with uncertainty and ambiguity. • Recognizes that there is a moving target. • Builds meaningful relationships. • Engages people throughout the process. • Is adaptable. • Welcomes challenges. • Is open to change. • Trusts emergence. • Lives with paradox. • Takes comfort in unanticipated consequences. • Expects criticism. • Does not see self as an expert.

(Continued)

	Rational Planning	Interpretive Planning
Planners' skill sets	• Conceives plan from beginning to end. • Sees goal as a vision and reaches for it. • Crafts causal program hypotheses. • Identifies appropriate measurements. • Translates program needs into resource plan. • Understands budgeting; can construct and defend it. • Knows EBP and can explain how it's being used. • Has strong research skills. • Can develop an information system.	• Trusts instinct and intuition. • Engages with intentionality. • Learns through action, ongoing reflection, careful observation, and attention to details and timing. • Asks hard questions. • Works well with others. • Maintains boundaries. • Sees things in complex ways, with attention to what is left out. • Works in concert with others to surface countertruths or disconfirming data. • Recognizes others.

CHAPTER 6

Program Planning in Diverse Cultural Contexts

If one does not decipher the pattern of basic assumptions that may be operating, one will not know how to interpret the artifacts correctly or how much credence to give to the articulated values. In other words, the essence of a culture lies in the pattern of basic assumptions, and once one understands those, one can easily understand the other more surface levels and deal appropriately with them.

—Edgar H. Schein, *Organizational Culture and Leadership*

Chapter Outline

Culture and Context
    Defining Culture
    Elements in Culture Development
    Cultural Competence
    Skills of the Culturally Competent
Challenges to Culturally Competent Human Service Programming
    Understanding Empiricism
    Recognizing Realism and Interpretivism
    Responding to Accountability Demands
Cultural Competence and Program Planning

Planning with Sensitivity to Difference
    Groups Different from the Mainstream
    Within-Group Differences
Planning with Sensitivity to Inclusion
Planning with Sensitivity to Context
    Planning across Multiple Organizational Settings
    Issues When Practicing Internationally
Summary
Conclusion
Exercises

Assumptions upon which the chapter is built:

- Sensitivity to cultural context requires the ability to use different approaches to planning.
- Planning requires cultural competence, even when working within one's own culture.
- Planning requires flexibility and courage to recognize the power dynamics in an expert model of planning, knowing when to be the expert and when to engage in a process in which all participants are experts.
- Complex systems and complex problems require complex responses.
- Interpretive planning is a responsible alternative way to capture complexity.

In Chapter 2, we referred to programs as containers for idea implementation. There, we defined programs and projects, services and interventions. We examined different types of programs and then we placed them in organizational contexts. In doing so, we suggested that organizations hold programs; but the program containers are not necessarily well protected and safely stored. If programs are nested within organizations (sometimes within multiple organizations), then it is important to recognize that no matter how large the organizational container and how wide the organizational impact, programs are rarely protected from the larger environment. Programs must continue to be relevant at the local level even if the organizational container is operating within a diverse, global context. The potential to do great good is always possible if program planners design programs with sensitivity to the people for whom, and the cultures within which, implementation will occur. There is also the potential to do great harm if these contextual considerations are not recognized.

This potential for good or harm is magnified in a world in which technology allows one almost instantaneously to find out about programs in any corner of the globe. In addition, with the push to "replicate" programs that appear to work based on empirical evidence, there is the potential for a planner to take what is a very useful idea in one place and uncritically attempt to implement it in an entirely different context. If that context is different, then is the program still feasible? Will it "fit" within the receiving culture?

In the previous chapter, we compared the different approaches to planning. We identified how sometimes there is a better fit of one approach with a particular time, a context, or a need in which the planner is immersed. We also demonstrated how the different approaches can interface—sometimes a very prescriptive approach leads to an emergent approach, and vice versa. However, one important difference is that, from a rational planning perspective, one standard of quality is *replicability*, being able to generalize a program to another setting. From an interpretative perspective, generalization is never a consideration because it is not possible; however, program *dissemination* is. Planners using either the prescriptive approach or the emergent approach want to solve problems but go about it differently, using different assumptions, skills, and expectations. We think knowing when to use which approach is a way of being culturally sensitive.

In this final chapter, we focus on the importance of context and the program planner's need to maintain sensitivity to culture and differences. We also examine the issues of twenty-first-century planning practices with special attention given to the challenges of programs developed in one context being replicated in or disseminated to other parts of the world.

CULTURE AND CONTEXT

Much has been written about culture, so much so that the term is often used as if everyone knows what it means. Yet, even scholars studying culture have different definitions. Therefore, we need to define what we mean by culture in the context of program planning.

DEFINING CULTURE

While sociologists and anthropologists have been defining culture for decades, a current definition that is very relevant to this discussion is provided by Rothman (2008). He defines *culture* as a "set of values, beliefs, and practices grounded in a common history and experiences shared by a group, which it views as distinct and different from that of other groups" (p. 8). Rothman points out that "culture is context-sensitive, and may be viewed broadly or narrowly in various contexts and situations" (p. 8). Culture requires some grounding in relationships that come from values and beliefs as well as their operationalization through practices and experiences. Grounding can occur within whole communities, in small groups, within organizational units, across large organizations, and even in networks of organizations. The context may be geographical or institutional. It may be created by a sense of connection and commonality through shared language, religion, ethnicity, identity, or ideology. To have a culture, there must be something significant that links individuals together. Knowing and understanding what links people to one another or bonds whole communities is necessary to practice in a culturally competent manner.

Martin (2002) selected 12 different definitions from the organizational culture literature to illustrate how definitions vary (pp. 57–58). Some definitions focus on ideation—emphasizing the cognitive aspects of culture—whereas others take a materialist focus—the tangible artifacts. Other definitions focus on both the ideological aspects (values and assumptions) as well as their material manifestations. Still other definitions assume that culture is "shared" (culture transcends time and space), just as others assert the uniqueness of culture (no two cultures are alike). Rational and interpretive planning may use different views of culture, and those differences are important when enacting culturally competent planning. Table 6.1 illustrates those different views.

Many of the differences vis-à-vis culture resemble the differences between ethical absolutism and ethical relativism that were investigated in Chapter 5. As was seen with the different approaches to ethics, different views of culture are neither right nor wrong, just different. These differences hold important implications for practice.

ELEMENTS IN CULTURE DEVELOPMENT

Usually, when one thinks of another culture, one imagines those exotic places where people look and sound very different from what one experiences on a day-to-day basis. Typically, one thinks of traveling in order to experience other cultures. For planners, that

Table 6.1

Different Views of Culture

Rational Planning	Interpretive Planning
Material manifestations (artifacts, behaviors) are primary, although cognitive manifestations are recognized.	Cognitive manifestations (values and assumptions) are primary, although material manifestations are recognized.
Culture is believed to be shared (agreed upon) within a group.	Culture has different, unique, and varied meanings within a group.
Culture is ingrained, through slowly changing universal assumptions.	Culture is changing, evolving, as groups change and develop.
Planners use cultural guides.	Cultural guides may become the planners (e.g., indigenous people plan).
There is a role for expert planners, even if they are not part of the culture.	There is no single expert role; everyone has expertise to contribute.
As long as culture is considered, there can be predetermined outcomes.	Culture is not only considered, but is of primary importance as culture changes and evolves, affecting goals as it does so.
Dominant cultures have something to offer other cultures.	There are many mutual learning ways and opportunities within cultures.
A program developed in one culture can be replicated elsewhere as long as it is done in similar cultures.	Findings from a program developed in one culture may be helpful elsewhere, as long as assumptions from one context are not superimposed on another. Final determination of appropriateness is in the receiving culture.

might be the first step in cultural competency development, but there are important aspects of culture that can be experienced and learned closer to home, in organizations and communities known to the planner.

Schein (1992) introduces three elements to the development of culture. First is *socialization* in which new members are inducted into the culture. If the group is relatively new, this socialization process may not be as institutionalized as it would be for a fully developed culture. Second is *behavior*, those actions and interactions that can be observed between members of the culture, between groups, and between individual members and groups. It may be that these behaviors are artifacts or deeply held beliefs, but it is important to look for patterns to determine if there is congruence between behavior and beliefs. Third, within any community or organization, there may be several cultures existing simultaneously; at any time, there may be distinctive *subcultures* within the same larger unit. Even when there is divisiveness among subunits of culture, and accompanying disagreements and conflict, when there is great need, such as from external threat, common assumptions consistent across subgroups will link units and create cohesiveness.

For example, a program planner was hired for a newly formed coalition of community agencies that had come together to respond to concerns about the number of homeless persons in an urban environment. The planner quickly realized there was an opportunity to get in on the groundwork of the planning process because no set policies and procedures existed. Socialization of new member agencies was fairly loose, as each brought new expertise to the table. The inclusion of homeless individuals and families in the planning process, though quite difficult and time-consuming, kept the group attuned to what was important (and what was not). The coalition was new and had such diversity and so many perspectives and agendas within it that it was often difficult to make any progress. Many participants began to grumble with frustration about the lack of movement.

However, when the local chamber of commerce formed a task force to force the city to relocate homeless people from the business district, the coalition surprisingly and immediately united. To the person, coalition members were opposed to this strategy because it was what they considered an "out of sight, out of mind" approach. In light of this common "enemy," the coalition rallied, and drafted a statement to take to the chamber. It was clear that a developing culture of the newly formed coalition had caused members to coalesce around common assumptions and values in reaction to the chamber's initiative.

A new set of *cultural norms* had been created in the consensus among participants. The planner used this newfound synergy to move the group forward with the planning process so that a viable alternative program plan could be offered. She sensed that the group was now ready to really plan, and now it was her job to determine which planning approach would be best suited for the new coalition culture in this sociopolitical context.

Another important element in culture development for planning is *context*, that situation, setting, or environment in which planning is conducted. The context may be an informal affiliation or group of individuals or organizations, a formalized organization, a community, or an institution. It may be ideological or geographical; it may be both. Whatever the context, there will be present either an emerging, developing culture or an established culture. The planner overlooks context at his or her own peril and to the detriment of the planning. Recognizing context involves cultural competence.

CULTURAL COMPETENCE

Cultural competence as an ideal makes perfect sense but represents difficult challenges, as the planner must deal with constituencies and competing demands and expectations. Competent multicultural practice is not easy in a known context. The challenges are even greater when the context is not a known organizational or community environment.

Cultural competence requires awareness, or what is commonly termed *cultural awareness*. This awareness includes the planner's culture as well as the "other." Cultural competence requires the practitioner to acquire knowledge about diverse groups. This knowledge must go beyond the simple stereotypes. For example, in certain cultures, it is disrespectful to look someone directly in the eye; or a firm handshake may be a sign of respect in some cultures, while in others it is considered rude, and a soft grasp is preferred. Deeper knowledge and skill development than these examples are needed to practice effectively. For the planner, this requires important elements such as understanding how people provide and manage information, how people communicate and make decisions, how they respond to outsiders, and how they deal with perceived or conferred power.

Additionally, cultural competence requires awareness of one's own personal or professional preferences and how they may differ from the context in which one practices. These differences are surfaced, described, and understood for what they are; they are not judged or criticized, but accepted as present in the context and necessarily bridged for planning success. *Ethnocentrism*, belief in the superiority of one's own culture, must be absolutely avoided if one is to be able do the work. Understanding traditions, values, family systems, socioeconomic issues, attitudes regarding social services and social policies, as well as important historical experiences, including the effects of prejudice and oppression, is not possible if the planner stands in judgment. For the planner, the relationship building required for appropriate decision-making rests on the ability to cross the borders of difference (Harper-Dorton & Lantz, 2007). These borders can be crossed with cultural competence.

Mastering another language is helpful in acquiring cultural competence, but it is not enough alone. For example, speaking Spanish is an important step to cultural competence; it is not an indication that someone is competent to practice with any Spanish speakers because those speakers represent myriad differing cultural responses to managing relationships, communication, and power. In addition, cultural competence involves attending to other important and sometimes subtle differences. Nonverbal and "body language" signals as forms of communication also come into play. Areas requiring special consideration and sensitivity for competent practice include cultural-based attitudes and behaviors toward: diversity; racism, sexism, and homophobia; discrimination and oppression; and ethnic, gender, and sexual orientation groups. Recently, an understanding of ethnic competence has included social and economic justice (Lum, 2005). In fact, for Lum, social and economic justice are only possible through ethnically competent changes such as those proposed through culturally competent planning. According to Lum, cultural competence is a mastery of a particular set of knowledge, skills, behaviors, and attitudes that create policies and programs built on an understanding of values and social class. Then policies and programs can address the cultural needs of individuals, families, groups, and communities.

SKILLS OF THE CULTURALLY COMPETENT

It is important to understand the interpersonal and organizational functions that culture represents in order to plan competently within it (Atkinson, Coffey & Delamont, 2003).

Following Lum, the culturally competent planner can acquire knowledge about the culture of interest the same way one learns about any subject: through study. Thorough investigation of available literature is always a way to accumulate knowledge and develop a sensitivity to the culture and the potential diversity within a particular culture. Certainly, attempts at acquiring the language of the culture will also aid competent communication. Learning the logic of the language helps one understand the logic-in-use in the culture. Linear, Anglo-Saxon-based languages (English and German, among others) provide different clues to reasoning and problem-solving than those available in more circular languages, such as the romance languages (French, Spanish, and Italian, among others). If one lacks language facility or the time to acquire the language, then cultural interpreters are essential to developing cultural competence. Professional colleagues or friends who are members of the culture of interest can help the planner not only learn about the culture but prepare for practice within it. Cultural "guides" can be worthwhile throughout the planning process to help the planner prevent or deal with cultural issues that may arise. These cultural interpreters can sometimes aid the planner in skill development relating to attitude and behavioral changes necessary to acculturate in a new culture.

The planner intent on becoming culturally competent must enter the culture of interest because it is only inside the culture that true cultural understanding becomes possible. Campbell and Gregor (2004), in their text on institutional ethnography, provide excellent guidance about how to do this in an organization. We recommend their work for details about data collection and developing the requisite interpersonal relations with organizational informants.

Two techniques of ethnographic research are important for entry into a different culture, and can enhance further understanding that will aid the planner to become culturally competent. These are: becoming a culturally competent interviewer and learning where to look in the cultural context (observation).

Culturally competent interviewing develops through informal conversational interviews (Ruben & Babbie, 2005, p. 447). In many cases, there is an assumption that culturally competent interviewing only occurs when the interviewer is of the same culture as the one being interviewed. This seems to suggest that communication across cultures is impossible. Others suggest that racial matching, though important, is no more important than interviewer competence (Jackson & Ivanoff, 1999). Previous experience, training in working within the culture, is also important. In addition to the help of cultural guides, informal conversational interviews will add to a planner's cultural competence. These informal conversations with a purpose (Lincoln & Guba, 1984) usually result from observations within the context that suggest where to look for clarifying information.

Much has been written about observation as a way of gaining information. In ethnographic research, this activity is generally known as *participant observation* (Marshall & Rossman, 1995). However, Gold (1969, pp. 30–39), in a classic work, explicates four different roles an observer might play. To gain insight, one might become a complete participant, a participant-as-observer, an observer-as-participant, or a complete observer. Each has much to offer, but each also represents specific challenges to the planner wishing cultural understanding.

From our perspective, the richest source of information to move toward cultural competence comes from a combination of the role of observer-as-participant and guided conversations with selected informants. During observations, the planner becomes aware of issues or questions. Ethically, it is made clear that he or she is both an observer and participant and is engaging in conversations to acquire relevant information to maximize an understanding of what is being observed and what people think about it. The planner engages in asking and listening. Lofland (1995, p. 56) calls this role a "naturalistic investigator." The planner, recognizing cultural ignorance, enters into these conversations with a purpose (Lincoln & Guba, 1984). The purpose is to be taught. The planner is a watcher and asker, a student, in search of elaboration so as not to make erroneous assumptions based on personal cultural assumptions. The skills of observing and interviewing improve with practice, and understanding culture enough to become competent within it takes time.

CHALLENGES TO CULTURALLY COMPETENT HUMAN SERVICE PROGRAMMING

Planning based on a cultural worldview as presented here brings us almost full circle to the philosophical discussions that started our discussion about planning in Chapter 1. We return to that now in the hopes that after reading this text, some of the philosophical issues are now more relevant. We are particularly interested in those philosophical aspects that might inform some of the current challenges to human services programming worldwide. We do this because, like Kuhn (1970), we believe the revolution in what constitutes knowledge and the way social science works to be incomplete.

As science has evolved, much has happened for the good, including technological advances in communication and the movement toward more open societies; but there remain many social and economic problems to address through human service programming. Three areas are particularly challenging in culturally competent program planning: (1) understanding empiricism, (2) recognizing realism and interpretivism, and (3) responding to accountability demands. In examining each of these areas, we return to the philosophical and epistemological consequences of differing worldviews, as well as further elaboration of positivism and interpretivism, which directly applies to the planner's ability to manage planning in the multicultural world of the twenty-first century.

UNDERSTANDING EMPIRICISM

Regardless of philosophical criticisms to the contrary, there continues to be strong reliance on an empirical approach to knowing in social science. Knowledge is assumed to be produced through observation and evidence so that "real" knowledge is developed from that which can be observed. Positivists remain intent on measurement and numbers. Post-Positivists admit that words may be data, too. Hess (1980) calls this approach an empirical philosophy composed of several dimensions: naïve realism, universal scientific language, and the correspondence theory of truth. Empiricism understood in this way suggests that systematic inquiry (science) is able to capture the external facts of the world in propositions (if/then statements) that are true if they correspond to the facts as measured, and false if they do not.

The assumptions about empiricism have been subjected to criticism and challenged with theoretical and experimental findings. It is certainly beyond this discussion to lay out all the criticisms, but the basic result of the critique is the view that positivism is an inadequate or incomplete conceptualization of what science is, especially social science. For planners, this is particularly important since in positivism there is focus on discovery over justification and on fact over theory; and with this, an overdependence on "operationalism" has developed. When there is demand to operationalize all variables, the approach to "coming to know" is restricted because it causes one seeking knowledge to attend to sensations (that which is measurable) over meanings (feelings) or implications. The culturally competent planner knows that what is measurable may not tell the full story.

The most important result of the criticisms of positivism, for planners, is that the positivistic view of science has not been able to deal with the emergent through its demands for empirical formulations. The surprises in planning are evident even when the practices are not cross-cultural in nature. Up until now, most program planners have been given planning tools congruent with the Western positivist approach to empiricism, based on valid research, as true knowledge is "above all (if not solely), the question of method and its systematic application" (Bauman 1978, pp. 15–16). Now, with the emergence of the global economy and the feeling that the world has gotten smaller, understanding the criticisms of empiricism and positivism is important to being culturally competent.

The currently dominant methods for program planning, rational planning, and prescriptive approaches reflect the limits of empiricism and positivism. As planners cross the borders of difference, it is evident that there is no single tangible reality; instead, there is a multiplicity of realities, constructed internally and externally by individuals and groups. What is learned depends on where one looks and what questions one asks. What is true at one time and place is not necessarily true in another time and place. Sometimes (maybe even most of the time), there is no clear linear causality because the planner sees effects without causes, and causes without effects. Finally, even the methodologies or planning tools used sets of values.

Until the scientific revolution takes us to a more holistic approach to coming to know both facts and meanings, we think the best advice for the program planner is to listen to the seductive call for empirical certainty but to temper that with an ability to manage ambiguity as well. The planner does this by using the appropriate planning tool at the appropriate time in the evolution of an idea in a particular context. From our perspective, this is an ethical and culturally sensitive strategy for planning.

RECOGNIZING REALISM AND INTERPRETIVISM

Closely related to empiricism, realism, particularly naïve realism, takes the position that there is an external world that can be totally described by science. Further, there is a belief that that which one knows exists independently of one's mind, so that understanding is abstracted from this independent reality "out there." This approach to the knowable has led some philosophers and scientists to hold a mechanistic view of the world. According to Schwartz and Ogilvy (1979, p. 72), this view assumes that there is a fundamental level of reality, or basic building blocks, and through science we understand these small particles and the set of forces that govern them. This is important because once that is known at the fundamental level, laws that govern reality can be discovered. Laws can be applied on a larger scale, becoming universal laws. This leads to a second important assumption: that we, as observers, can be isolated from experiments and from the world, thus producing objective descriptions. From the discussion of empiricism, you may see that this is not always possible.

Realism, however, is not just a position of empiricists. Some Post-Empiricists, Post-Modernists, and Post-Positivists subscribe to the same definition of realism, recognizing that entities exist independent of being perceived or independent of our theories about them (Phillips, 1987)—but with a twist. This alternative position recognizes and allows a distinction between what is believed to be true as opposed to what is really true. Realism for them allows "at least in principle, a standard by which all human societies and their beliefs can be judged; they can all have beliefs about the world, which turn out to be mistaken" (Trigg, 1985, p. 22). This kind of realism allows the planner to take what stakeholders believe into account and use it as a referent point for judgment about the accuracy of the depiction of that believed reality. Whether or not the belief is "correct" or "real" or "objective" has meaning. Even when there is a mistaken belief, that belief has meaning and significance to be taken into account in the planning process.

This approach to realism takes the planner into practical *multiculturalism* and into assuming that there are both simple and complex realities. There is diversity and interactivity (complex), not just a reality constructed from the sum of it parts (simple). This allows for uniqueness. This approach to realism takes the planner from a hierarchical to a heteroarchical concept of order, in which there can be many orders operating side by side.

Most importantly, this approach to realism moves the planner seeking just objectivity to being able to choose (and interpret). This is an interpretive perspective. Cultural competence allows bridging between cultures. Where one looks affects what one sees, and a particular focus may give only partial results. The whole picture could require multiple perspectives. With a perspectival view, plans can more easily deal with diversity, openness, and complexity, the cornerstones of culturally competent practice. Even with apparent certainty that comes from objectivity, planning decisions must be based on what seems reasonable. Sometimes what is reasonable comes from meaning, not facts; thus there is a need to recognize and use both rational and nonrational thought in decision-making. This moving from realism to interpretivism brings us to the great accountability challenge in culturally competent planning practice.

RESPONDING TO ACCOUNTABILITY DEMANDS

In Chapter 5, we compared accountability in light of different approaches to planning. As you may recall, there were different challenges for rational and interpretive planning. In addition, there are accountability demands that impact planning regardless of which approach one is taking.

"Accountabalism," a term coined by the marketing consultant, David Weinberger (2007), relates to the emphasis on accountability in all aspects of organizations and programs. From his perspective, this focus on accountability is superstitious thinking that supports practitioner and public denial about just how little control we have over organizations and programs, in particular, and the environment, in general. It is probably understandable that the automatic reaction to serious scandals in public and private sectors has been to ward off unethical behavior through attention to precision. With this precision we are further lulled into the belief that there is a right and a wrong way to operate, a right and wrong answer to every decision, and that through demands for precision, we can measure everything exactly. Our earlier philosophy of science discussion relates to the depth of belief in this myth. The Enron scandal and others like it demonstrate how difficult this attention to accountability really is: systems do go wrong with unethical individuals; but controls in place do not always prevent future disasters, if the individuals are bent on unprincipled practice.

Our worry is about the unintended consequences from over-attention to misplaced accountability in which there is such great precision in detailing regulations and oversight that planners' hands are tied in designing innovative programs. This attention to detail can hamper creativity in program design and subsequent implementation. There is also the demand of what we are calling contradictory accountability, which occurs when programmatic policies and directives are helpful to one group but actually contradict what is helpful to another group. In human service programs in which there are multiple constituencies to whom one is accountable, there will inevitably be difficulties in balancing accountabilities, and times during which being accountable to one group means countermanding the demands of another.

We agree with Weinberger (2007), that accountability requirements reduce complexity, while also increasing detail. Creative, responsive organizations resist being boxed into regulating procedures and routines because responsiveness requires innovation and adaptability that will undoubtedly require breaking those rules and procedures. Forms, reporting, and documentation inhibit agility and set up a force field against change.

We advance accountability by urging clarity and responsibility, regardless of the approach to planning, instead of using an accountability shield to relieve the planner of the hard work of critical thinking and ethical decision-making. We assume that in situations where close control is mandated, responsible use of resources and useful feedback can become important for all stakeholders in the process. Yet there are also times when close control is neither possible nor good for responsible planning. In those times, resistance to overcontrol, based on critical thinking and cultural competence, must be asserted and acknowledged to bring balance to the planning process.

CULTURAL COMPETENCE AND PROGRAM PLANNING

From our perspective on culturally competent program planning, planning is delivered in a series of nested cultures, all requiring cultural competence to assure quality services. First, the program planner must engage in the planning process with a full understanding of his or her cultural background. Second, the programmer must understand both the organizational and contextual cultures where planning is occurring. Third, regardless of the means employed in planning (rational or interpretive planning), it is important to acknowledge the different cultures or subcultures represented by the stakeholders in the planning process.

This attention to nested cultures is important to underscore an appreciation of differing value systems, beliefs, and behaviors in each. This sets the stage for the difficult work of multicultural practice. When cultural issues of all participants are appreciated, the cultural preferences of the majority will not be adopted without critical testing, preventing cultural differences from being understood as synonymous with cultural inferiority. This will add to the complexity of the process, but it will also add immeasurably to both the relevance and the effectiveness of the program plan.

For the planner, this is impossible without support of an organizational tether, within which planning practice occurs. No matter how sensitive the planner, culturally competent work is not possible without organizational supports from culturally competent organizations. Organizational values that support cultural competence include:

- Respect for the unique, culturally defined needs of diverse client populations
- Acknowledgment of culture as a prevailing factor in shaping client behaviors and values
- Understanding when values of cultural groups may come into conflict with societal or organizational values
- Belief that diversity within cultures is as important as diversity between cultures
- Acknowledgment and acceptance that cultural differences exist and have an impact on how services are both delivered and received
- Recognition that an understanding of individual, family, and community can differ from culture to culture and within cultural subgroups
- Focus on the domestic unit as a primary and preferred point of intervention or inclusion in some cultures
- Respect for the family as indispensable to understanding the individual
- Respect for cultural preferences that value process rather than product and emphasize harmony or balance in one's life over achievement
- Recognition that minorities may be forced to adapt and manage by being bicultural, which may create complex behavior issues
- Advocacy for culturally competent services

When practicing in another culture, whether that is in an organization, a neighborhood, or another country, to be culturally competent is to honor and respect the cultural collective values and to recognize individual values within the larger context.

We now identify three ways in which the program planner engages in culturally competent planning: (1) planning with sensitivity to difference; (2) planning with sensitivity to inclusion; and (3) planning with contextual sensitivity. Planning with sensitivity to difference requires awareness of cultural characteristics that need to be considered. Planning with sensitivity to inclusion suggests there are potential consumers who should be a part of conceptualizing any program that will affect their lives. Planning with sensitivity to context recognizes the nuances of the situation, the setting, or the environment, including how the placement of the program will enhance or limit the implementation. All three are important for competent practice, regardless of the approach selected.

PLANNING WITH SENSITIVITY TO DIFFERENCE

Cultural competence includes cultural sensitivity, but that sensitivity must be nuanced. Planning with sensitivity to difference includes thinking about tailoring programs to fit the needs of groups of people not of a dominant culture, perhaps in a culture with which the planner is unfamiliar. It also recognizes that planning with sensitivity requires responsiveness to differences within groups that are often assumed to be fairly homogenous.

Groups Different from the Mainstream

Weaver (2005) tells the story of trying to develop a culturally sensitive assessment tool to use with Tamil refugees who fled the civil war in Sri Lanka and relocated to North America. Without an appropriate assessment, it was impossible to plan programs that would be culturally sensitive. The project team located a tool that had been used with various population groups and that had been translated into a variety of languages. They knew it would need to be appropriately reframed with careful consideration for cultural and gender norms of the Tamils. A team of helping professionals and Tamils worked together to review the tool; consider what needed to be asked; and to take care to use culturally sensitive approaches to privacy, confidentiality, and respect for human dignity. For example, based on gender norms, a female interviewer would administer the tool to women, and a male interviewer would do the same with men. In addition, in order to be respectful of individual preferences and provide options, the team offered to locate interpreters for interviewees or to allow interviewees to bring their own interpreter. They did this even though Tamils being interviewed in the pilot project were fluent in English.

The project team recognized that Tamils are Hindu, and understood that Hinduism emphasizes community and interdependence as foundational to well-being, unlike the individualism and autonomy in Western cultures of team members. They also learned that individuals are expected to persevere through hardship and avoid unpleasantness. Assuming, for example, that a woman in an Asian patriarchy culture such as Tamil would likely not reveal that she had been victimized, and since the assessment dealt with torture and trauma, including sexual assault, the helping professionals planned for complete confidentiality by having as few people as possible involved in the interviewing process. When the assessment process began, the planners were totally surprised. "We found that the respondents did not want to discuss issues of trauma and torture in a one-to-one format. Rather, they openly discussed sensitive issues in the presence of family members, and the women discussed their experiences with trauma in front of male family members and through a male interpreter" (Weaver, 2005, p. 242). In this example, the planners used an emergent approach, responsively engaging potential consumers in every phase of the process. The participants became the planners' cultural guides. Even when the team was prepared to respond to the cultural needs of Tamil refugees in determining service needs, they found assessment was more complicated than expected. While trying to protect refugees and provide privacy, they unwittingly could have caused further hurt by separating the women from their community support. By recognizing their own biases, and responding flexibly, they learned, "There is a lesson for all of us that we constantly need to be willing to discard our assumptions when the voices of our clients carry different messages" (Weaver, 26, p. 243).

This example might suggest that in planning for those outside the mainstream, emergent planning is the only sensitive approach. But whereas rational planning might not work in the situation just described, it can be just as culturally sensitive. Likewise, a prescriptive approach could be particularly appropriate when culturally appropriate assessment tools exist for Tamil refugees, or if in the planning process there are identified certain needs that require specific ongoing interventions. But no matter the approach used to proceed, it is important to factor in inclusiveness so those outside the mainstream can continue to inform the process.

Within-Group Differences

When members of a population group are part of the mainstream culture, there may be diversity within the group. Sensitivity to heterogeneity within groups is required so as not to miss important cues that point to needed alterations in interventions. Cultural competence respects that one size does not necessarily fit all. Here we are thinking about consumer groups or target groups for service, but the same would be true for groups of identity or other natural groups.

Melbin, Sullivan, and Cain (2003) bring home this point in their discussion of transitional supportive housing programs designed for battered women. Some programs have specified time limits for the use of the housing while others provide housing until permanent homes can be located. Typically, programs offer supportive services including counseling, housing assistance, employment location, child care, and transportation. Although early on, shelter programs were designed with consumer input, many current transitional housing programs are planned without a great deal of consumer input, despite "the plethora of research that has supported the benefits of using consumers' needs to guide the delivery of services" (p. 447). Given the lack of consumer voices in planning for transitional housing, Melbin and her colleagues decided to conduct focus groups to directly ask battered women what they needed. They also asked advocates, coalitions, and provider networks all over the country about best practices and policies, only to be told that there were no standard protocols or practices, often forcing providers "to make up the rules as they went along" (p. 447). It would seem housing providers were engaged in emergent planning, taking one step at a time, and were eager to learn from what the focus groups might tell them.

The researchers explored "perspectives about guiding principles, eligibility issues, rules and regulations, safety protocols, and services as a means of assisting agencies that provide services to battered women to design the most helpful and supportive programs possible" (Ibid., p. 447). Battered women in the focus groups were not in agreement about what was most useful. What some women rated as most helpful, others rated as least helpful. The majority did agree that supportive staff are essential and certain services are useful, including child care, transportation, referrals to other agencies, and rent subsidies. It became clear that needs unique to individual clients in transitional housing require offering a wide range of services so that women could "shop" among a menu of services they might need. Some need support groups; others do not. Some require clear, somewhat rigid protocols; others want few, and flexible, rules. Findings suggest assumptions cannot be made about which package of services an individual needs. The authors call for recognizing within-group differences related to individual women's needs: "It is only by acknowledging the individuality of each woman's experience that we will create effective solutions to the complex housing needs of battered women" (Ibid., p. 459).

Another population group with high heterogeneity comprises caregivers of older people. Smith and Toseland (2006) provide advice to planners developing telephone support programs for this group. When considering effectiveness for individual users, the authors discovered telephone support groups had strong positive results for adult children caregivers by providing both social and emotional support. These caregivers, as a result of the service, experienced reduced depression and less stress over time, increasing knowledge about services and accessing services from others. These same effects were not present for spousal caregivers. The disparity of findings points out differences within caregiver groups. First, spouses who are typically retired and live at home might appreciate the respite of attending a face-to-face support group. Adult children generally do not live with the care recipient, and work outside the home, making them more amenable to a phone conversation than a meeting, attendance at which would have added one more responsibility. In addition, adult children's relationships with older parents are qualitatively different from relationships among spouses. Even though they are all caregivers, planning the same intervention for all does not recognize the needs of different subgroups within the caregiving population.

Some may question how these two examples represent cultural sensitivity. However, embedded in difference are nuances

regarding individual experiences that reflect Rothman's (2008) definition, which includes sets of values, beliefs, and practices
grounded in a common history and shared experiences, which
are viewed as distinct and different from that of other population
groups. Both the battered women and the elder caregivers have
specific experiences that have led them to be distinct from other
population groups, as a whole. Our point is that planners must not
overlook within-group differences, or they risk expensive and frus-
trating off-targeted program implementation.

Within attention to difference is an assumption of the positive
aspects of diversity. Planners seeking to be culturally competent
must also aspire to manage the diversity present in most contexts
worldwide. Given the development of a world economy and
ongoing and widespread technological advances, it is almost impossible to find a "pure" culture. So to add to the complexity of
culturally responsive planning, next we investigate the challenges
of planning for inclusion.

Planning with Sensitivity to Inclusion

When inclusion is part of the planning discussion, the focus is
generally on some minority population whose needs are overlooked
by majority society. While this is certainly an important part of
sensitivity to inclusion, we focus on an example that provides a
picture of the complexity that must be faced when inclusion involves
multiple needs and multiple cultures within the same intervention.
We do this to underscore the challenges of multicultural work even
when the planner is clearly sensitive to culturally competent planning. An example showcases how important it is to include persons
of all ages in program planning targeted to entire communities.

Although the United Nations Convention on the Rights of the
Child contains a set of participation clauses intended to recognize

the rights of children and youth to be a part of planning programs for their own well-being, children and youth are often planned *for*, rather than *with*. However, one way the U.N. principle of inclusiveness is achieved is in the Growing Up in Cities project of the United Nations Educational, Scientific, and Cultural Organization (UNESCO). This project has spread across six continents and in more than 50 sites (Chawla & Driskell, 2006, p. 185).

Chawla and Driskell (2006) report on one of the sites in Sathyanagar, on the outskirts of Bangalore, India. Sathyanagar is considered to be a slum. Project staff work with 38 children (18 girls and 20 boys) ages 10 to 14, who represent a cross section of the community's linguistic and religious groups. Children have different schooling options, but all work either in their homes or nearby. The project engages the children in a series of activities in which they learn how to conduct one-on-one interviews and participate in a series of small group activities, including walking tours of the area, taking photographs, and focus group discussions. Children talk about their living environments and the challenges they face, but their stories also speak "of young people with an astonishing degree of resilience . . . Although Sathyanagar ha[ve] little financial capital, in the eyes of the project children it [is] rich in social and cultural capital" (p. 189).The children in Sathyanagar are not naive. They share stories of neglect, lost opportunities, and corruption. They also reveal "misguided development agencies and mismanaged nongovernmental groups," in which the concept of participation is touted but the rhetoric does not always fit with steps in the planning process.

Even though the intent of the participation is for the young people to develop project goals that will guide the planning of needed programs in the community, potential funding agencies often see "small projects with community-determined outcomes . . . as both risky and ineffective" (Ibid., p. 192). "Tangible, measurable outcomes (maps, plan documents, education materials, capital improvements) need to be identified in the proposal. Community participation [is] of course paramount, but only as a vehicle for implementing predefined project outcomes" (Ibid., p. 193).

The various reports from the UNESCO Growing Up in Cities sites from around the world reveal several lessons learned. First, adults simply do not fully understand young people's issues and priorities. Second, even young children can participate in meaningful community evaluation and generate feasible recommendations. Third, if adults and children work together, young voices can be heard, and there can be a role for influencing decisions that will affect their well-being.

This project is reminiscent of the AIDS Orphans and the Pig Intervention project discussed in Chapter 5. Child-headed households could easily be disregarded in the planning process, being composed of children. However, without attention to their perspectives, planners risked dire consequences to the pig industry nationally in unintended consequences, resulting from not understanding the children's preferences. Their inclusion required being sensitive to the cultural nuances that bond them together as children. In attempting to plan on their behalf and with genuine interest in their well-being, planners overlooked their perspectives, with almost disastrous results.

With or without cultural sensitivity, excluding important stakeholders in the problem identification and in problem resolution sets up difficult challenges to overcome for planning and implementation. Unintended negative consequences are sure to accrue. Good intentions, many times based on erroneous cultural assumptions, will not overcome the challenges created when the minority voice goes unheard by the majority.

PLANNING WITH SENSITIVITY TO CONTEXT

Whether it is within an organization, at the intersection of multiple organizations, or in communities, cultural norms and values define

context. Lazzari, Amundson, and Jackson (2005) conducted a qualitative study of an innovative arts project funded by the federal
Office of Juvenile Justice, in collaboration with a regional art
museum and a county detention center in the western United
States. Planners for this project were aware that female juvenile
offenders constitute more than a quarter of arrests of young people
each year, representing the more rapidly growing segment of the
juvenile justice system, and that "young women are more likely to
have multiple diagnoses and major neurological abnormalities and
to be at a greater risk of suicide" than their male counterparts
(p. 170). Of these offenders, females of color from disadvantaged
backgrounds are overrepresented in the system, primarily being
charged with status offenses such as truancy, running away from
home, or incorrigibility. Clearly, the confined nature of detention
facilities represents limits to programming; but in addition, myths
and stereotypes about female offenders can limit sensitivity within
population group needs in programs and interventions. "Gender-
specific programs are an exception, rather than a rule because most
detention centers are designed on the basis of male models of
incarceration" (p. 171).

So, in addition to the challenges of gender differences within the
offender population, the limits of what was possible in incarceration represent challenges for culturally sensitive planners. In the
program that Lazzari, Amundson, and Jackson studied, a professional artist who was attending to gender issues guided the young
women in producing individual and collective painting, sculptures,
poems, and other works of art. Within-group diversity was apparent. The young women came to the center having committed a
variety of offenses; having wide-ranging life experiences; being of
different age groups and at different developmental stages; and
coming from varying ethnic and cultural backgrounds. Context
constraints required the project to be focused and short term.

A detention center is often disruptive; but more important, because the young women's lengths of stay varied, any long-term intervention continuity would be broken. The program posed challenges not only for the planners but also for those planning to evaluate it.

The evaluators interviewed 31 participants and the artist, and observed the arts project over a period of time. Findings revealed the importance of the relational nature of the program as the young women connected to one another, to the artist, to the artwork, to their families, and to themselves. The evaluators concluded that the artist and the work were pivotal in facilitating those connections. This underscores the need for gender-responsive programming for incarcerated young women, given women's relational needs. Art is a relational intervention, but it also provides an opportunity for self-expression in a tightly controlled, freedomless environment. Planning for the individual in her environment (the detention center) and recognizing the culture in which she must live (at least for a short time) illustrates planning with contextual sensitivity.

Let's look at another example. There is likely no more challenging environment for contextual sensitivity than when end-of-life care is the program and the institution is the one in which individuals face the inevitability of their mortality. Here again, good intentions are not sufficient to assure planning with sensitivity to context. Even the most culturally competent planner can benefit from the experiences of others. This is especially true when the reports on model programs are transparent in revealing the lessons learned and challenges encountered.

Kramer and Auer (2005) report a case study of the challenges involved in offering an end-of-life care program to older persons with low incomes and multiple comorbid chronic conditions. Advanced chronic disease is incredibly unpredictable in its progression. The precise moment of death, and the conditions in which that death will occur, is a totally unique human experience. Thus, end-of-life care teams are often caught off-guard when sudden changes either precipitate death or when a medical crisis completely diverts staff's regular focus on chronic care management. Kramer and Auer (2005) reveal the challenges of the emotional context by showing that when ill patients get better, staff experience a feeling of euphoria, which is quickly dispelled when the patient dies shortly thereafter. "Team members expressed how frequently deaths caught them off-guard while they were distracted by acute care needs or complications" (Kramer & Auer, p. 654).

Recognizing specific contextual needs, Kramer and Auer make recommendations for end-of-life care programming. Going beyond culture—that is, the United States medical care system, which denies death—they recommend planning programs to "routinize and normalize end-of-life- planning" so that it is not introduced only when a person is perceived to be near death. Additionally, such planning assists everyone involved in maintaining "a panoramic view" that keeps staff mindful of the bigger picture (including death) during acute care episodes (p. 654).

Barriers associated with culture and languages were also encountered in working with elders and their families. Not only did cultural competency need to be enhanced for staff, but it was recommended that cultural liaisons be enlisted. "Hispanic community leaders served as mediators and helped to facilitate discussions with families. Native American tribal leaders facilitated teams' understanding of the Native American cultural community, and an intermediary from the Hmong community helped identify interpreters outside the home and community" (Ibid., p. 658).

This program evaluation discovered similar cultural insensitivity as that found in the program targeting Tamil refugees. Culturally appropriate assessment tools were needed to assess older people at the end of life and their caregivers. Health care professionals were very individualistic, focusing on the older person rather than on the family. Rather than "patient-centered care," there was often a desire by the patient and his or her family to engage in a collective or communal decision-making process (Ibid., p. 658).

Planning for an end-of-life program requires institutional sensitivity as well. Institutional settings have their own cultures, making it imperative that planners and implementers alike recognize the differences and the impact those differences can have on patients and their families. For example, when an older person is in the hospital, medical staff will do everything they can to prolong life; but when a patient is moved to a hospice unit, the intent is to provide comfort care. These represent not only different goals but very different institutional cultures with opposite interventions. The responsibility is with the culturally competent program planner to determine what is feasible and appropriate in the context.

PLANNING ACROSS MULTIPLE ORGANIZATIONAL SETTINGS

The preceding discussion about end-of-life care began to surface the challenges in interorganizational planning involving a constellation of provider organizations with differing organizational cultures. Regardless of the need or social problem, the program planner engaged in community-based program planning will be working with multiple stakeholding institutions representing very different cultural perspectives.

Wahab (2005) reveals some of the challenges faced in a project to divert prostitution. The First Offenders of Prostitution Program (FOPP) was started by an ex-San Francisco sex worker who founded Standing against Global Exploitation with the collaboration of the police department and the district attorney's office. The program, targeting first-time prostitution offenders, spread quickly in the United States, Canada, and Europe. Designed to help offenders avoid the legal system altogether, diversion programs are seen as "an increasingly popular form of restorative justice in contemporary criminal justice" (p. 204).

One of the replication programs, the Salt Lake City Prostitution Diversion Program, was evaluated by Wahab, using qualitative methods, to understand how sex workers were served by the program and how stakeholders viewed their relationships with one another. The major institutional stakeholders were the Harm Reduction Project of Salt Lake City, the Salt Lake City Prosecutor's Office, and the Salt Lake Valley Health Department. Thirty-one participants were interviewed, observational field notes were taken, and written program materials were reviewed. The most consistent theme identified was the unlikely and difficult working relationship between the criminal justice system and the Harm Reduction Project. They differed on important aspects regarding appropriate programming, such as: including urine analyses; whether to impose sanctions and consequences for providing "dirty" urine analyses; how much participant information to share with legal bodies; and more. These organizations held similar goals but had different sets of assumptions as to how to go about what they wanted to do.

The planner working with organizational cultures with opposing worldviews can recognize that he or she will not be able to change what are tantamount to ethnocentric cultures but can still act as a bridge between the cultures and, as Wahab points out, keep dialogue open even in the face of the inevitability of conflict because through dialogue, respect for alternative perspectives may emerge. Possible resulting consensus positions can be even more powerful than those held separately.

ISSUES WHEN PRACTICING INTERNATIONALLY

The bridging that planners do in connecting disparate organizational cultures may be a good way to imagine the enormous challenges of international planning practices. Two of us are returned Peace Corps volunteers with experience in planning and organizing in emerging nations, and we offer the following thoughts based on our experience.

First and foremost, planning in an international context requires gaining entry and achieving endorsement by community leaders for the planning process. This is possible only if the planner has become a culturally competent interviewer who has learned what is important to the planning process by learning where to look.

Second, the planner in an international context must take guidance from international community developers and community organizers who know that once entry is gained, it must be maintained by nurturing gatekeepers through appropriate individualized contacts and culturally acceptable personal touches. Bridging happens through respectful, trusting, and, in most cases, personal relationships. No planner gathers suitable stakeholders and fashions a culturally sensitive planning process without thorough understanding of the culture and the people within it. It is necessary to elaborate on what is being observed so that true understanding is achieved and erroneous assumptions are avoided. Most times, this is possible only through strong, trusting relationships and information provided by planners' cultural guides.

Relationship building includes dealing with the inevitable language problems. The most effective planners on the international scene are not only steeped in knowledge about the culture and practices of those with whom planning work is being done, but they are also able to communicate accurately and effectively. The first and preferred way is through language fluency. If fluency is not possible, then at least beginning language competence, supported through interpreters, is acceptable. Sole reliance on others for translations and interpretation will lead to misinterpretations, potential manipulations of the planner, cultural biases on both sides, and general barriers to trust and respect. If an interpreter is the only means of communicating with stakeholders, then it is important to vary interpreter services in order to triangulate information.

Finally, throughout the text, we have attempted to make it clear that neither of the two approaches to planning presented is correct and the other incorrect. However, depending on the cultural context in which an approach is used, one approach may be more culturally congruent than the other. Cultural congruence is an important factor because program planning cannot be separated from organizational, community, and societal contexts (O'Connor & Netting, 2007). In some countries, assumptions congruent with prescriptive planning approaches will hold based on political or accountability reasons. In others, when stability is desired, it may be important to begin planning in highly rational ways to neutralize political pressures that have caused programs to operate in a more emergent fashion. In other international arenas, emergent approaches are compatible with the existing cultural approaches to problem-solving. It is the planner's responsibility to think and be sufficiently cognizant of the sociopolitical and cultural situation to choose the approach appropriate for the setting. The application of prescriptive planning approaches may extinguish that which is powerful and unique in the situation. By transporting Western prescriptive planning into a sociocultural context containing unique views of social problem elements and resources, solution alternatives may be limited, making a prescriptive approach culturally or technologically inappropriate. On the other hand, application of prescriptive approaches may be exactly what is required to assure stability and sustainability.

SUMMARY

In this chapter, we focused on the importance of culture and context. Culture has been defined in many ways, but our point in this chapter is that culture may be viewed differently in rational and in interpretive planning. In the former, culture may be viewed in terms of its material manifestations (e.g., artifacts and behaviors), whereas in the latter, it may focus more on cognitive elements (values and assumptions). Both are important, even though the emphasis may shift, depending on whether one is using a prescriptive or an emergent approach to program planning.

Cultural competence is important to program planning because the planner or planners must have some understanding of the context within which they are working. Not only does cultural competence require cultural awareness, but it also requires a deep understanding leading to action. Thus, a culturally competent planner must be a good interviewer (be able to listen to different voices with unexpected messages), be an observer of human behavior within the planning context, be willing to learn, and then be able to synthesize. During the process, culturally competent planners sometimes actively participate and, at other times, actively observe. We suggest that the richest source of information to move toward cultural competence comes from a combination of the role of observer-as-participant and from engaging in guided conversations with selected informants.

Contextual variables must be considered in culturally competent practice. These include developmental and family-oriented needs of stakeholders; professional skills, practice, and approaches guiding planning practice; research and knowledge building from the literature and from the cultural context; organizational and contextual diversity; and delivery of program planning services. From this perspective, planning occurs in a series of nested cultures. We returned to a discussion of positivism and interpretivism to extend our understanding of the challenges of managing planning in the multicultural world of today.

We provided examples from the literature of how planning with a sensitivity to difference may occur. Planning with groups different from the mainstream was illustrated through Weaver's (2005) story about Tamil refugees fleeing the civil war in Sri Lanka and relocating to North America. In this example, the planners needed an emergent approach to be responsive to potential consumers. Planning within-group differences was illustrated by examining Melbin, Sullivan, and Cain's (2003) study of designing transitional housing for battered women, and by focusing on Smith and Toseland's study of developing a telephone support program for caregivers of elders. Both battered women and elder caregivers have specific experiences that have led them to be distinct from other client groups.

Planning with sensitivity to inclusion was illustrated through a UNESCO initiative in which young children were actively part of the planning process. This was similar to the AIDS Orphans and Pig Intervention project in Chapter 5. Planning with contextual sensitivity was emphasized in an innovative arts project that occurred in a women's detention facility, followed by a case study of an end-of-life program that revealed the importance of including staff, clients, and family members in planning processes. Planning across multiple settings was emphasized as well, using the Salt Lake City Prostitution Diversion Program as an exemplar.

These many examples from the literature, as well as experience in international practice, were used to reveal how no one model of planning is correct or incorrect. They also remind the reader how important it is to be aware of the basic underlying assumptions that guide culturally competent program planning practice.

CONCLUSION

We leave you with the words of one of our graduates who called and asked if we might consult with her team in a national training program designed to translate the latest mental health research into practice. The graduate's training program was nested in a large corporation composed mostly of business and helping professionals, and it seemed that communication was always a challenge across geography and between professional cultures. As we shared the contents of the book we were writing, we could not see the faces of the team members because we were on a conference call, but as we talked about the possibility that they might be using language from two different worldviews, often straddling the line between rational and interpretive planning, we heard these words of exclamation: "As a team we are overwhelmed with emotion about the years we have put into something, and that our experience is not singular . . . it is so wonderful and moving to know that this is hard *not* because we are doing it wrong, but rather because it is hard, and that instead we are doing it well."

Culturally competent planning, attentive to the differences in prescriptive and emergent approaches, is hard. That is why it takes skill and dedication. We chose to write this book as a way to extend our strong commitment to social justice and out of a concern that current planning technology, though well intended, might not be enough to provide planners with what they need to design the socially just human service programs they desire.

EXERCISES

Exercise 1: A Program Targeting African American Youth

In an example of planning for inclusion, Harvey and Hill (2004) tell the story of the Africentric Adolescent and Family Rites of Passage Program in Washington, DC. The program, funded by the U.S. Center for Substance Abuse Prevention, was planned to target African American young men between 11.5 and 14.5 years old. They were targeted because of their high rates of detention, suspensions, and expulsions from schools, accompanied by high incidences of substance abuse and antisocial behavior. The program was planned to intervene across several levels in their lives—individual, peer group, family, and community. Based on a strengths perspective, the intent was to increase self-awareness, respect, and emotional strength through the use of African-based rituals and principles of Nguzo Saba (unity, self-determination, collective work and responsibility, cooperative economics, purpose, creativity, and faith) (p. 68).

Of critical importance to the intervention was the inclusion of parents in the program, with attention to parenting skills, community involvement, racial identity, cultural awareness, parental advocacy, and attendance at PTA meetings. Five themes that stakeholders repeatedly identified as contributing to program success were that it was "holistic, family-oriented, Africentric, strength-based, and had an indigenous staff" (p. 73). Without the inclusion of the entire family system, the program would not have worked; but with inclusion of parents alongside youth, it is working.

For a program targeting this population group, the involvement of family members supports the youth; moreover, the family members receive attention and support themselves. Parents in this program often comment that the focus on Nguzo Saba is helpful to them, as well, because it reinforces their African heritage and is sensitive to who they are as African Americans.

- What is illustrated by this program about cultural awareness?
- If you were to design a similar program, what assumptions would you bring to the planning process?
- What would you need to know about culture in this situation?
- Given what you know about rational and interpretive planning, how might your knowledge guide what you do?

(Continued)

Exercise 2: Developing Standards for Cultural Competency
Think about standards that might be developed to guide program planners in being more culturally competent. For example, one profession has a set of standards that include themes such as self-awareness, cross-cultural knowledge, cross-cultural skills, empowerment and advocacy, among others (NASW, 2001).

- What themes might be featured to create a guide for the program planner who wants to be culturally competent?
- Do those themes lead to specific principles that could be developed? (Note: Think of themes as key concepts—for example, cultural sensitivity—and principles as the operationalizing of these concepts.)

Glossary

action planning: Design that serves as a guide for decision-making about detailed tasks in a plan; also known as program design.

advocacy planning theories: Approaches that guide planning responses to group interests recognizing pluralities of needs and demands.

advocacy program(s): Support activities systematically aimed at influencing decision-making when situations needing attention are perceived to be unjust or unresponsive. Advocacy programs can be focused on case (individual) or cause (collective) problem-solving.

analyzing: Using available data from various sources and an appropriate framework to fully examine, as far as time and resources allow, a situation.

approach: A method used to go about planning.

auspice: Referring to being under the protective umbrella or wing of another group or organization.

autonomous ethics: A perspective that holds that human beings can and should determine the moral rules.

behavior: Comprising those actions and interactions that can be observed between members of a culture, between groups, and between individual members and groups.

British Empiricists: Philosophers who took the position that knowledge about the environment came from experience or sense data.

case: An individual person, organization, or community, as in case problem-solving or case advocacy.

cause: A concept originating with Aristotle, who was trying to frame the fundamental nature of things. Usually discussed as *efficient cause* (any power or agent that effects a result), *final cause* (the purpose or end for which anything is produced), *formal cause* (the ideal standard according to which a thing or event is produced), and *material cause* (the means undertaken to produce a formal cause). In positivistic research, efficient cause is of most interest. In advocacy, final cause is generally the focus. In problem-solving, cause is related to problems of the collective.

collaboration (collaborative): More than one person, group, or organization working in tandem to solve a problem or seek an opportunity.

condition: Identification of what is; a factual description.

constituencies: Various groups that are engaged in, or have an investment in, the planning process.

constraints: Those elements in an organization or its environment that cannot be changed.

constructivist research: An interpretive, alternative model of emergent inquiry that attends as much to the inquiry process as the product produced. The research design is based on a hermeneutic process of consensus building and the iterative surfacing of issues, concerns, and concepts, which are documented and tracked and serve as the basis of a negotiated outcome, a case study report.

context: That situation, setting, or environment in which the planner is planning.

Continental Rationalists: Philosophers taking the position that what is known about nature could be reasoned by one's intelligence, as opposed to other philosophers who take the position that knowledge about the environment comes from experience or sense data.

contingencies: Those elements in an organization or its environment about which negotiation and compromise are required.

critical thinking: A careful consideration of alternative views and claims and the willingness to alter one's perspective in light of evidence that refutes a cherished assumption or position.

cultural awareness: Being sensitive to cultural differences.

cultural competence: Having awareness of a culture and being able to act with sensitivity and understanding within that cultural setting about how people provide and manage information, how people communicate and make decisions, how they respond to outsiders, and how they deal with perceived or conferred power.

cultural norms: Ways of thinking and behaving created in consensus among participants.

culturally competent interview: Conversation with a purpose guided by the interviewer's knowledge or understanding of the beliefs and norms of the context to suggest not only what to look for in the conversation but also the appropriate ways in which to conduct the interview and engage the intervewee in the conversation. Previous experience in, exposure and sensitivity to, and training in working within the culture, as well as the use of cultural guides, are important elements to assure competence in this type interviewing.

culture: The customary values, beliefs, social forms, and/or material traits shared by a group that are seen by the group and others as different.

data: Numbers or words that stand alone without meaning. Once pieces of data are connected, they become information.

decision-making: Process of arriving at a solution that ends uncertainty or dispute; to make a choice or judgment.

deduction: A reasoning process that moves from a more abstract meaning to meanings that are subsumed by it; going from the general to the particular.

demonstration: A project that is used to show how one might go about addressing a condition or problem and which may lead to a more formalized program once the results are known.

determinism (determinist): Refers to limitations placed on events or behaviors and framed in terms of antecedents and consequences. The type of determinism is dependent on the type of cause that is of interest. With efficient cause, the assumption is that everything is entirely determined by a sequence of causes.

direct service program(s): Activities focusing specifically on needs of clients.

discovery: A dimension of emergent planning, and part of the planning process achieved through ongoing participation, and consisting of utilizing multiple data sources and valid and complex data.

dissemination: Using various mechanisms to spread information from research results or ideas from other sources to those who are interested or should otherwise be informed.

emergent approaches: Alternative approaches to program planning using emergent logic, which attempts to remove barriers to innovation through intense interactions, networking, and information exchange among those with a stake in change, based on the assumption that they should be empowered to create and re-create as new discoveries occur using nonlinear, unpredictable strategies. Program planning using these approaches, based on assumptions of interpretive planning, consists of several predictable dimensions, the specific content of which cannot be known in advance: engagement, discovery, sense-making, and unfolding.

emergent logic: Nonlinear, circular, or holistic patterns of thought using induction over deduction whereby engagement with others leads to a process in which discovery occurs and a tentative understanding or sense-making regarding a problem evolves.

emic: Providing an insider's view or perspective.

engagement: The first dimension of emergent planning. Engagement comprises the entry part of planning and consists of an ongoing process connecting with multiple perspectives, developing mutual respect through relationship building, and resulting in understanding the conflicts and complexities of the context in which planning is occurring.

epistemology (epistemological): Assumptions related to what can be known and how scientists can be expected to come to know it.

ethical absolutism: In this text, refers to an approach whereby the planner learns to apply preestablished rules to situations, to deduce what to do, to assume that these principles are universal, and to order the principles so that any conflict of principles can be resolved. Also called the *ethics of principles.*

ethical conduct: Carrying out one's role in a manner consistent with a set of principles, values, and moral assumptions.

ethical egoist: A person who maximizes the good for himself or herself without regard to the consequences.

ethical quandary or dilemma: A situation in which two equally important principles or values are opposed to one another.

ethical relativism: Rejecting a system of fixed moral codes, believing that ethical decisions can only be justified based on the context of a decision or the consequences created as a result of the decision. Results, not motivations, are the focus.

ethical utilitarian: Seeking the greatest good for the largest number, regardless of what happens to those left behind.

ethics: Principles of behavior based on beliefs or values, constitutive of personal and professional moral codes.

ethnocentrism: Belief in the superiority of one's culture.

ethnographic approach: A qualitative research design first developed in sociology based on the assumption that the context of the phenomenon under investigation shapes the reality of the phenomenon. Qualitative methods such as interviews and observations are used to understand the phenomenon within a particular situation.

etic: Providing an outsider's view or perspective.

evidenced-based practice (EBP): Practice guided by research results or measurable outcomes.

expressed need(s): Demands or needs presented by current and potential program participants.

feminist model of planning: An approach to planning aimed at assisting women in demystifying the planning process through elimination of power dynamics, and rejecting dominant linear models in favor of multidimensional thinking, intuition, and feelings.

force-field analysis: Examining the driving and restraining forces that are influencing a possible change.

formative evaluation: Monitoring and documenting the process of program implementation, rather than attending to only the program result, outcome, or impact.

forward-sequence planning: An interpretive type of planning that begins by asking where one can start rather than what one wants as a final result. Forward-sequence planning is the opposite of reverse-order planning of the rational type in which one works toward a predetermined goal.

generalization: The ability of a truth to hold across time and circumstance.

goal(s): Overriding visionary statements that are agreed upon by decision-makers and planners, and from which measurable objectives can be derived.

grand tour activities: Informal qualitative research methods developed in anthropology and sociology whereby the researcher collects information in context through questioning and observing without a particular focus or plan in order to get a sense of the context prior to engaging in more formal data collection activities.

hermeneutic process: In the sense of Gadamer, a circular conversation among and between interested parties (including texts and other data sources) wherein perspectives and insights are shared, tested, and evaluated.

heteronomous ethical systems: A perspective that holds that moral rules are derived from sources outside of human beings, such as through divine origins.

hierarchy (hierarchical): Thoughts, persons, or things arranged in a graded order, as in a descending order of power.

historicity: What is known about the deep context of a situation and how it developed.

human agency: A belief that humans engage in certain inferential processes (induction) and act independently on that basis.

human service program(s): Organized effort to enhance the social, emotional, physical, and/or intellectual well-being of a targeted segment of society.

impact: Outcome or goal; result of planning that solved a problem.

incremental decision-making: An approach to deciding where each step is not radically different from previous steps so that stakeholders are not unduly overwhelmed with or threatened by rapid change. If steps taken are upsetting to participants, then steps can easily be retraced because major change has not occurred. This approach allows decision-makers to resolve differences and maintain relationships with various stakeholders in the process, and involves continuous political balancing and rebalancing.

incremental planning theories: Planning theories guiding compromises between groups toward the most expedient decision.

induction: A reasoning process moving from lower to higher levels of abstraction; going from the particular to the general.

information: Data about which some meaning can be given.

information system: Systematic mechanism for data collection so that data can be translated through analysis into information that can be useful.

initiative: Program concepts or ideas guided by preferences rather than legal requirements.

input(s): Raw materials and resources, including knowledge, skills, expertise, human resources, fiscal resources, facilities, and equipment.

interpretive planning: Context-embedded planning that emerges in response to the particulars of the situation, the understandings and inclinations of the stakeholders to the process, and the resources at hand.

interpretivism: A perspective informed by the desire to understand the world as it is at the level of subjective experience, within the realm of individual consciousness and subjectivity. The perspective sees the social world as an emergent social process that is created by the individuals concerned. Reality, then, is little more than a network of assumptions and intersubjectively shared meanings that hold only as long as meaning is shared.

irrational thought: Mental processes that do not include reasoning and/or any identifiable logic.

Lady Boards of Managers: All-female governing boards, whose members were founding, chartering, governing, administering, and managing beneficent organizations in the United States as early as the early 1800s and continuing through the turn of the twentieth century.

learning organization: An organization committed to learning from experiences and using the results of those experiences in decision-making, even if doing so changes what was originally expected or designed.

line item: An approach to budgeting in which dollar measures of input items are each listed on their own lines. This is referred to as a *line-item budget*.

logic model: A systems-based approach to program design that shows how client needs or conditions can be addressed by the delivery of particular program services. The process includes problem/need identification; establishing the goal; writing objectives; and identifying inputs, methods, results, and outcomes.

logical empiricism: A philosophical perspective that establishes verifiability as grounds for judging whether a question or issue has meaning. Empirical observation and measurement is the basis of this approach's measure of good scientific investigation.

logical positivism: Built on the same assumptions of logical empiricism that all knowledge must be based on observable things and events.

macrointerventions: Sets of coordinated or linked actions at the system level, often engaging numerous participants in organization, community, or policy arenas.

mandate: Requirements expressed by a funding source or other public pressure; usually based on regulatory or legal requirements.

model: A conceptual structure consisting of various dimensions or parts that can be used to guide a particular type of practice in a regularized direction; generally based on similar assumptions, and constructed in similar ways as theories.

multiculturalism: Relating to, reflecting, or adapting to diverse cultures; assumes there are both simple and complex realities, that there are many ways of viewing truth and the world through diverse cultural lenses.

natural science: An approach to describing things by reducing all formal and final cause explanations to material and efficient cause explanations, based on the assumption that natural forces work toward a purpose, and the cause can be identified using natural scientific methods.

needs assessment: Determining what is absent and necessary for problem resolution or improved quality of life.

nomothetic: An approach to description of behavior and things based on what is generally the case. This approach relies on lawlike generalizations that describe everything exactly the same way for all time. Individual differences are minimized and commonalities are emphasized.

nonrational planning: Planning designs not based on linear models of logic. Usually based on induction rather than deduction, taking a more holistic, rather than reductionistic approach to what should be learned and decided in the planning process; also understood to be interpretive planning or an emergent approach to planning.

nonrational thought: Speaks of a logic that is not linear, but instead tends to be circular and able to consider the most tangential aspects of a thought process. Nonrational reasoning is reasoning by metaphor and analogy rather than by if/then statements.

normative needs: Needs known by those working in the field.

objective or objectivist perspective: Belief that social reality has concrete existence above and beyond the individual and that reality can be understood by all under the right circumstances.

objectives: Measurable statements containing time frame, target of the change, results to be achieved, criteria by which results will be documented, monitored and/or measured; can be process (during implementation) or outcome (impact) objectives.

objectivity: Refers to constructs with meanings that transcend the individual who frames the relationship intended, and, therefore, may be understood by all individuals who expend the proper effort. Objective meanings can be understood by anyone who sincerely examined the contents at issue because social reality has concrete existence above and beyond the individual.

ontology (ontological): Perspective on the nature of reality; what is real. Asks the question Is it above and beyond individual knowledge or is it based on individual consciousness without regard to the outside world?

organization(s): Social unit(s) with a purpose.

outcome(s): The actual changes in the client's quality of life; can be immediate, intermediate, or final/ultimate (as in impacts).

outcome evaluation: Objective assessment of the effects of programs on the target populations.

output(s): The products, such as units of service provided.

participant observation: Listening and observing as a participant in the planning process, asking appropriate questions and informing others that one is both a part of and an observer of the planning process.

perceived needs: Needs not yet formally expressed by those with the need. Sometimes called *felt needs* because they are recognized by the person but not known to others.

phronesis: Practical wisdom in balancing the complexity of situations and maintaining consistent moral aims.

pilot(s): Also known as a demonstration, in which the process of discovery is intended to lead to new programmatic approaches.

pilot projects: Demonstration programs in which the objectives are subject to change. Pilot projects are designed to search for unexpected outcomes and to change on an as-needed basis.

positivism: A perspective generally understood to be the same as the logical positivist or logical empiricist, in which theoretical propositions are tested or built according to rules of formal logic to create scientific knowledge.

postpositivism: Within the tradition of positivism, a perspective that recognizes the value-laden and interactive nature of the research process, so that direct correspondence or direct, objective knowledge of forms are eliminated. Though generalizability remains the goal, more subjective approaches using qualitative methods are recognized as possibly acceptable ways of scientific knowing.

prescriptive approaches: Traditional approaches to program planning using linear logic and based on the assumptions of rational planning, which attempt to solve problems using logic or problem-solving models in planning.

problem(s): A judgment that something needs to change; also known as *problem identification.*

problem analysis: Use of needs assessment data to help determine what must change for a problem-solving outcome to be achieved.

problem-solving: A process in which one engages in trying to find a solution (or solutions) to a problem. Depending on the situation, problem-solving can occur in both rational and interpretive planning, but how one goes about the process will look different.

problem-solving model: Similar to the logic model for program planning and geared at addressing needs or conditions. This model includes problem/need identification; establishing the goal; writing objectives; and identifying inputs, methods, results, and outcomes. Note This is a rational planning approach, unlike the more generic concept of a problem-solving process.

problem-solving process: Using critical thinking or other means of analysis to understand a vexing or perplexing situation in order to change it for the better. Depending on the way the process is used, it can be a rational or an interpretive process.

problem statement: Written qualitative expression of a situation, followed by a quantitative expression of size and scope of situation, ending with a desired course of action.

process evaluation: Assessment of the way a program is being mounted or delivered; attention is given to the quality of the process of implementation. Also known as *formative evaluation.*

program(s): Structural container for long-term commitments, consisting of mainstream, alternative, hybrid, direct service, and advocacy approaches that include services and/or activities designed to directly or indirectly address human needs; set of activities designed to fulfill a social purpose.

program design(s): Activities that staff or the implementing organization intend to deliver or undertake on behalf of consumers/beneficiaries. Also called *action planning* because it serves as a guide for decision-making about details and tasks.

program hypothesis: Series of if/then statements that articulate what must be undertaken to achieve change.

program planning: Conscious strategy developed to facilitate problem-solving in human services; mechanism to move toward idea implementation to achieve goal.

program theory: Integrated statement of framework describing what is to be undertaken programmatically, from which can be drawn the design, specifications, activities, observable measures, and measurable outcomes, as well as aid in determining whether program success is possible.

project(s): Set of activities with a purpose, but more time-limited and flexible than a program.

radical planning theories: Planning built on assumptions that the system in which planning is occurring is oppressive, and, therefore, only through empowerment of individuals and groups is transformative change possible.

rational planning: Planning based on linear problem-solving in which a step-by-step process moves toward a predetermined goal.

rational thought: Linear reasoning or logic based on if/then statements; based on moving forward with purpose toward a pre-identified goal based on the assumptions that one can know the problem if one analyzes it well enough; that one can solve a problem if a clear direction of how to proceed can be identified; and that there are logical ways in which to move through this problem-solving process.

realism (Realist): The philosophical view that the context of one's mind, that which one knows, exists independently of one's mind; understanding of anything is abstracted from an independent reality.

reason: Inferential processing of information leading to decisions regarding actions.

reductionism: A mechanism, based on positivist assumptions about reality and how one comes to know it, that aims to reduce complexity to the most definable and controllable elements.

relative needs: Comparison between one set of needs and others.

replicability: Capability to reproduce a program in another setting based on the assumption that what works in one context can be generalized to another.

request for proposals (RFP): An initiative issued by a funding source to solicit applications for funding.

reverse-order planning: Establishing a goal and then backtracking to fill in the actions that need to occur to arrive at the selected goal. Opposite of forward-sequence planning.

satisficing: Decision-making within boundaries; using available knowledge. Recognizing that everything cannot be known about a situation, and moving ahead with a decision based on what is known and what is possible.

scenario planning: Planning through play metaphors where a script or story of change is developed.

science of muddling through: Growing out of an assertion that, at least in public institutions, a myth existed that decision-making was a linear, sequential process; instead, decisions are made in a halting incremental way with periods of recycling, iteration, and reformulation. The process is a nonlinear one and highly political.

Search Conference: Participatory planning model based on democratic principles which dictate that all stakeholders be included in the planning process.

sense-making: A dimension of emergent planning that focuses on what is discovered in the planning process. Consists of compromise, consensus-based decision-making, and valid and complex decisions with hallmarks of contextual responsiveness.

sense-making theory: Demonstrates how stimuli are placed into some kind of framework to explain surprises, seek information, make connections, ascribe meaning, and suggest action; includes rules of perceiving, interpreting, believing, and acting, all based on an understanding or meaning construction.

service(s): Direct intervention in a way that will address human need.

situational ethics: Achieving good and avoiding evil, or at least gaining more good for assuring the balance of good over evil. There is no absolute standard for decision-making; everything is relative to the specific context.

social constructivist theory (constructivism): Assumes that reality is constructed based on intersubjectively achieved meaning that cannot generalize beyond the time and context of the encounter; that there are no fundamental causes, but instead networks of relationships that produce multiple and simultaneous shaping in the construction of reality. Focus is on cognitive schemas that construct the subject's experience and action and lead to new interpretive frameworks or structures.

social learning theory: Assumes that what is known or assumed to be real is a product of the context within which learning occurs rather than in reaction to some immutable truth.

socialization: Inducting new members into a culture, its expectations, and behavioral norms.

staff development and training program(s): Activities targeting staff by providing knowledge and skills for better direct service provision or for performing at a higher capacity.

stakeholders: Individuals who have an interest (a stake) in the planning process.

strategic planning: Rational, goal-oriented guidance for a course of planned change, typically within an organization or community setting.

strategy: A general direction taken, designed to achieve an end. Usually consists of multiple tactics.

subculture(s): Cultures existing within larger cultures, in which values and norms differ from those of the larger culture.

subjective or subjectivist perspective: Assumes that social reality exists primarily in the human consciousness (a product of one's mind). Meanings are private and cannot be extended beyond the individual who has framed the meaning, making generalizability impossible.

subjectivity: Refers to constructs with meanings that are somehow private and, therefore, incapable of being extended beyond the individual who framed the meaningful relationship intended. Subjective meanings cannot be totally understood, even when one sincerely examines the contents at issue because social reality exists primarily in the individual's consciousness or mind.

summative evaluation: Evaluation designs informed by a problem-solving approach that sets out in advance details of implementation and expected results regarding the problem at hand. The degree to which the problem is solved is the focus of summative evaluation.

support program(s): Activities intended to assist direct service or staff development and training programs, including but not limited to performing functions such as advocacy, research and development, and fundraising.

synoptic planning theories: Rational theories guiding rational decisions and step-by-step activities.

synoptic rationality: Centralized, linear decision-making filtered through administrative hierarchy.

tactic(s): Planned action(s) for achieving an end.

throughput: The service delivery, or how the intervention target's condition is intended to change; includes service definitions and tasks (activities) and the method of intervention (the technology employed and the ways services are delivered).

transactive planning theories: Approaches that guide maintenance of as much face-to-face mutual learning as possible, as a means of achieving fundamental change.

truth: A fact or reality related to actual existence and capable of being verified. In traditional science, truth must also be established to exist across time and context.

typology: A group of related categories or "types." Belonging to a class considered to possess properties or characteristics of that class.

unfolding: A dimension of the emergent planning model, the planning product, that occurs in the context of the problem-solving process. Consists of assessment and identification of program options and possibilities; continual learning; and continuous attention to complexity, which results in continuous revisioning of the planned program as the planning process continues to reverberate as the program continues to unfold.

units of service: Services that can be delivered and measured as episodes or contact units, as material units, or as time units.

References

Atkinson, P., Coffey, A., & Delamont, S. (2003). *Key themes in qualitative research: Continuities and change*. New York: AltaMira Press.

Bauman, Z. (1978). *Hermeneutics and social science*. London: Century Hutchison.

Bickman, L. (1987). The functions of program theory. In L. Bickman (ed.). *Using program theory in evaluation: New directions in program evaluation* (pp. 5–18). San Francisco: Jossey–Bass.

Brager, G., & Holloway, S. (1978). *Changing human service organizations: Politics and practice*. New York: The Free Press.

Brody, R. (2000). *Effectively managing human service organizations* (2nd ed.). Thousand Oaks, CA: Sage.

Brooks, F. (2005). Resolving the dilemma between organizing and services: Los Angeles ACORN's welfare advocacy. *Social Work, 50*(3), 262–270.

Brown, E., deMonthous, P., & McCullough, A. (1976). *The access-casebook*. Stockholm: Teknisk Hogskolelitteratur I Stockholm AB.

Burrell, G., & Morgan, G. (1979). *Sociological paradigms and organizational analysis: Elements of the sociology of corporate life*. London: Heinemann.

Campbell, M., & Gregor, F. (2004). *Mapping social relations: A primer in doing institutional ethnography*. New York: AltaMira Press.

Chambers, D. E., & Wedel, K. R. (2005). *Social policy and social programs* (4th ed.) Boston: Allyn & Bacon.

Chawla, L., & Driskell, D. (2006). The Growing Up in Cities project: Global perspectives on children and youth as catalysts for community change. *Journal of Community Practice, 14* (1/2), 183–200.

Christie, C. A., Montrosse, B. E., & Klein, B. M. (2005). Emergent design evaluation: A case study. *Evaluation and Program Planning, 28*, 271–277.

Cohen, M. D., March, J. G., & Olsen, J. P. (1972). The garbage can model of organizational choice. *Administrative Science Quarterly, 17*(March), 1–25.

Cohen-Mansfeld, J., & Bester, A. (2006). Flexibility as a management principle in dementia care: The Adards example. *The Gerontologist, 40*(4), 540–544.

Comte, A. (1974). *The positive philosophy* (H. Martineau, trans.). New York: AMS Press. (Original work published, 1855).

Council on Social Work Education (2004, October). *Educational policy and accreditation standards.* Alexandria, VA: Author.

Deising, P. (1991). *How does social science work? Reflections on practice.* Pittsburgh: University of Pittsburgh Press.

Denzin, N. K., & Lincoln, Y. S. *Handbook of qualitative research.* Thousand Oaks, CA: Sage.

Dilthey, W. (1976). *Selected writings* (H. P. Richman, trans.). New York: Cambridge University Press.

Downs, A., Durant, R., & Carr, A. N. (2003). Emergent strategy development for organizations. *Emergence: Complexity and Organization, 5*(2), 1–19.

Easterling, D. (2000). Using outcome evaluation to guide grant making: Theory, reality, and possibilities. *Nonprofit and Voluntary Sector Quarterly, 29*(3), 482–486.

Edmond, T., Megivern, D., Williams, C., Rochman, E., & Howard, M. (2006). Integrating evidence-based practice and social work field education. *Journal of Social Work Education, 42*(2), 377–396.

Ellsworth, C., Hooyman, N., Ruff, R. A., Stam, S. B., & Tucker, J. H. (1982). Toward a feminist view of planning for and with women (pp. 146–157). In A. Weick & S. Vandiver (eds.), *Women, power, and change.* Washington, DC: NASW Press.

Faludi, A. (1993). *Planning theory.* Oxford, UK: Pergamon Press.

Fauri, D. P., Netting, F. E., & O'Connor, M. K. (2005). *Social work macro practice: Exercises and activities for policy, community, and organization interventions.* Pacific Grove, CA: Brooks/Cole.

Fay, B. (1996). *Contemporary philosophy of social science.* Oxford, UK: Blackwell Publishers.

Feldman, M., Bell, J., & Berger, M. (2003). *Gaining access: A practical and theoretical guide for qualitative researchers.* Walnut Creek, CA: AltaMira Press.

Fenno, R. (1978). *Homestyle: House members in their districts.* Boston: Little, Brown.

Fishkin, J. (1982). *Beyond subjective morality.* New Haven, CT: Yale University Press.

Fletcher, J. (1966). *Situation ethics, the new morality.* Philadelphia: Westminster Press.

Frankena, W. K. (1980). *Thinking about morality.* Ann Arbor, MI: University of Michigan.

Fraser, M. W. (2004). Intervention research in social work: Recent advances and continuing challenges. *Research on Social Work Practice, 14*(3), 210–222.

Freidmann, J., & Hudson, B. (1974). Knowledge and action: A guide to planning theory. *Journal of the American Institute of Planners, 40,* 147–166.

Freire, P. (1994). *Pedagogy of the oppressed: New revised 20th anniversary edition.* New York: Continuum.

Funnell, S. (1997). Program logic: An adaptable tool for designing and evaluating programs. *Evaluation News and Comment, 6*(1), 5–17.

Gadamer, H. (1989). *Truth and method* (2nd rev. ed.) (J. Weinsheimer & D. Marshall, trans.). New York: Crossroads.

Gilgun, J. F. (2005). The four cornerstones of evidence-based practice in social work. *Research on Social Work Practice, 15*(1), 52–61.

Glanz, K., & Rimer, B. K. (1995). Theory at a glance: A guide for health promotion practice. NIH pub. 95-3896. Bethesda, MD: National Institutes of Health-National Cancer Institute.

Gold, R. L. (1969). Roles in sociological field observation. In G. J. McCall & L. L. Simmons (eds.), *Issues in participant observation* pp. 30–39. Reading, MA: Addison-Wesley.

Goldbert, G. S. (1995). Theory and practice in program development: A study of the planning and implementation of fourteen social programs. *Social Service Review, 69*(4), 614–655.

Gordon, K. H. (1991). Improving practice through illuminative evaluation. *Social Service Review, 65*(3), 365–378.

Gray, M., & McDonald, C. (2006). Pursuing good practice? The limits of evidence-based practice. *Journal of Social Work, 6*(1), 7–20.

Guba, E., & Lincoln, Y. (1989). *Fourth generation evaluation*. Newbury Park, CA: Sage.

Hammersley, M., & Atkinson, P. (1983). *What's wrong with ethnography?* London: Routledge.

Hardcastle, D., Powers, P., & Wenocur, S. (2004). *Community practice: Theories and skills for social workers* (2nd ed.). New York: Oxford University Press.

Hardina, D. (2002). *Analytical skills for community organization practice*. New York: Columbia University Press.

Harper-Dorton, K., & Lantz. J. (2007). *Cross-cultural practice: Social work with diverse populations* (2nd ed.). Chicago: Lyceum Books, Inc.

Harvey, A. R., & Hill, R. B. (2004). Africentric youth and family rites of passage programs: Promoting resilience among at-risk African American youths. *Social Work, 49*(1), 65–74.

Hasenfeld, Y. (2000). Social welfare administration and organizational theory. In R. J. Patti (ed.), *The handbook of social welfare management* (pp. 89–112). Thousand Oaks, CA: Sage.

Hess, M. (1980). *Revolutions and reconstructions in the philosophy of science*. Bloomington, IN: Indiana University Press.

Hudson, B. M. (1979). Comparison of current planning theories: Counterparts and contradictions. *Journal of the American Planning Association, 45*(4), 387–398.

Imre, R. (1991). What do we need to know for good practice? *Social Work, 36*, 198–200.

Jackson, A. P., & Ivanoff, A. (1999). Reduction of low response rates in interview surveys of poor African-American families. *Journal of Social Service Research, 25*(1–2), 41–60.

Jewell, C., Davidson, L., & Rowe, M. (2006). The paradox of engagement: How political, organizational, and evaluative demands can hinder innovation in community mental health services. *Social Service Review, 80*(1), 3–26.

Kauffman, S. (1996). *At home in the universe: The search for the laws of self-organization and complexity*. Oxford, UK: Oxford University Press.

Kellogg Foundation. (2001). *Logic model development guide: Logic models to bring together planning, evaluation, and action*. Battle Creek, MI: W.K. Kellogg Foundation.

Kettner, P. M., Moroney, R. M., & Martin, L. L. (1999). *Designing and managing programs* (2nd ed.). Thousand Oaks, CA: Sage.

Kloss, L. L. (1999). The suitability and application of scenario planning for national professional associations. *Nonprofit Management & Leadership, 10*(1), 71–83.

Kramer, B. J., & Auer, C. (2005). Challenges to providing end-of-life care to low-income elders with advanced chronic disease: Lessons learned from a model program. *The Gerontologist, 45*(5), 651–660.

Kroeger, O., & Thuesen, J. M. (1988). *Type talk.* New York: Dell.

Kuhn, T. (1970). *The structure of scientific revolutions* (2nd ed.). Chicago: University of Chicago Press.

Lawlor, E. F., & Raube, K. (1995). Social interventions and outcomes in medical effectiveness research. *Social Service Review, 69*(3), 383–404.

Lazzari, M. M., Amundson, K. A., & Jackson, R. L. (2005). "We are more than jailbirds": An arts program for incarcerated young women. *Affilia, 20*(2), 169–185.

Lewis, J. A., Lewis, M. D., Packard, T., & Souflee, F. Jr. (2001). *Management of human service programs* (3rd ed). Belmont CA: Brooks/Cole.

Lincoln, Y., & Guba, E. (1985). *Naturalistic inquiry.* Beverly Hills, CA: Sage.

Lindblom, C. E. (1959). The science of muddling through. *Public Administrative Review, 19*(2), 79–88.

Loewenberg, F., & Dolgoff, R. (1992). *Ethical decisions for social work practice* (4th ed.) Itasca, IL: F. E. Peacock.

Lofland, J. (1995). Analytic ethnography: Features, failures, and futures. *Journal of Contemporary Ethnography, 24*(1), 30–67.

Lum, D. (ed.). D (2005). *Cultural competence, practice stages, and client systems: A case study approach.* Belmont, CA: Thompson Brooks/Cole.

Marshall, C., & Rossman, G. B. (1995). *Designing qualitative research.* Thousand Oaks, CA: Sage.

Martin, J. (2002). *Organizational culture: Mapping the terrain.* Thousand Oaks, CA: Sage.

Martin, L. L., & Kettner, P. M. (1996). *Measuring the performance of human service programs.* Thousand Oaks, CA: Sage Publications.

McCawley, P. F. (1997). *The logic model for program planning and evaluation.* Boise, ID: University of Idaho Extension.

McLaughlin, L. A., & Jordan, G. B. (1999). Logic models: A tool for telling your program's performance story. *Evaluation and Program Planning, 22*, 65–72.

McNeill, T. (2006). Evidence-based practice in an age of relativism: Toward a model of practice. *Social Work, 51*(2), 147–156.

Melbin, A., Sullivan, C. M., & Cain, D. (2003). Transitional supportive housing programs: Battered women's perspectives and recommendations. *Affilia, 18*(4), 445–460.

Merleau-Ponty, M. (1994). *Phenomenology of perception* (C. Smith, trans.) New York: Routledge and Kegan Paul.

Miller, S. J., Hickson, D. J., & Wilson, D. C. (1996). Decision-making in organizations. In S. R. Clegg, C. Hardy, & W. R. Nord (eds.), *Handbook of organization studies* (pp. 293–312). London: Sage.

Minkoff, D. C. (2002). The emergence of hybrid organizational forms: Combining identify-based service provision and political action. *Nonprofit and Voluntary Sector Quarterly, 32*(3), 377–401.

Mintzberg, H. (1987). Crafting strategy. *Harvard Business Review 65*(4), 66–76.

Mondros, J., & Wilson, S. (1994). *Organizing for power and empowerment.* New York: Columbia University Press.

Morrison, J. B., & Salipante, P. (2007). Governance for broadened accountability: Blending deliberate and emergent strategizing. *Nonprofit and Voluntary Sector Quarterly, 36*(2), 195–217.

Moxley, D. P., & Manela, R. W. (2001). Expanding the conceptual basis of outcomes and their use in the human services. *Families in Society, 82*, 569–577.

Mullen, E. J. (2006). Choosing outcome measures in systematic reviews: Critical challenges. *Research on Social Work Practice, 16*(1), 84–90.

Mulroy, E. A., & Lauber, H. (2004). A user-friendly approach to program evaluation and effective community interventions for families at risk of homelessness. *Social Work, 49*(4), 573–586.

National Association of Social Workers Standards for Cultural Competence in Social Work Practice (2001). www.naswdc.org/pubs/standards/cultural.htm. March 7, 2007.

Netting, F. E., Kettner, P. M., & McMurtry, S. L. (2008). *Social work macro practice* (4th ed.) Boston: Allyn & Bacon.

Netting, F. E., & O'Connor, M. K. (2005). Lady Boards of Managers: Subjugated legacies of governance and administration. *Affilia, 20*(4), 448–464.

Ibid. (2003). *Organization practice: A social worker's guide to understanding human services*. Boston: Allyn & Bacon.

Ibid. (forthcoming). Recognizing the need for evidence-based practices in organizational and community settings. *Journal of Evidence-based Social Work*.

Netting, F. E., O'Connor, M. K., & Fauri, D. P. (2007). Planning transformative programs: Challenges in translating social change into measurable action. *Administration in Social Work. 31*(4), 59–81.

Netting, F. E., O'Connor, M. K., & Singletary, J. (2007). Finding homes for their dreams: Strategies founders and program initiators use to position faith-based programs. *Families and Societies, 8*, 19–29.

O'Connor, M. K., & Netting, F. E. (2007). Emergent program planning as competent practice: The importance of considering context. *Journal of Progressive Human Services, 18*(2), 57–75.

Pawlak, E. J., & Vinter, R. D. (2004). *Designing and planning programs for nonprofit and government organizations*. San Francisco: John Wiley & Sons, Inc.

Phillips, D. (1987). *Philosophy, science, and social inquiry*. Oxford, UK: Pergamon.

Polanyi, M. (1958). *Personal knowledge: Toward a post-critical philosophy*. London: Routledge and Kegan Paul.

Pollio, D. E. (2006). The art of evidence-based practice. *Research on Social Work Practice, 16*(2), 224–232.

Posavac, E. J., & Carey, R. G. (1985). *Program evaluation: Methods and case studies*. Englewood Cliffs, NJ: Prentice Hall.

Quinn, R. E. (1998). *Beyond rational management*. San Francisco: Jossey-Bass Publishers.

Quinn, R. E., Faerman, S. R., Thompson, M. P., & McGrath, M. R. (2003). *Becoming a master manager: A competency framework* (3rd ed.) Hobokon, NJ: John Wiley & Sons, Inc.

Rehm, R., & Cebula, N. (2000, May). *Search conferences for participatory planning*. Retrieved on March 13, 2005, from: www.peopleincharge .org/Search%20Conferences%20For%20Participatirve%20 Planning.

Rehner, J. (1994). *Practical strategies for critical thinking.* Boston: Houghton-Mifflin Co.

Robinson, J., & Pillemer, K. (2007). Job satisfaction and intention to quit among nursing home staff: Do special care units make a difference? *The Journal of Applied Gerontology, 20*(1), 95–112.

Rodwell, M. K. (1998). *Social work constructivist research.* New York: Garland.

Rothman, J. C. (2008). *Cultural competence in process and practice: Building bridges.* Boston: Allyn & Bacon.

Savaya, R., & Waysman, M. (2005). The logic model: A tool for incorporating theory in development and evaluation of programs. *Administration in Social Work, 29*(2), 85–103.

Schein, E. H. (1996). *Organizational culture and leadership* (2nd edition). San Francisco: Jossey-Bass.

Schneider, R. L., & Lester, L. (2001). *Social work advocacy.* Belmont, CA: Brooks/Cole.

Schwartz, P., & Ogilvy, J. (1979). *The emergent paradigm: Changing patterns of thought and belief.* Analytical Report 7, Values and Lifestyles Program. Menlo Park, CA: SRI International.

Senge, P. M. (1990). *The fifth discipline: The art and practice of the learning organization.* New York: Doubleday.

Smith, T. L., & Toseland, R. W. (2006). The effectiveness of a telephone support program for caregivers of frail older adults. *The Gerontologist, 46*(5), 620–629.

Spradley, J. (1979). *The enthnographic interview.* New York: Holt, Rinehart, and Winston.

Stone, D. (1997). *Policy Paradox.* New York: Norton.

Strauss, A., & Corbin, J. (1998). *Basics of qualitative research techniques and procedures for developing grounded theory* (2nd ed.). Thousand Oaks, CA: Sage.

Sullivan, W. M. (2005). *Work and integrity.* San Francisco: Jossey-Bass.

Trigg, R. (1985). *Understanding social science.* Oxford, UK: Basil Blackwell.

Tyson, K. (1995). *New foundations for scientific social and behavioral research: The heuristic paradigm.* Boston: Allyn & Bacon.

U.S. Department of Health and Human Services, Office of Minority Health. (2001). National Standards for Culturally and Linguistically

Appropriate Services in Health Care. Executive Summary. Prepared by IQ Solutions, Inc. Rockville, MD.

Unrau, Y. A., Gabor, P. A., & Grinnell, R. M. Jr. (2001). *Evaluation in the human services*. Itasca, IL: F. E. Peacock.

Wahab, S. (2005). Navigating mixed-theory programs: Lessons learned from a prostitution-diversion project. *Affilia, 20*(2), 203–221.

Weaver, H. N. (2005). Reexamining what we think we know: A lesson learned from Tamil refugees. *Affilia, 20*(2), 238–245.

Weick, K. (1998, September/October). Improvisation as a mindset for organizational analysis. *Organization Science 9*, 543–555.

Ibid. (1995). *Sensemaking in organizations*. Thousand Oaks, CA: Sage.

Weinberger, D. (2007, Feb.). The HBR list: Breakthrough ideas for 2007. *Harvard Business Review, 12*(12).

Westley, F., Zimmerman, B., & Patton, M. Q. (2006). *Getting to maybe: How the world is changed*. Canada: Random House.

Wheatley, M. J., & Kellner-Rogers, M. (1996). *A simpler way*. San Francisco: Berrett-Koehler Publishers.

Witkin, S. L., & Harrison, W. D. (2001). Whose evidence and for what purpose? *Social Work, 46*(4), 293–296.

Index

Page numbers followed by *t* indicate tables

access. *See* gaining entry
accountabilism, 229
accountability
  budgeting and, 99, 103–4
  challenges related to, 97–99, 155–57, 165
  contradictory, 230
  data collection and, 98, 100–102, 113
  information systems and, 99, 100–103
  international planning practice and, 247
  interpretive planning and, 154–62, 165, 166–67, 192, 198–201, 229
  planning approach selection and, 176, 192, 198–201, 207–8
  program planning issues and, 49, 99, 103–4, 113, 192, 198–201, 207–8
  rational planning and, 71, 72, 96–104, 113, 192, 198–201, 229
  types of, 100*t*
ACLU, 47
ACORN (Association of Community Organization for Reform Now), 48
action, reflection as, 154
action planning
  definition of, 253
  See also program design
activities, rational planning and, 74, 76, 78, 88
adaptability, 163
Adards nursing home (Australia), 37, 38
advance planning, 105, 113
advocacy organizations, 47–48
advocacy planning theories, 16–19, 21*t*, 23, 27, 128
  definition of, 253
advocacy programs, 34–35, 47–48, 49
  definition of, 253
African American youth, 250–51
Africentric Adolescent and Family Rites of Passage Program (D.C.), 250–51
after-school programs, 36
AIDS Orphans (case example), 173–76, 182–83, 201, 240, 249
ambiguity
  cultural competence concerns and, 227

interpretive planning and, 162, 164, 165–66, 167, 172, 202
Amundson, K. A., 241
analyzing, 182, 183
  definition of, 253
approach, definition of, 253
Area Agency on Aging, 45
  case example, 119–25, 133, 139–53, 157–59, 206
Aristotle, 188
arts projects, 241–42, 249
assessment, culturally sensitive, 233–35, 243
Association of Community Organization for Reform Now (Los Angeles), 48
audiences, logic models and, 74
Auer, C., 242, 243
auspice, definition of, 253
autonomous ethics, 190
  definition of, 253
Ayers (Vienna Circle member), 7

balance, 232
banking model, accountability and, 207–8
Barnard, Chester, 71
battered women programs, 236–37, 238, 249
behavior
  biculturalism and, 232
  cultural competence and, 231, 238
  cultural development and, 219
  definition of, 253
beliefs
  behavior and, 219
  critical thinking and, 184
  cultural competence and, 231, 238
  realism and, 228
benchmarks, 135, 157, 208
benefits, rational planning and, 78
Berkeley, George, 7
Bester, A., 37–38
biculturalism, 232
blueprint planning mode, 70
body language, 222
British Empiricists, 7
  definition of, 253

Brody, R., 126
Brooks, F., 48
budgets, 71, 99, 103–4, 107, 108–9
bureaucratic models of organizing, 24

Cain, D., 236, 249
Campbell, M., 223
capacity building, 18, 34
caregivers, for older people, 237–38, 249
Carnap, Rudolf, 7
Carr, A. N., 126
case, definition of, 253
case problem-solving, 35
cause, definition of, 254
cause advocacy, 47, 48
cause problem-solving, 35
census data, 79
Center for Substance Abuse Prevention,
    U.S., 250
CFS (child and family services), 38–39
Chambers, D. E., 18, 36, 46, 84, 92
change
    advocacy planning and, 19, 47–48
    interpretive planning and, 132, 141,
        147, 156, 160, 163, 165, 202
    logic of play/life and, 134
    program success and, 33
    radical planning and, 19, 20
    strategic planning and, 20, 24
    surety issues and, 24
    transactive planning and, 20
character, ethics of, 188
Chawla, L., 239
child and family services, 38–39
Children's Street Education Program
    (Brazil), 61–69, 78–81, 92, 93t, 94, 95,
    101, 102, 103
chronic pain (case exercise), 51–57
circles, 136–37
    as planning metaphor, 5–16, 25, 27
    planning theory and, 16–25
    scientific perspectives and, 7–9
    tentativeness and, 24–25
circular reasoning, 2, 6, 12, 14, 27. See also
    nonrational thought
clarity of expression, 183
client fees, 103
client satisfaction scores, 90
coalitions, 23–24, 42
codes of ethics, 188–89
Cohen, M. D., 132
Cohen-Mansfield, J., 37–38
collaboration, 14

definition of, 254
    interpretive planning and, 127, 141–42,
        146, 153
    Lady Boards of Managers and, 131
    logic model and, 110
communication
    cultural competence and, 221–24,
        246–47
    interpretive planning and,
        135
community-based program planning,
    244
community mental health services, 40
community needs, 44, 49
community organizing, 150, 178
comparing, critical thinking and, 182–83
competence
    becoming oriented and, 180
    See also cultural competence
complexity
    cultural issues and, 214, 228, 229, 238
    interpretive planning and, 137, 140,
        142, 152–54, 156, 166, 172, 214
compromise, 17, 145–46, 155
computing, critical thinking and, 182, 183
Comte, Auguste, 8
conditions, 24, 81
    definition of, 254
conflict, 19, 99, 142, 188
Connecticut Peer Engagement Specialist
    Initiative, 126
consciousness, 163, 164
consensus building
    interpretive planning and, 19, 135, 141,
        142, 144, 145–46, 147, 155, 165, 200
    Lady Boards of Managers and, 131
    transactive planning and, 18–19
consequences
    advance identification of, 105, 113
    program hypotheses and, 85–86, 89
    unintended, 98, 160, 163, 176, 230, 240
constituencies, 18, 230
    definition of, 254
constraints, 42
    definition of, 254
constructivism. See social constructivist
    theory
constructivist research, 161
    definition of, 254
contact logs, 158
containers, programs as, 32–33, 41,
    214–15
context

becoming oriented and, 180
budgets and, 108–9
cultural, 213–52
culture development and, 220
definition of, 254
engagement and, 137, 139, 141
gaining entry and, 178
international, 245–47, 249
interpretive planning and, 118, 133–34,
    136, 137, 139, 141, 144, 145, 147–48,
    156, 165, 202
organizational, 32, 33, 39–43, 49
planning approach selection and, 172,
    178, 180
political, 60–61, 103, 107, 144, 147, 152,
    165, 176, 207, 247
sensitivity to, 214, 216, 233, 240–44, 249
Continental Rationalists, 7
definition of, 254
contingencies, 42
definition of, 255
contingency planning, 105
contracts, 103
contradictory accountability, 230
contributions, revenues and, 104
control, 75, 230–31
cooperation, 131
coordinating, critical thinking and,
    182, 183
coping, 38–39
copying, critical thinking and, 181, 182,
    183
correspondence theory of truth, 226
counseling, 38–39
courage, 162
credibility, gaining entry and, 177, 181
critical thinking
    definition of, 255
    ethical decision-making and, 170, 172,
        176, 188, 191–92
    gaining entry and, 178–79
    interpretive planning and, 152, 166,
        172, 185–87, 197–98
    planning approach selection and, 170,
        171–72, 176–77, 180–88, 191–92,
        197–98, 205, 207
    questions to ask, 184–85
    rational planning and, 185–87, 196
cultural awareness, 221, 248
    definition of, 255
cultural competence, 39, 176, 214, 217,
    220–52

accountability demands and, 225,
    229–31
definition of, 255
exercises, 250–52
human service programs and,
    225–31
international planning practice and,
    245–47, 249
multiple organizational settings and,
    244–45, 249
program planning and, 231–47, 248
realism and interpretivism and, 225,
    227–29, 248
sensitivity to context and, 233, 240–44,
    249
sensitivity to difference and, 233–38,
    241, 248–49
sensitivity to inclusion and, 233,
    238–40, 249, 250–51
service provision and, 38–39
skills needed for, 222–25, 248
understanding of empiricism and,
    225–27
cultural interpreters/guides, 223, 224,
    235, 243, 246
culturally competent interviews, 223–24,
    246, 248
    definition of, 255
cultural norms, 220
    definition of, 255
culture, 213–52
    context and, 216–25
    definition of, 216–17, 255
    development of, 217–20
    human service program challenges
        and, 225–31
    interpretive planning and, 172, 216,
        217, 218t, 235, 247–48
    organization practice and, 42
    planning approach selection and, 205
    program planning concerns and,
        231–47
    rational and nonrational thought and,
        14–15
    rational planning and, 172, 207, 216,
        217, 218t, 235, 247–48
    sensitivity to context and, 214, 216, 233,
        240–44, 249

data
    definition of, 255
    information vs., 101

data collection
interpretive planning and, 118, 135,
144–45, 161
rational planning and, 78, 79, 98,
100–102, 113
Davidson, L., 40, 126
decision-makers, 110, 113
budgets and, 107
emergent approaches and, 126–27
evidence-based practice and, 107
program hypotheses and, 86
social change programs and, 47
support programs and, 35
decision-making, 110, 112, 255
budgeting and, 103, 107
cultural competence and, 221
deductive vs. inductive reasoning
and, 6
definition of, 255
ethical, 170, 171–72, 176–77, 180,
187–92
garbage can model and, 132
incremental, 129, 259–60
interpretive planning and, 127, 129,
130, 135, 140, 141, 145–47, 158, 165,
200
nonrational thought and, 2, 12–16, 229
political context issues and, 60–61
program design and, 91–96, 113
rational planning and, 71–72, 190–91
rational thought and, 2, 12–16, 69,
71–72, 229
deduction, 6, 7, 8, 14
definition of, 256
deductive (linear) reasoning, 6, 10, 12, 13,
27
demand. See expressed needs
dementia care programs, 37, 38
democratic decision-making, 72
demographics, 82
demonstrations, 2
definition of, 256
incremental planning and, 17, 18
details
interpretive planning and, 163
rational planning and, 105, 113
determinism, 10, 256
definition of, 256
dialogue
learning and, 151, 152
multiple organizational settings
and, 245
difference, sensitivity to, 233–38, 248–49

non-mainstream groups and, 233–35,
249
within-group differences and, 235–38,
241, 249
direct service programs, 34, 39, 46, 48–49,
80, 256
definition of, 256
discovery
definition of, 256
documentation of, 158, 159
information validity/complexity and,
144–45
interpretive planning and, 118, 133,
134, 135–37, 140, 143–45, 158, 159,
161, 171, 192
multiple data sources and, 144
discrimination, 222
dissemination, 215, 216
definition of, 256
diversion programs, 244–45, 249
diversity, 222, 228, 229, 232, 248
within groups, 235–38, 241
documentation, 157–61, 166
domestic unit, 232
Driskell, D., 239
Durant, R., 126

Easterling, D., 74
EBP. See evidence-based practice
economic justice, 222
effectiveness-based program planning,
16–17, 38, 76, 125
efficiency, interpretive planning and, 165
Ellsworth, C., 23
emergent approaches, 26, 126, 171
accountability and, 154–62
cultural sensitivity and, 235, 236, 249
decision-makers and, 126–27
definition of, 256
dimensions of, 133–54, 192–205
historical overview of, 129–32
international planning practice and,
247
logic of, 133–38, 171
power dynamics management and, 18
problem-solving and, 14
transactive planning and, 19–20
See also interpretive planning
emergent evaluation, 158–59, 160–62
emergent logic, 11
definition of, 257
emic, 10
definition of, 257

empathy, 141, 142
empiricism
    cultural competence and, 225–27, 228
    evidence and, 7–8, 200, 206
    See also logical empiricism
employee-related expenses, 104
empowerment, 19, 24
end-of-life programs, 242–44, 249
endowments, 104
engagement
    complexity of, 137, 140, 141–42
    context of, 137, 138, 141
    definition of, 257
    documentation of, 158, 159
    interpretive planning and, 118, 133,
        135–43, 158, 159, 161, 163, 165, 171,
        192, 194–95
    methods for achieving, 142–43
    multiple perspectives and, 137, 139–40
    mutual respect and, 137, 138, 140–41
    paradox of, 40
    rational planning and, 194–95
    relationship building and, 137, 140–41
Enron scandal, 230
episode (contact) units, 94
epistemology, 11
    definition of, 257
equipment maintenance, 104
ERE. *See* employee-related expenses
ethical absolutism, 170, 188, 189–90, 196,
        199, 200, 217
    definition of, 257
ethical conduct, 188, 191
    definition of, 257
ethical decision-making
    critical thinking and, 170, 172, 176, 188,
        191–92
    planning approach selection and, 170,
        171–72, 176–77, 180, 187–92, 200–201,
        202, 205, 207
    questions to ask, 191
ethical egoist, 190
    definition of, 257
ethical quandary or dilemma, 188, 191
    definition of, 257
ethical relativism, 170, 188, 189–90,
        197–98, 200, 217
    definition of, 257
ethical utilitarian, 190
    definition of, 257
ethics
    autonomous, 190, 253
    definition of, 258

heteronomous systems of, 190, 259
    observation issues and, 224
    planning approach selection and, 170,
        172, 176, 187–91
    professional, 188–89
    situational, 190, 268
ethnicity, 222
ethnocentrism, 221
    definition of, 258
ethnographic approach, 143, 145, 179
    definition of, 258
ethnographic research, 223, 224
etic, 10
    definition of, 258
evaluation
    emergent, 158–59, 160–62
    formative, 157, 158, 160, 166, 200, 208,
        258
    goals and objectives and, 87
    interpretive planning and, 155, 156,
        157–62, 166, 200, 208
    logic model and, 99
    measures for, 90
    programs and, 38, 74, 75, 109, 110, 113,
        199
    summative, 157, 200, 208, 269
    See also outcome evaluation; process
        evaluation
evidence, 183, 200
evidence-based practice, 3
    accountability issues and, 97–98, 199,
        200
    definition of, 258
    outcome measurement and, 73, 107,
        109
    rational planning and, 73, 82, 97–98,
        107, 109, 199
experience, knowledge and, 7
expert model of planning, 17, 214
experts
    critical thinking and, 184
    interpretive planning and, 140, 166
expressed needs, 78–80, 141
    definition of, 258
expression, clarity of, 183

Faerman, Sue R., 169
failure, interpretive planning and, 161,
        163
faith-related programs, 41–42
Faludi, A., 70
family, 232, 251
Fay, B., 8–9

feedback, 164
feminist model of planning, 23–24, 27, 128
    definition of, 258
Fenno, R., 179
final (ultimate) outcomes, 88
First Offenders of Prostitution Program (FOPP), 244–45
fitness landscape, 135
flexibility
    becoming oriented and, 180
    interpretive planning and, 163
    as program design principle, 37–38
Food Stamp Program, 44
force-field analysis, 82
    definition of, 258
forecasting techniques, scenario planning and, 22
formal organizations, 43
formative evaluation
    definition of, 258
    interpretive planning and, 158, 160, 166, 200, 208
forward-sequence planning, 126, 171
    definition of, 258
foundations, 74
founders, programs and, 2, 27, 41
Freidmann, J., 71–72
Freire, P., 207–8
function, programs and, 35
funding, 110, 113, 199, 205–6
    budgeting issues and, 103–4, 107
    data collection and, 101
    for differing program types, 46–47
    interpretive planning and, 156, 166, 200
    needs assessment and, 80
    organizational structure issues and, 42, 49
    program design and, 95
    program hypotheses and, 86
    as program planning impetus, 45
fundraising programs, 34, 49, 103
future studies, 129–30

Gabor, P. A., 35, 38
gaining entry, 176, 177–79, 180, 181
garbage can model, 132
gatekeepers
    gaining entry and, 178
    international planning practice and, 246
gender, 222, 234, 241–42. See also women

generalization, 10
    definition of, 258
goals, 27
    critical thinking and, 185–86
    definition of, 259
    interpretive planning and, 171
    logic model and, 76, 87, 99
    organizational, 40
    programs and, 38
    rational planning and, 60, 69–70, 75, 76, 87–91, 99, 113, 171, 192, 202
    strategic planning and, 20
Gold, R. L., 224
Goldberg, G. S., 2
good, ethical decision-making and, 190
Government Accounting Standards Board, 72
Government Performance and Results Act, 72
government programs, 2, 17, 27
    Food Stamp Program, 44
    Medicare, 33
    outcome-based measurement and, 74, 205–6
    Senior Nutrition Program, 44
grand tour activities, 179, 181
grants, revenues and, 104
    definition of, 259
grassroots groups, 42, 44
grassroots programs, 2, 33
Gregor, F., 223
Grinnell, R. M., Jr., 35, 38
group interests, 18, 103
Growing Up in Cities project (UNESCO), 239–40, 249
Gues, Aries de, 22

Hahn (Vienna Circle member), 7
"hand" benefit programs, 46
harmony, 232
Harm Reduction Project of Salt Lake City, 245
Harvey, A. R., 250
Hasenfeld, Y., 15
Health and Human Services Department, U.S., 70
health care, 73, 74
hermeneutic process, 14
    definition of, 259
Hess, M., 226
heteronomous ethical systems, 190
    definition of, 259
Hickson, D. J., 129

hierarchy, 14, 24
  definition of, 259
Hill, R. B., 250
historicity, 14
  definition of, 259
homelessness programs, 70, 219–20
homophobia, 222
hospice programs, 36, 111, 244
host organizations, program design
  and, 92
Hudson, Barclay, 16, 17, 19, 20, 71–72,
  129–30
human agency, 8, 9
  definition of, 259
human service organizations, 39–40, 44
human service programs, 34, 49
  accountability and, 98, 225, 229–31
  budgeting and, 104
  cultural competence challenges and,
    225–31
  definition of, 259
  intervention strategies and, 82, 84,
    86–87
  outcome measurement and, 97, 107,
    109
  planner skills and, 107, 109, 172
  rational planning and, 86–87, 97, 107
  realism and interpretivism and, 225,
    227–29
  understanding empiricism and,
    225–27
Hume, David, 7
hybrid scenario planning, 22

immediate outcomes, 88
impact, 71
  definition of, 259
  logic model and, 76, 87, 88, 99
implementation
  accountability and, 230
  interpretive planning and, 136, 137,
    141, 154, 156
  rational decision-making and, 72
improvisation, 146, 147
inclusiveness
  cultural sensitivity and, 235
  interpretive planning and, 139, 140
  planning approaches and, 18, 25
  Search Conference and, 23
  sensitivity to, 233, 238–40, 249, 250–51
  transactive planning and, 19
incremental decision-making, 129
  definition of, 259–60

incremental planning theories, 16–19,
  21t, 27, 128
  definition of, 260
induction, 6, 7, 8, 14
  definition of, 260
inductive reasoning, 6, 12, 27
Industrial Revolution, 24
informal organizations, 43
information
  data vs., 101
  definition of, 260
  exchange of, 134
  tracking of, 153
information gathering
  becoming oriented and, 179
  interpretive planning and, 141, 143,
    144–45, 171
information system, 71, 99, 100–103
  definition of, 260
initiative
  definition of, 260
  program planning and, 44–46, 49
innovation, 134, 180, 230
inputs
  definition of, 260
  logic model and, 76, 86
  program design and, 92
  rational planning and, 76, 82, 84, 86, 92,
    97–98, 105
insider demands, 176
institutional sensitivity, 244
intelligence, reasoning and, 7
interactions, interpretive planning and,
  134, 135, 137, 140–41
interest groups, 103
intermediate outcomes, 76, 88
international planning practice, 245–47,
  249
interpersonal skills, 179
interpretive planning, 26, 112, 126,
  117–68, 171
  accountability and, 154–62, 165,
    166–67, 192, 198–201, 229
  analysis and, 135, 139–40, 161, 164,
    171
  approach selection and, 170–208
  case example, 119–25
  complexity and, 137, 140, 141–42,
    152–54, 156, 166, 172, 214
  consensus building and, 19, 135, 141,
    142, 144, 145–46, 147, 155, 165, 200
  critical thinking and, 152, 166, 172,
    185–87, 197–98

culture and, 172, 216, 217, 218t, 235, 247–48
decision-making and, 127, 129, 130, 135, 140, 141, 145–47, 158, 165, 200
definition of, 260
dimensions of, 133–54, 192–205, 215–16
discovery and, 118, 133, 134, 135–37, 140, 143–45, 158, 159, 161, 171, 192
discussion questions, 167–68
documentation and, 157–61, 166
engagement and, 118, 133, 135–43, 158, 159, 161, 163, 165, 171, 192, 194–95
ethical decision-making and, 190–91
evaluation and, 155, 156, 157–62, 166, 200, 208
feminist model of planning and, 24
historical overview, 129–32
international planning practice and, 247
learning and, 140, 151–52, 156–57, 161
logic of emergence and, 133–38, 171
mind-sets for, 154, 162–63, 166
problem statements and, 148, 149–50
program design and, 118, 127, 141, 185
program dissemination and, 215
skills needed for, 162, 164–65, 166, 172, 192, 201–5
strengths and challenges of, 165–66
transactive planning and, 19–20
unfolding and, 127, 135–37, 148, 150–54, 158, 159, 161, 171, 192
See also sense-making
interpretivism, 22–23, 26
cultural competence and, 225, 227–29, 248
definition of, 260
emergent approaches and, 128
nonrational thought and, 12, 14, 27, 128
positivism vs., 6, 9–12
intervention
design documents, 158, 159
indirect, 46
inputs and, 82, 84
macro, 39, 49, 261
program design and, 94
programs and, 32, 38–39
rational planning and, 76, 82, 84–87, 94, 110–12, 113, 192
interview, culturally competent, 223–24, 246, 248, 255
intuition, 144, 163
scenario planning and, 22

Invisible People. See Area Agency on Aging
irrational thought, 9
definition of, 260
nonrational thought vs., 2, 7, 16

Jackson, R. L., 241
Jewell, C., 40, 126
Juvenile Justice, U.S. Office of, 241
juvenile offenders, female, 241–42

Kauffman, Stuart, 135
Kellner-Rogers, Myron, 117, 134
Kettner, Peter M., 16–17, 31, 72, 74, 78, 85, 88, 90, 94, 103
Kloss, L. L., 22
knowledge , development of, 7–8, 26, 27, 225–26
Kramer, B. J., 242, 243
Kroeger, O., 181, 183
Kuhn, T., 225

Lady Boards of Managers, 130–32
definition of, 261
language skills, 221–23, 243, 246–47
Lauber, H., 70
Lawlor, E. F., 73, 74, 98
Lazzari, M. M., 241
leadership, 141, 162
learning
continual, 151–52, 156–57
interpretive planning and, 140, 151–52, 156–57, 161
mutual, 140
learning organization, 22–23, 130, 151–52
definition of, 261
lessons learned chronology, 158
level of functioning scales, 90
Lindblom, Charles, 18, 71, 129, 130
linearity, 5–6, 11, 70
linear reasoning, 6, 10, 12, 13, 27
linear thinking
logic models and, 60, 98–99
mind-set and, 104–5
line item, 103, 104
definition of, 261
lines, 5–25, 27, 136–37
linked services, 37
listening, 181, 183
Locke, John, 7
Lofland, J., 224
logical empiricism, 7–9
definition of, 261

logical positivism, 7–9
  definition of, 261
logic model, 8, 26
  accountability and, 97, 98–99
  definition of, 261
  of interpretive planning, 133–38, 171
  of language, 223
  linear thinking and, 60
  mind-set and, 105
  outcomes and, 88, 97
  programs and, 38, 74
  program theory and, 84, 105
  sequence of, 76
  See also rational planning
logic of play/life, 134
long-term outcomes, 88
luck, 180
Lum, D., 222

macrointerventions, 39, 49
  definition of, 261
managed care, 72
mandate, 44–46, 49, 80
  definition of, 261
March, J. G., 132
Martin, J., 217
Martin, Lawrence L., 31, 72, 78, 85, 88, 90, 94, 103
material units, 94
McGrath, Michael R., 169
measures, outcome, 73, 90–91, 96–97, 107, 109, 198, 205–6
Medicare, 33
medium-term outcomes, 88
Melbin, A., 236, 249
methodology, 8
methods journals, 158, 159
micromanagement, 131
Miller, S. J., 129
mind-set
  interpretive planning and, 154, 163, 166
  planning approach selection and, 201–5
  rational planning and, 104–5, 113
Mintzberg, Henry, 1
mission, strategic planning and, 20
mission statements, 87
model, 2, 26
  definition of, 262
  See also logic model; problem-solving model
morals, 187–90. *See also* ethics

Moroney, Robert M., 31, 72, 78, 85, 88, 94, 103
Mulroy, E. A., 70
multiculturalism, 228
  definition of, 262
  practice of, 42, 231, 238, 248
multiple perspectives
  critical thinking and, 184
  cultural competence and, 229
  ethical conduct and, 189
  interpretive planning and, 137, 138–40, 144, 165
mutual respect, 137, 138, 140–41, 144

naïve realism, 226, 227
National Association for Chronic Pain Control (case example), 51–57
National Performance Review, 72
naturalistic investigators, 224
natural science
  cultural competence and, 225, 226, 227–28
  definition of, 262
  ethical conduct and, 189
  key aspects of, 8
  positivism and, 11, 226
  reason and, 7–9, 11
needs
  community, 44, 49
  expressed, 78–80, 141, 258
  normative, 78–80, 262
  perceived, 78–80, 141, 263
  relative, 78, 79–80, 266
needs assessment
  definition of, 262
  rational planning and, 71, 76, 78–80, 113, 192
  transactive planning and, 19
nested cultures, 231, 248
Netting, F. E., 34
networking, 134
Nguzo Saba, 251
nomothetic, 10
  definition of, 262
nonlinear reasoning. *See* circular reasoning
nonprofit groups, 34, 42, 49
nonrational planning, 24, 32–33, 38, 133
  definition of, 262
  See also interpretive planning
nonrational thought, 26, 27
  decision-making and, 2, 12–16, 229
  definition of, 262

nonrational thought (continued)
  interpretivism and, 12, 14, 27, 128
  irrational thought vs., 2, 7, 16
  program planning and, 2, 6, 12, 172
  thought process comparison, 13t
nonverbal communication, 222
normative needs, 78–80
  definition of, 262
norms, cultural, 255
numerical counts, 90
nutrition programs, 44

objective (objectivist) perspective,
    definition of, 263
objectives, 38
  as data collection guide, 102
  definition of, 263
  program hypothesis assessment and,
    106–7
  rational planning and, 76, 85, 87–91, 99,
    106–7, 113, 125, 192
  strategic planning and, 20
objectivity, 9, 75, 139, 229
  definition of, 263
observation, 223–26, 248
O'Connor, M. K., 34
Ogilvy, J., 228
ontology, 11
  definition of, 263
openness, 229
operating costs, 104
operationalism, 226
oppressed groups, 19, 20, 222
order, 229
organizational auspice, 92, 94
organizations
  accountability and, 229–30
  cultural competence and, 231, 232,
    244–45
  definition of, 49, 263
  formal vs. informal, 43
  interpretive planning and, 129–30
  Lady Boards of Managers and, 130–32,
    261
  programs and, 32, 33, 39–43, 49, 214–15
  rational planning and, 105, 113
  values of, 232
orientation, 176, 179–81
outcome evaluation, 200
  definition of, 263
  health care and, 73, 74
  rational planning and, 73–74, 81, 85,
    109, 199, 206

outcomes
  definition of, 263
  interpretive planning and, 156, 160,
    206
  logic models and, 74, 76, 87, 99
  measurement of, 73, 90–91, 96–97, 107,
    109, 198, 205–6
  objectives and, 85, 88–90
  as programming basis, 76
  rational planning and, 76, 199
  types of, 88
outputs, 74, 76, 86, 87, 94, 97, 99
  definition of, 263
outreach, perceived needs and, 79
outsider demands, 176

paradox
  of engagement, 40
  interpretive planning and, 172, 202
paradoxical thinking, 189
participant observation, 224
  definition of, 263
participatory planning, 23, 128
partnership, 131
patience, 105, 113
Patton, M. Q., 135
Pawlak, Edward J., 17, 34, 59
peer mentor programs, 126–27
perceived needs, 78–80, 141
  definition of, 263
performance-based programming, 76
persistence, becoming oriented and,
    180
personal service programs, 19
pet-facilitated therapy programs, 111
philosophy, 7, 8, 187, 188, 190
phronesis, 188
  definition of, 264
Pig Intervention (case example), 173–76,
    182–83, 201, 240, 249
pilot, 2
  definition of, 264
pilot projects, 17–18, 36
  definition of, 264
planned change model, 24, 26
policy analysis, 150
political context
  budgeting and, 103, 107
  decision-making and, 60–61
  international planning practice and,
    247
  interpretive planning and, 144, 147,
    152, 165

planning approach selection and, 176,
207
Popper, Karl, 8
Positive Philosophy, The (Comte), 8
positivism, 26, 128
cultural competence and, 225, 226–27,
248
definition of, 264
interpretivism vs., 6, 9–12
postmodernism critique of, 9
rational thought and, 12–13, 27, 71
science and, 11, 226
See also logical positivism
postage and shipping, 104
Post-Empiricists, 228
postmodernism (Post-Modernists),
9, 228
postpositivism (Post-Positivists), 10, 226,
228
definition of, 264
power issues
advocacy planning and, 18
budgeting and, 103
expert model of planning and, 214
gaining entry and, 178, 181
interpretive planning and, 141, 142,
144, 147, 150
practitioners, organizational structure
and, 42, 43
prescriptive approaches, 26, 59–116, 125,
132, 171
accountability and, 96–104
case example, 61–69
cultural sensitivity and, 235
definition of, 264
dimensions of, 75–96, 192–205
history of, 71
international planning and, 247
limitations of, 60
planners utilizing, 60, 172
problem-solving and, 14, 60
See also rational planning
principles, ethics of, 188
printing and publications, 104
prisoner advocacy programs, 47–48
problem analysis
definition of, 264
rational planning and, 71, 75, 76, 80–82,
99, 106, 113, 192
problem/problem identification, 81
definition of, 264
interpretive planning and, 139–40, 141,
144–45, 146, 147, 153

rational planning and, 75, 76, 80–82,
113, 192
problem-solving, 27, 110, 171, 207
critical thinking and, 182, 183
deductive vs. inductive reasoning and,
6
definition of, 264
differing assumptions and, 12
political context and, 60–61
rational vs. nonrational approaches to,
7, 12–16, 24, 25, 70, 71
support programs and, 35
problem-solving model, 24, 25, 26, 112,
125, 171
definition of, 265
problem-solving process, definition of,
265
problem statements
definition of, 265
interpretive planning and, 148, 149–50
rational planning and, 78, 82, 83–84
process
cultural preferences for, 232
in interpretive planning, 135–36, 137,
140, 147, 161, 165, 171
process evaluation, 74, 200
definition of, 265
process logs, 159
process objectives, 85, 88–90
professional ethics, 188–89
professional fees, 104
professional growth *See* staff
development and training programs
professional standards, 99
program approach selection, 169–212
accountability concerns and, 176, 192,
198–201, 207–8
approach dimensions comparison, 176,
192–205
approach similarities, 172, 176–92
approach type comparisons, 210–12*t*
becoming oriented and, 176, 179–81
case example and analysis, 172, 173–76
critical thinking and, 170, 171–72, 176–
77, 180–88, 191–92, 197–98, 205, 207
decision issues for, 205–8
discussion questions and, 208–10
ethical decision-making and, 170, 171–
72, 176–77, 180, 187–92, 200–201, 202,
205, 207
gaining entry and, 176, 177–79, 180, 181
mind-sets and, 201–5
skills and, 170, 176, 201–5

program design, 32
  accountability and, 99, 199–200, 230
  critical thinking and, 185
  decision-making and, 91–96, 113
  definition of, 265
  flexibility and, 37–38
  interpretive planning and, 118, 127,
    141, 185
  rational planning and, 76, 84, 91–96,
    109, 113, 185, 192
  skills needed for, 71
  throughputs and, 94–96
program hypothesis, 85–86, 88–90, 102–3,
    106–7, 198
  definition of, 265
program logic. See logic model
program planning
  accountability and, 49, 99, 103–4, 113,
    192, 198–201, 207–8
  budgeting and, 71, 99, 103–4, 107,
    108–9
  cultural issues and, 213–52
  definition of, 265
  for different program types, 46–48
  discussion questions and, 28–29
  existing plan obsolescence and, 5
  line and circle metaphors for, 5–16, 25,
    27, 136–37
  mandates/initiatives and, 44–46, 49
  multiple organizational settings and,
    244–45, 249
  nonrational approaches to, 2, 38
  organization size as factor in, 2
  practical guides for, 46
  program impetus and, 32, 43–48, 49
  rational thought and, 2, 6, 69
  sensitivities in, 214, 216, 233–44,
    248–51
  theory approaches to, 16–25
  as unfolding process, 3–5
  See also interpretive planning; program
    approach selection; rational
    planning
programs, 31–57
  accountability and, 229–30
  case exercise, 51–57
  as containers, 32–33, 41, 214–15
  definition of, 34, 48, 265
  discussion questions, 49–50
  evaluation of, 38, 74, 75, 109, 110, 113,
    199
  inherited, 2, 27

  organizational context and, 32, 33,
    39–43, 49
  planning experience variation and, 2,
    27
  program planning/impetus for, 32,
    43–48, 49
  projects vs., 32, 36–38, 49
  public, 2, 17, 27
  redesigning of, 2
  revenues and, 103–4
  service/interventions and, 32, 38–39
  types of, 34–36, 35t, 48–49
program theory, 84–85, 105
  definition of, 266
projects
  definition of, 36, 266
  programs vs., 32, 36–38, 49
  service/interventions and, 32
public agencies, 34, 42, 49
public programs. See government
    programs

qualitative research, 200
quality standards, 95
quantitative research, 200
quantitative scenario planning, 22
Quinn, Robert E., 153, 169

racism, 222
radical planning theories, 16–19, 21t, 27,
    128
  definition of, 266
Rand Corporation, 22
rapport, 178
Rationalists, 8–9
rational planning, 16–17, 19, 26, 27,
    59–116, 125, 171
  accountability and, 71, 72, 96–104, 113,
    192, 198–201, 229
  approach selection and, 170–208
  budgets and, 71, 99, 103–4, 107, 108–9
  case example, 61–69
  critical thinking and, 185–87, 196
  culture and, 172, 207, 216, 217, 218t,
    235, 247–48
  definition of, 266
  dimensions of, 75–96, 192–205, 215–16
  discussion questions, 114–16
  empiricism, positivism, and, 227
  engagement and, 194–95
  ethical decision-making and, 190–91

evidence-based practice and, 73, 82, 97–98, 107, 109, 199
goal and objective writing and, 76, 87–91, 99, 113, 192
historical overview of, 71–75
international practice and, 247
intervention strategy selection, 76, 82, 84–87, 113, 192
linearity in, 70
logic model and, 70, 74, 75–78, 86, 87, 96, 97, 109–13, 125, 171
mind-set for, 104–5, 113
needs assessment, 71, 76, 78–80, 113, 192
problem definition and analysis, 76, 80–82, 99, 106, 113, 192
program design, 76, 84, 91–96, 109, 113, 185, 192
programs as containers and, 32
replicability and, 215
skills needed for, 106–9, 113, 192, 201–5
strengths and challenges of, 110–12
summative evaluation and, 157, 200, 208, 269
unexpected results and, 111–12
rational thought, 9, 26, 27
costs and benefits of, 7, 13
decision-making and, 2, 12–16, 69, 71–72, 229
definition of, 266
positivism and, 12–13, 27, 71
program planning and, 2, 6, 69, 172
synoptic, 71, 269
thought process comparison, 13*t*
Raube, K., 73, 74, 98
reading, critical, 184
realism (Realist), 10, 225, 227–29
definition of, 266
naïve, 226, 227
reality, 9, 11, 228
multiple views of, 227
reason
definition of, 266
human behavior/understanding and, 8–9
science and, 7–9, 11
reasoning
circular, 2, 6
critical thinking and, 183
linear, 2, 6
reductionism, 9, 10
decision-making and, 13, 14, 15
definition of, 266

interpretivism and, 11
linear thinking and, 24
strategic planning and, 20
reflection
action as, 154
critical thinking and, 182
reflexive journals, 159
regulation, 2, 17, 230
Rehner, J., 184
relationship building
becoming oriented and, 179
cultural competence and, 221, 246
engagement and, 137, 140–41
gaining entry and, 177–79, 181
international planning practice and, 246
interpretive planning and, 137, 140–41, 144, 163
relative needs, 78, 79–80
definition of, 266
relativism. *See* ethical relativism
religion, ethical conduct and, 189, 190
replicability, 215, 216
definition of, 267
reputation by association, 177, 181
requests for proposals, 45
definition of, 267
research and development programs, 34
resilience, 162
resource inventories, 79
resource plans, 107
resources
interpretive planning and, 135, 156
logic model and, 74, 76
program design and, 92, 94
rational planning and, 76, 92, 94
respect
cultural competence and, 232, 233, 245
mutual, 137, 139, 140–41, 144
responsiveness, 163, 230, 233
retrospection, interpretive planning and, 133, 137, 145
revenues, 103–4
reverse-order planning, 70, 112, 171
definition of, 267
RFPs. *See* requests for proposals
Rothman, J. C., 216, 238
Rowe, M., 40, 126

salaries, 104
Salt Lake City Prosecutor's Office, 245
Salt Lake City Prostitution Diversion Program, 245, 249

Salt Lake Valley Health Department, 245
sampling, systematic, 161
Sathyanagar, India, 239–40
satisficing, 14
    definition of, 267
Savaya, R., 84
scenario planning, 22, 27, 128
    definition of, 267
Schein, Edgar H., 213, 218–19
Schlick (Vienna Circle member), 7
Schwartz, P., 228
science. *See* natural science
science of muddling through, 18, 129
    definition of, 267
scripts, 22
Search Conference, 23, 27, 128
    definition of, 267
self-awareness, gaining entry and, 179
self-knowledge, 184
self-presentation, 179–80
Senge, Peter M., 5, 130, 152
Senior Nutrition Program, 44
sense data, 7
sense-making, 25
    contextual responsiveness and, 147–48
    decision-making and, 146–47
    definition of, 267
    documentation of, 158, 159
    interpretive planning and, 118, 127,
        130, 133, 135–37, 145–48, 158, 159,
        161, 171, 192
sense-making theory, definition of, 267–
    68
service definition, 94
Service Efforts and Accomplishment
    initiative, 72
services
    definition of, 268
    linked, 37
    programs and, 32, 38–39
    units of, 94–95
service tasks, 94
setting, programs and, 35
sexism, 222
sexual orientation, 222
SFA initiative, 72
shared vision, 144
short-term outcomes, 88
Simon, Herbert A., 71
situational ethics, 190
    definition of, 268
skills
    budgeting, 107

cultural competence and, 222–25, 248
human service program planners, 107,
    109, 172
interpersonal, 179
interpretive planning and, 162, 164,
    166, 172, 192, 201–5
language-related, 221–23, 243, 246–47
planning approach selection and, 170,
    176, 201–5
program design, 71
rational planning and, 106–9, 113, 192,
    201–5
Smith, T. L., 237, 249
Smithville Friendly Visiting Program, 33
social change programs, 47–48
social class, 222
social constructivist theory, 127, 153
    definition of, 268
socialization, 218–19
    definition of, 268
social justice, 222
social learning theory, 127
    definition of, 268
social policy, 44
social problems, 36, 60, 171
social reality, 9, 11
social responsibility, 155
social science, 8, 10, 225–26
sociology, 8
"soft benefit" programs, 46
Spradley, J., 179
staff
    budgeting for, 104
    data collection by, 100–101
    program design and, 92, 94
staff development and training
        programs, 34, 39, 46–47, 48–49
    definition of, 268
    professional growth and, 170
stakeholders, 18, 110
    accountability and, 99, 158–59, 161
    becoming oriented and, 180, 181
    cultural competence related to, 231,
        240, 244, 245, 248
    definition of, 268
    engagement and multiple, 137,
        139–40
    gaining entry and, 177, 178, 181
    incremental decision-making and, 129
    interpretive planning and, 118, 129,
        134, 137, 139–40, 141, 146, 152, 154,
        158–59, 161, 165, 171
    program design and, 95

program planning and, 43–44, 99
Search Conference and, 23
standardized tests, 90
Standing against Global Exploitation, 244
status, gaining entry and, 178, 181
strategic planning, 20, 24, 27
 definition of, 268
strategic thinking, 153
strategy
 definition of, 269
 macro-level, 39
 programs and, 41
Street Educators. *See* Children's Street
  Education Program
subculture, 219
 definition of, 269
subjective (subjectivist) perspective,
  definition of, 269
subjectivity, 10–11, 139, 140, 159
 definition of, 269
Sullivan, C. M., 236, 249
Sullivan, W. M., 188
summative evaluation, 160, 200, 208
 definition of, 269
support, interpretive planning and, 164
support programs, 34–35, 48–49, 269
 definition of, 269
surety, 24–25
surveys, 79
sustainable community development, 18
synoptic planning theories, 16–17, 21*t*,
  27, 75, 112
 definition of, 269
synoptic rationality, 71
 definition of, 269
synthesizing, critical thinking and, 182,
  183, 185
systemic-level change, 19, 20
systems theory, 105, 113

tactics
 definition of, 269
 macro-level, 39
 strategic planning and, 20
Tamil refugees, 233–35, 243, 249
target population, 35–36
teen pregnancy programs, 45
telephone support programs, 237, 249
tension, interpretive planning and, 154,
  165
tentativeness, 24–25
theory-based evaluation. *See* logic model
theory of action. *See* logic model

third-party payments, 103
Thompson, Michael P., 169
throughput, 76, 94–96
 definition of, 270
Thuesen, J. M., 181, 183
time, attention to, 118, 145
time-series analysis, 22
time units, 94
top-down hierarchy, 24
Toseland, R. W., 237, 249
Total Quality Management (TQM), 72
transactive planning theories, 16–20, 21*t*,
  23, 27, 128
 definition of, 270
transformative program planning, 47–48
transitional housing programs, battered
  women, 236–37, 249
travel costs, 104
troubleshooting, 129–30
trust
 becoming oriented and, 180
 ethics and, 188
 gaining entry and, 177, 179
 interpretive planning and, 140, 141,
  163, 167
truth
 correspondence theory of, 226
 definition of, 270
 differing assumptions of, 12
 engagement and, 139
 interpretive planning and, 139, 155
 interpretivism and, 11
 nonrational thought and, 14
 rational thought and, 13
 realism and, 228
typology, definition of, 270

ultimate outcomes, 88
uncertainty
 interpretive planning and, 162, 164,
  165, 167
 interpretive thinking and, 132
 rational decision-making and, 71–72
understanding, interpretivism and,
  10–11
unfolding
 complexity and, 152–54
 continual learning and, 151–52
 definition of, 270
 documentation of, 158, 159
 interpretive planning and, 127, 135–37,
  148, 150–54, 158, 159, 161, 171, 192
 options and possibilities, 150–52

United Nations Convention on the Rights of the Child, 238–39
United Nations Educational, Scientific, and Cultural Organization, 239–40, 249
United Way, 103–4, 205
units of service, 94–95
    definition of, 270
universal scientific language, 226
Unrau, Y. A., 35, 38

validation procedures, 8
validity checks, 145
values
    cultural competence and, 221, 222, 231–33, 238
    ethical quandaries/dilemmas and, 188
    organizational, 232
Vienna Circle, 7
Vinter, Robert D., 17, 34, 59
voluntary associations, 42
volunteers, 92

Wahab, S., 244, 245
Waysman, M., 84
Weaver, H. N., 233, 249
Wedel, K. R., 18, 36, 46, 84, 92
Weick, Karl, 130, 133, 146
Weinberger, David, 229, 230
Westley, F., 135, 153–54
Wheatley, Margaret J., 117, 134
Wilson, D. C., 129
within-group differences, 235–38, 241, 249
Wittgenstein, Ludwig, 7
women
    feminist model of planning and, 23–24
    as juvenile offenders, 241–42
    Lady Boards of Managers, 130–32, 261
writing, critical, 184

Zimmerman, B., 135

Made in the USA
San Bernardino, CA
14 August 2018